Moorish Architecture

in Andalusia

Marianne Barrucand · Achim Bednorz

Moorish Architecture

in Andalusia

TASCHEN

KÖLN LONDON MADRID NEW YORK PARIS TOKYO

Cover Photo:
Madînat al-Zahrâ', Salón Rico

© 2002 TASCHEN GmbH
Hohenzollernring 53, D-50672 Köln
www.taschen.com
Original edition: © 1992 Benedikt Taschen Verlag GmbH
Edited and produced by Rolf Taschen, Cologne
Layout by Peter Feierabend, Berlin
Cover design: Jiménez & Casagrande, Frankfurt/Main
English translation by Michael Scuffil, Leverkusen

Printed in Italy
ISBN 3–8228–2116–0

Contents

1237–1492   The Rule of the Nasrids

The Architecture of the Nasrids

Conclusion

Introduction

The contrast between the desolate ruined castles on the heights of the sun-baked mountain landscape, and the palaces in the cities, with their cool patios, babbling fountains and scented blossoms testifying to a lifestyle of elegant sophistication – this contrast has stimulated the imagination of the northern European ever since the days of the Romantic movement. Since Washington Irving, one of the earliest and most sympathetic Hispanophiles, whose Alhambra Tales of 1832 achieved worldwide renown, the traveller in Andalusia has set out on a search for a dream and fairy-tale world in which Almanzor, Boabdil and Carmen live, love and suffer according to other, alien laws. "Andalusia" – for the northern European the word signifies an Orient with all the magic of the Islamic Orient but without its drawbacks. Its customs and usages, even today occasionally reminiscent of the Middle Ages, remind him of North Africa and the Near East, while its modernization nevertheless preserves him from any unpleasant surprises.

Andalusia is a land in which Islam and Christianity fought the good fight, as they respectively saw it, and half-heartedness had no place in the battle. It is a land of crusade, in which the Imam disappeared to be replaced by the Grand Inquisitor, and where processions of penitents wind their way through one-time *sûqs*, and where, for all the intolerance and all the hatred between the two religions and the two civilizations, a shared culture developed to inspire the imagination.

In the second half of the 19th century, the romantic approach gave way to the scholarly, while the first half of the 20th witnessed the appearance of magnificent compendia in the fields of Andalusian language, history, literature and art, which, though continually expanded and enriched, are still valid even today. Today, the once Islamic Spain is the subject of intensive research; it is still too early to formulate any comprehensive new theses, but scholars are nevertheless faced with the constant task of integrating the results of the research of recent decades into the living panorama left us by the old masters.

Geographically and administratively, the name Andalusia (Andalucía) refers today to the south-western region of Spain, comprising the provinces of Almería, Málaga, Cádiz, Huelva, Seville, Cordova, Jaén and Granada. Three geomorphological units can be clearly distinguished: in the centre, the marl and sandy valley of the Guadalquivir, bounded by hills and opening onto the Atlantic in sandy, marshy monotony; in the north,

Granada, Alhambra
View from the "Hall of the Two Sisters" to the belvedere of the Linderaja, formerly the "House of 'A'isha". The accuracy of this engraving is remarkable; it takes superb account of the gradation of the rooms, to which this architecture owes much of its charm.

PREVIOUS DOUBLE PAGE:
Ruined Castle of La Guardia de Jaén
Under the Romans, and perhaps much earlier, the hilltop was the site of a fortified settlement. On top of the Roman walls first Visigothic, then Arab and finally Christian walls were erected; it is almost impossible to establish the date of the individual remains. The towers bear witness to a life that was continually under threat in an area which for centuries was disputed between Christian and Islamic rulers.

11

the Sierra Morena, the southern foothills of the Iberian Meseta, a thinly populated mountain region, whose sole source of wealth lies in a few copper, coal, mercury and lead mines; and in the south, the mighty Sistema Penibético, stretching from Gibraltar in the west to Cape Nao in the east. The Lower Baetic Cordilleras divide the Guadalquivir Valley from a series of parallel valleys, dry to the east around Guadix and Baza, but in the neighbourhood of Granada irrigated and thus extraordinarily fertile (the Vega). High mountain ranges in the south (Sierra de Ronda, Sierra Nevada, Sierra de los Filabres) leave room along the coast for small irrigated plains. The most important area – historically and economically – is the rich Guadalquivir valley, the cradle of the three cities of Cordova, Seville and Cádiz.

Originally, al-Andalus comprised the whole of Islamic Spain, which from the 8th till the 10th century included by far the greater part of the Iberian peninsula. Its northern border followed approximately the course of the Duero, while being bounded to the east by the Pyrenees. In other words, theoretically at least, material evidence of Islamic culture should be present in the whole of this area. In this book, therefore, "Andalusian" is synonymous with "Ibero-Islamic" or "Islamo-Hispanic", and by "Andalusia" is meant the whole of Islamic Iberia.

Until recently, the origin of the name al-Andalus presented something of a mystery. It appears for the first time five years after the Islamic conquest, on a coin bearing the bilingual inscription "Span(ia)" – in Latin – and "al-Andalus" – in Arabic.[1] Subsequent Arabic historians and geographers traced it back to some "ante-diluvian" aboriginal population, while European scholars linked it "in some way or other" to the Vandals: "Vandal" had somehow developed into "al-Andalus". This derivation is etymologically impossible, but historical considerations have also prevented the idea from carrying any conviction, since the Vandals, along with the Alani and Suebi, occupied Andalusia for only a short time (411–429) before setting sail for North Africa. Heinz Halm[2] has recently demonstrated that "al-Andalus" is simply an Arabization of the Visigothic name for the for-

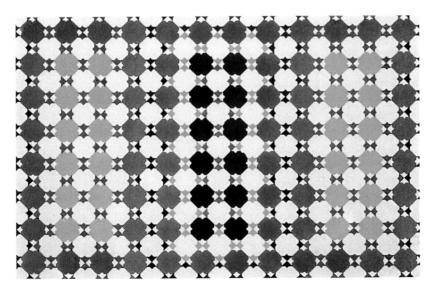

Granada, Alhambra: coloured drawing of a faïence mosaic

12

mer Roman province of Baetica. The Visigoths had dominated the region from 468 until the Islamic conquest of 711. Like their Germanic predecessors, they too had allocated the conquered land by lot. "Sortes Gothica" was the name given to the lots drawn by the individual lords, and also to the lands they thus acquired. The singular form, "Gothica sors", can be found in nearly all the written sources, couched without exception in Latin, as the term for the Gothic Kingdom as such, while its Gothic equivalent, "landa-hlauts" ("land-lot") quickly, and so to speak spontaneously, became "al-Andalus" (which also explains the conspicuous Arabic definite article "al-").

Along with the country itself, the Muslims took over from their immediate predecessors not only its name, but also elements of their art. The development of Hispano-Islamic art was at first a fusion process, in which Visigothic, Romano-Iberian, Romano-Syrian, Byzantine and Arabic elements combined to form a new and autonomous style, which in turn provided the stimulus for other artistic directions. It is impossible to understand post-8th-century Christian and Jewish art in Spain without taking their Islamic component into account. In Mozarabic churches (i.e. Chris-

Granada, Alhambra: Lion Court
The Lion Court was once a garden, and the dense, albeit untidy, vegetation in this romantic 19th century print is more in accord with its original condition than are the present-day gravel-beds.

13

tian churches erected under Islamic rule), the relationship with contemporary Islamic architecture is already evident, but Andalusian architecture comes to real fruition in the churches and palaces built after the Reconquista. From the purely Islamic stucco ornamentation of the monastery of Las Huelgas near Burgos (which at no time during its whole existence has ever been in Islamic hands), from the Chapel of St Ferdinand in the Grand Mosque in Cordova – both dating from the 13th century – via the Alcázar of Pedro the Cruel in Seville, dating from the 14th century, and the Aragonese church towers of the 15th century, right up to the railway stations of southern Spain, built in the late 19th and early 20th centuries: Spanish architecture is characterized through and through by interlocking multi-lobed arches, decorative masonry-work, and colourful glazed bricks.

The *Mudéjar* style is the term used when speaking of Islamic forms created under Christian rule; the setting may be a magnificent palace chapel or a cathedral, or it may equally well be a humble village church. Mudéjar (from the Arabic *mudajjan*: "domesticated") was originally a pejorative term used by those Muslims who fled after the Reconquista to describe those who stayed behind. Mudéjar art in Spain displays an infinite variety; every region has its own version, influenced by local traditions, by the taste of the client, and not least by his financial potential. The one common denominator of all mudéjar art is the crispness of its inventory of Islamic forms. The reappearance of medieval styles in southern Spain towards the end of the 19th century, however, has nothing to do with the mudéjar phenomenon, but rather with the same historicism which gave rise, for example, to the Palace of Westminster.

Andalusian art in general, and her architecture in particular, has left a permanent reminder not only in Christian Spain and in such art throughout the world as has been influenced by Christian Spain, but has also had a continuing effect on Islamic art. The exchange and interplay of forces between Andalusia and North Africa, characteristic of the period of Islamic hegimony on both shores of the Mediterranean, was followed on

Granada, Alhambra: coloured drawing of a faïence mosaic

Tarifa: School and Leisure Centre in an "ancient" setting
Castellated walls, pools in rectangular inner courtyards, single-storey buildings with shady galleries, faïence to give a colourful touch, horseshoe arches, palm-trees: all these are elements of the domestic architecture of southern Spain even today.

Arcos de la Frontera: panoramic view of the ancient hilltop city
The old settlement was destroyed by the Vandals, but achieved a new prosperity under the Moors. In 1250 Arcos was taken by Alfonso X.

A ruined castle near Arcos de la Frontera

the North African side by centuries of imitative creativity. Almost the whole of Moroccan art of the past few centuries has been produced in the wake of Granada. While Tunisia and Algeria became outposts of Ottoman art following the Turkish conquest, Morocco remained unshakably loyal to her Andalusian heritage.

Thus for centuries after its own demise, Ibero-Islamic architecture continued to leave its mark both on non-Islamic Iberian and on non-Iberian – i.e. North African – Islamic architecture. By what factors in its own development can this posthumous dynamic be explained? Before we come to consider this theme, a few further remarks on the special position of Iberian Islam would not be out of order.

From a purely Spanish point of view, there have been many attempts since the 19th century to present Andalusian culture as a specifically Iberian creation. The theory of the more or less basic Spanishness of the cultures which arose on Spanish soil has long dominated Spanish historiography. However this may be, there can be no doubt whatever that the Spanish Muslims regarded themselves first and foremost as Muslims who happened to live on the Iberian peninsula, and not at all as Islamic Spaniards. The term "Ishbâniya" was applied only to the Christian part of the country, while the Islamic part was called al-Andalus, a term whose geographical application was subject to variation. At first it referred to the major part of the peninsula, while by the 15th century it was restricted to the small Kingdom of Granada. One can with reasonable confidence deny the presence of any territorially-based national feelings on the part of Spanish Muslims; their deeper sense of identity was based rather on their membership of a tribal and religious community. Even the innumerable alliances formed during the course of the centuries with Christians in times of danger – including, incidentally, the period of the crusades in the Near East – do not alter the fact that the "alien" was, on principle, the non-Muslim, Spanish or not as the case might be.

Górmaz: Citadel
The complex measures about 380 metres in length and 50 metres wide (at its broadest point), and occupies a ridge above the Duero valley. Its ground plan is determined by the lie of the land. It guarded a broad plain in the northern frontier area of Islamic Spain at a time when the latter had reached its maximum size.

Teruel: general view and details of the Torre del Salvador
This most famous of the town's mudéjar towers dates from the 13th century. During the Moorish period Teruel was for a time part of the petty kingdom of Albarracín, until it was reconquered by Alfonso II of Aragón in 1171. Mudéjar is the description applied to Islamic forms produced under Christian rule.

These facts notwithstanding, al-Andalus was perceived within the Islamic world as a unit apart, and her inhabitants wrote proud verses glorifying the beauty of their adopted homeland, verses which came to acquire highly specific forms.

And like Hispano-Islamic literature, Hispano-Islamic architecture also developed an individuality of form; but just as it is impossible to appreciate this literature without a knowledge of the Arabic language, so it is likewise impossible to isolate this architecture from the totality of Islamic architecture as a whole. The form and functions of the buildings are determined first and foremost by Islam; their Spanishness is secondary. Moreover, the vocabulary of forms employed by Andalusian architects between the 11th and 13th centuries was determined in part by influences from North Africa, giving general currency to the terms Hispano-Maghrebian or Hispano-Moorish art.

"Moors" (from the Greek *mauros*, "dark") was the name given by Lucian to the aboriginal non-negroid population of West Africa. Today the term is applied indiscriminately to the people of North Africa, consisting for the most part of aboriginal Berbers and Arab immigrants. "Maghreb" (Arabic, "West") is used in the Arabic world to mean Algeria and Morocco, while in French it generally includes all the states of North Africa other than Egypt.

One could spend hours discussing the most appropriate way to pigeonhole this architecture in some classificatory scheme. Whether it is described as Moorish, Hispano-Islamic or Hispano-Maghrebian, it is clear that none of these attributes does justice to a reality in which Arabic, Spanish and Berber elements subjected each other to mutual influence of varying intensity on the fertile soil of Islam, and in so doing gave rise to unparalleled peaks of achievement.

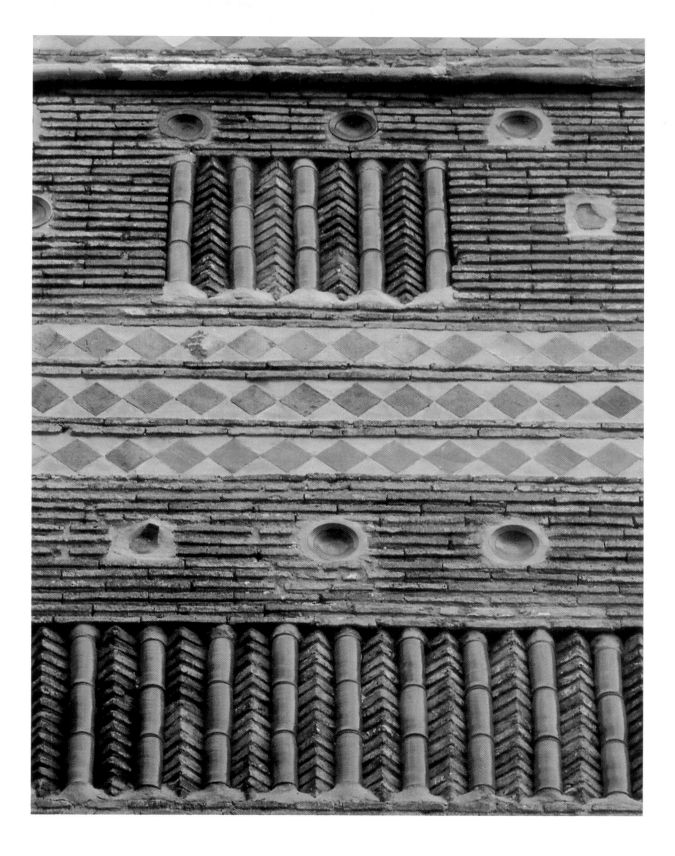

710-912

Events up to the End of the 9th Century

By the beginning of the 8th century, the weakness of the once mighty Visigothic kingdom was plain for all to see. A small, vastly wealthy upper class, composed of the Germanic aristocracy and the descendants of the Ibero-Roman *noblesse de robe*, was confronted by an impoverished rural population and a growing mass of serfs. The increasing economic and social tensions found their expression, *inter alia*, both in anti-Jewish pogroms and in ever more draconian laws against fugitive slaves, which were nonetheless impotent to stop the continuing flight. The towns too were impoverished, having lost their privileges and their former power. And while the monarch had quite extraordinary wealth at his disposal, his authority was minimal. Court intrigues and internecine murder had led to a chaotic situation, whose origins lay in part in the old Gothic system of elective kingship, which recognized no dynastic succession to the throne; the only criterion of eligibility was membership of the Gothic nobility. Each of the rival clans maintained their own retinues, who, on the victory of an opponent, were massacred, if possible to the last man. At the same time, the King seems not to have had a regular and reliable army at his disposal. In theory, every free man owed a duty of military service to the ruler, but by the end of the 7th century, the ruler no longer had the means to enforce compliance. As a result, claimants to the throne turned to foreign powers in order to achieve their ambitions. Athanagild called on Byzantium for help, Sisenand the Franks, Froia the Basques, and finally, in the year 711, Akhila and his brothers, the sons of Wittiza, the last king, appealed to the Muslims of North Africa for assistance against the usurper Roderic.[3]

Although the Gothic period ended in bloodshed and misery, it would be wrong to pronounce an entirely negative judgement upon it. It was, after all, the period during which Spain was united administratively for the first time, and it also saw not only the Iberian peninsula's conversion to Christianity, but also its thoroughgoing Romanization in respect of language and law. The Germanic Visigoths played the role of a catalyst in this process. Later historians came to glorify this period as that which saw the birth of a Spanish national sentiment.[4]

There are just a few, mostly very modest churches – basilicas and centrally-planned buildings as well as simple rectangular halls – in existence today to provide us with some evidence of Visigothic religious architecture.[5] They are built of handsome dressed stone, following the noble "more gothico", as St Isidore of Seville called it (as opposed to the "more gallicano", a combination of wood with bricks and mortar). While the plan and elevation of the churches point to an oriental influence, the building technique is of frankly Roman lineage. A number of forms owe nothing to other traditions, however, in particular the constantly-recurring horseshoe arch. The ornamentation represents one of the various branches of late Roman provincial art, which, despite its undoubted initial impression of monotony, nevertheless does display marked local variations. Thus the geometric ornamentation of Visigothic buildings shares definite elements of folkart. Here, as in the floral and leaf patterns as well as the figurative decoration, we see a tendency towards the filling up of spaces, and a treatment of volumes which can only be called careless. The repertoire of vegetable forms, with its acanthus, vine and laurel leaves, is certainly Roman in origin, even though the technical quality of the work shows a marked deterioration when compared with earlier periods.

Other well-known material evidence of this culture is to be found in its liturgical apparatus, where Byzantine and Coptic influence is unmistakable, and in its golden, heavily bejewelled votive crowns. The "Germanic" tradition, with its tendency towards colourfulness and abstraction, is more obvious in these votive crowns, as well as in humbler metal objects of everyday use (such as pins, brooches, needles, buckles and rings), than in architecture and sculpture, which look more to Rome for their inspiration.

Visigothic art was the recipient of influences of the widest possible variety: Germanic folk culture, Byzantine court culture, Ravennese, Ibero-Roman and even Afro-Roman elements are all present, fused into an ultimately simple yet individual artistic language, which in its turn was to have a decisive influence on the art of Islamic Spain.

The Islamic Conquest

The Religious Message

Muhammad appeared in early 7th-century Mecca at first as one prophet among several. His monotheistic, egalitarian message of eternal salvation through Islam, "surrender" to the will of God, found a rapid echo, however, which elevated its messenger to a unique status. The Koran (Qur'ân), the sacred text of this new religion, is the Word of God, and like God himself eternal. It was conveyed to Muhammad by the Archangel Gabriel, so that he might proclaim it to mankind ("*Iqra'*!" – "Recite!" – was the command of the angel to the Prophet). The new message promises every human being eternal bliss, provided he or she believes in the one merciful God, Allah, and keeps His commandments. These are based essentially on the "Five Pillars of Religion": the profession of faith ("There is no God but God, and Muhammad is His Prophet"), the five daily prayers (*salât*), the religious tax (*zakât*), keeping the annual month of fasting (*Ramadân*), and the pilgrimage to Mecca once in a lifetime (*hadj*). In comparison with the polytheism then prevalent in Arabia, the demands of Allah did not

seem oppressive. Moreover, Muhammad promised that those who fell in the Holy War against the Infidel would proceed directly to Paradise, which is described in great detail in the Koran as a place of physical pleasure; other mortals, by contrast, will have to wait for the Last Judgement before gaining access. The growing success of his preaching forced Muhammad to flee from the hostile Mecca establishment in September 622 and to take refuge at the oasis of Yathrib, about 360 kilometres to the north. This oasis was later given the name Madîna.[6] The settlement at Yathrib constituted the first Islamic state, with the Prophet at its head, exercising both spiritual and temporal authority.

The message of Muhammad was directed in the first place towards the inhabitants of Mecca, and then to the Arabians as a whole. It is quite probable that towards the end of his life the Prophet himself included the whole of mankind in his programme of salvation. However that may be, the Koran, the Word of God, was proclaimed in Arabic, thus securing the pre-eminent position of the Arabs in the new religion, whatever its universalist claims.

Mecca, the birthplace of the Prophet and one of the Holy Places of Islam
The city was a centre of trade and pilgrimage even before Muhammad. The Kaaba, the cubic structure covered with a black cloth in the middle of the great courtyard, has been a religious shrine since the earliest days of Islam. According to the Koran, the sacred Black Stone was built into the walls of the Kaaba by Abraham himself and Ishmael his son. Mecca lies in the midst of desert scenery, and lives from pilgrimage. Its present-day architecture has nothing in common with that of early Islam. Only in the case of the Kaaba itself has the original form been respected whenever it has been restored.

Gibraltar – Jabal Târiq (Târiq's Mountain)
Târiq ibn Ziyâd, a converted Muslim of – probably – Berber descent, was the Syrian Caliph's viceroy in Tangier, and directed the Islamic conquest of Spain. Although he was not to see the fruits of his military exploits, at least his name was immortalized. Gibraltar, famed in Antiquity as one of the "Pillars of Hercules", was for centuries, and remained until very recently, an important military base on the Spanish coast, controlling as it does the exit from the Mediterranean to the Atlantic Ocean.

The Expansion of Islam

The echo of the new religion was amplified many times over by the military victories which quickly ensued. Attempts have been made to present the idea of the Holy War as a rationalization of the raids and skirmishes which were the order of the day on the Arabian peninsula, and these attempts are not altogether misguided. Certainly religious motives were intermingled with economic and political calculations, giving the movement a dynamic which within a short period led to the conquest of large regions of Asia and North Africa.

The Holy War was not simply aimed at a choice between "death or the sword". The Koran accorded the "People of the Book" (*Ahl al-kitâb*) a special status as "protected persons" (*Dhimmî*); in other words, monotheists whose teaching was contained in sacred texts of revelations were permitted to continue to practise their religion in the Islamic state on payment of a special poll tax. The defeated polytheistic tribes of Arabia, then, had no choice but to be converted, but things were different as far as those peoples were concerned who before the Islamic conquest had been part of the Byzantine Empire. Here it was both simpler and more profitable to preserve the existing social and administrative structures, while at the same time collecting the tax. In the case of conversion, which – if only on economic grounds – became more and more frequent, the new Muslims (*mawlâ*, plural: *mawâlî*) would entrust themselves to, and become dependent upon, an already Islamicized Arabian tribe. This *mawlâ* relationship created a link between the rulers and the new Muslims which was to have a continuing effect for generations. And in Spain post-750 quite especially, the effects were to be far-reaching.

The Islamic expansion did not follow the rules of a centrally-planned military campaign in the modern sense. It proceeded, rather, by leaps and bounds, often being carried forward by the most recently conquered and Islamicized tribes. It directed its energies at first in a northerly and easterly direction, in other words towards Syria and Iran/Iraq. Between 640 and 642, Egypt was taken, but various subsequent expeditions towards the west achieved no lasting success at first. Only in 670 was Kairuan founded as a base in the struggle against the local Berber tribes, who were putting up a ferocious resistance. 698 saw the fall of the Byzantine city of Carthage, and from the beginning of the 8th century onwards, joint Arab and Berber armies advanced across Algeria towards Morocco. The command of these joint armies remained always in Arab hands. The newly conquered areas of the Maghreb were placed in 708 under the administration of the governor of Ifrîqiya in modern Tunisia, a Syrian named Mûsâ ibn Nusayr, who was directly responsible to the Caliph in Damascus.

From Morocco, the Muslim armies turned not towards the south, where they would have found themselves in familiar surroundings, but towards the north, which promised considerably more wealth, but could only be reached by means of a sea-crossing which at first they found very difficult.

The Conquest of Spain

In the summer of 710, a small body of men under the command of Tarîf ibn Mâlik, a Berber, landed to the west of Gibraltar, at a point later known as Tarifa. This first reconnaissance was promising, so in the following spring a 7000-strong army crossed the Straits in ships provided by the Visigothic faction headed by Akhila. This overwhelmingly Berber force was led by Târiq ibn Ziyâd, a freedman of Mûsâ ibn Nusayr, and probably

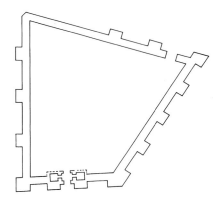

ADJACENT AND ABOVE:
Tarifa: Alcazaba with ground plan
Tarifa, a 10th-century fortress, played an important part in the defences of the south coast.

LEFT:
View from Tarifa towards the African coast

himself a Berber, though another source says he was Persian. It is from him that Gibraltar takes its name (*Jabal Târiq*, "Târiq's Mountain"). Târiq had previously been Mûsâ's representative in Tangier and was no doubt well informed about the internal problems of the disintegrating Gothic kingdom. Roderic, who at the time of Târiq's landing was away in the north fighting the Basques, hastened south immediately, where he was easily defeated on 19th July 711 near Algeciras (on the Rio Barbate) by the Islamic army in alliance with his Visigothic opponents. Following this victory, Târiq met no further organized resistance: Cordova and the Visigothic capital Toledo fell that same summer. In the summer of 712 Mûsâ ibn Nusayr himself crossed the Straits with an army of 18 000 men, consisting largely of Arabs. He occupied first Seville and its surroundings, and then Mérida. It was not until the summer of 713 that he joined up with Târiq, while his son meanwhile took Niebla and Beja. Arab sources lay some stress on Mûsâ's envy of Târiq's successes. In any case, Mûsâ made a triumphal entry into Toledo, where he took up residence in the Visigothic palace, which was famous for its wealth. The conquest of Spain proceeded the following summer with Mûsâ's advance on Oviedo via Soria and the upper Duero valley, and Târiq's campaign on the upper Ebro as far as Galicia. In the meantime, court intrigues led the Caliph to recall both Mûsâ and Târiq to Damascus to explain their conduct. Spain was left under the command of 'Abd al-'Azîz, one of Mûsâ's sons. Mûsâ himself probably ended his days in a Syrian prison, while Târiq was also last heard of in the Orient.

Under 'Abd al-'Azîz, present-day Portugal in the west and Catalonia and Narbonne in the east were also taken by the Muslim armies. Málaga, Elvira (the later Granada) and Murcia all surrendered. The treaty concluded with the Gothic Prince of Murcia is still extant: it guarantees the Goths sovereignty, freedom of worship, and economic autonomy in exchange for an annual tribute. 'Abd al-'Azîz is thought to have married Roderic's widow; he settled in Seville, where he was murdered by order of the Caliph in 716. By then, the Islamic conquest of Spain was more or less complete.

The events of the next forty years are confused. Arab sources tell of countless quarrels, skirmishes and revolts among the various groups of conquerors. These latter had come to Spain and settled there as self-contained units, so to speak; in other words, their tribal allegiances were preserved. In consequence, the population of Andalusia was extraordinarily heterogeneous; society was fragmented, and the central government was unable to enforce its authority. Southern Arabians confronted Northern Arabians (hence the famous conflict between the tribes of the Kalb and the Qays), Medinans confronted Damascenes, Berber confronted Arab. Governors followed each other in rapid succession, most remaining in office for hardly more than six months. The remoteness and isolation of Andalusia, which had no common border with any other Islamic state, made any effective intervention on the part of Damascus impossible. In spite of all this, campaigns continued to be undertaken on the eastern front during this period: from Narbonne to Avignon, and up the Rhône valley as far as Lyons; and from Pamplona via Bordeaux to Poitiers. The Battle of Poitiers and Tours of 732, in which Charles Martell inflicted a decisive

Area of Islamic influence on the Iberian peninsula

defeat on the Muslim army, figures large in French history books, which may well be justified by its importance from the Christian point of view; seen through Arab eyes, however, its significance may seem overestimated, in view of the fact that it was neither the first nor the last Arab excursion into France. Be that as it may, 751 saw the recovery of Narbonne by Pepin, effectively putting an end to Arab activity north of the Pyrenees.

Christian countermeasures on the Iberian peninsula itself took shape in Asturias under Alfonso I (739–757), from where Galicia and also parts of Old Castile roughly as far as the Duero were soon reconquered. Alfonso I did not command the necessary strength, however, to hold the depopulated areas in the south of Asturias, which remained a kind of no-man's-land between the southern fastnesses of the Asturian kingdom and the northernmost fortresses of al-Andalus. The Duero was the approximate major axis of this debatable area, which remained subject for centuries to attacks both from the north and from the south.

Earlier Christian historians discerned a direct line of descent from Al-

FOLLOWING DOUBLE PAGE:
Buitrago: north façade of the citadel
Buitrago, a picturesque fortified town on the road from Madrid to Burgos, guarded one of the most important passes of the Sierra de Guadarrama. The Muslims built a fortified town there to block any Christian invasion from the other side of the pass. After the Christian reconquest, at the end of the 11th century, Buitrago's walls were repaired, but the Islamic armies never penetrated so far to the north again. All that remains of the citadel is the outer wall with its five towers, of which several can be seen here.

27

fonso I to the fall of Granada in 1492. For them, the germ of the destruction of al-Andalus was already present in this 8th-century kingdom of Asturias and Galicia, which from the point of view of Arab historians represents no more than one border problem among many.

The Emirate

The Umayyad Family

On his death in 632, Muhammad had left neither a son nor any clear instructions regarding his successor; the first Caliphs (*khâlifa*, "deputy") were chosen, more or less smoothly, from among the Prophet's companions. In 760, Mu'âwiya, a member of one of Mecca's richest families, which had converted relatively late to Islam, succeeded in seizing power and instituting a hereditary succession. This first Muslim Umayyad dynasty governed not from Medina, but from Damascus; by 740 their Islamic empire stretched from Spain in the west to Sind (in modern Pakistan) in the east.

Religious schisms, internal Arab quarrels, social discontents, economic problems, incompetence and bloody internecine feuds all exacerbated the existing basic difficulty of governing an empire that was simply too big for any centralized authority to administer effectively. Developments in Spain from 711 to 755 demonstrate more clearly than anything else the lack of understanding in Damascus for what was taking place on the periphery.

'Abd ar-Rahmân I

In 750 the Umayyads were toppled by the Abbasids, and almost all of the family were massacred. Just one of their number managed to escape, the barely 20-year-old Abû'l-Mutarrif 'Abd ar-Rahmân bin Mu'âwiya. His mother was a Nafza-Berber from northern Morocco, which explains why young 'Abd ar-Rahmân went immediately to North Africa. After wandering aimlessly for four years, he decided to seek his fortune in Spain, where, in Jaén and Elvira, many clients (*mawâlî*) of the Umayyads had settled, after coming to the country with units of Syrian cavalry. It was to these *mawâli* that the fugitive 'Abd ar-Rahmân turned, and he succeeded in winning their support. They were soon joined by other Arab groups, as well as by Andalusian Berbers. The prestige of the old ruling family was an effective weapon in the hands of 'Abd ar-Rahmân, significantly enhancing the appreciation of his doubtless outstanding personal qualities. The inhabitants of the distant province of al-Andalus had, after all, played no part in the turbulent events in the Near East, and their loyalties still largely lay with the deposed dynasty. In any case, 'Abd ar-Rahmân was able to enforce his claims against the governor and his supporters, and in May 756 he was proclaimed Emir of al-Andalus in the Grand Mosque in Cordova.

With 'Abd ar-Rahmân as ruler, Cordova became the capital of al-Andalus. The city walls were improved, and a number of smaller mosques erected. In 784/785, 'Abd ar-Rahmân built a new Emir's Palace (*dâr al-imâra*) on the banks of the Guadalquivir, and followed this up a year later with a new Grand Mosque alongside it. 'Abd ar-Rahmân, "the Immigrant" (ad-Dâkhil), maintained a lifelong attachment to his Syrian homeland; to the north-west of Cordova he built a summer palace surrounded by gardens, which he called al-Rusâfa, after the famous Umayyad palace near Palmyra. Poems by 'Abd ar-Rahmân are extant, and his nostalgia for Syria is quite apparent in them:

> "In Rusâfa I came upon a palm;
> here in these Western lands a sight so rare,
> I said: You stand alone, like me so far from home,
> you miss the children and our loved ones there;
> you have not grown tall in native soil.
> Like you I too must breathe the alien air."[7]

Nevertheless, neither he nor a single one of his successors ever tried to reconquer their Syrian homeland.

The literature of al-Andalus is inexhaustible in its praise of 'Abd ar-Rahmân, the "Falcon of the Umayyads". It puts the following words into the mouth of Abû Dja'far al-Mansûr, the Caliph in Baghdad: "The Falcon of the Quraish is 'Abd ar-Rahmân bin Mu'âwiya; he travelled over the sea, crossed the desert, and came to a country which was not of the Arabs. Left entirely to his own resources, he founded cities, gathered troops, and organized the government. Having lost his throne here, he acquired a realm there, and all by virtue of his clever mind and his brave heart . . . 'Abd ar-Rahmân all alone – his only helper was his cause, his only friend was his will – founded the emirate of al-Andalus, he conquered border castles, he brought death to the heretics and forced reluctant tyrants to do his will."[8]

A long reign enabled him to build up a powerful, affluent and well-organized state, and thus inaugurate 200 years of cultural splendour which were later glorified as inimitable and incomparable.

The New Umayyad State

'Abd ar-Rahmân's status in the Islamic world was new, to the extent that while he made no claim to the title of Caliph, nor formed any ideological basis for his rule, he yet exercised this rule in an autonomous fashion, answerable to no one.

The problems which were to beset the new Emir of al-Andalus for the whole of his life were first and foremost those of a country which by dint of its physical geography alone did not lend itself to centralized administration. It was too varied in character, its individual regions too small. Constant insurrections on the part of the various elements in the population made the organization of an army and the establishment of a reliable civil service the *sine qua non* of internal peace.

The heterogeneity of the Andalusian population meant that conflicts were inevitable. Even within the Arab upper class, those of the first wave (the *baldiyyûn*) were ill-disposed to later arrivals, the "Syrians" (shâ-miyyûn), the latter being economically privileged. Then there were the surviving members of the Umayyad family, whom 'Abd ar-Rahmân had called from the Orient to join him in Spain. At the same time, the ancient feuding between northern and southern Arabs had by no means been set aside. The hostility between the various Arab groups was thus based partly on tribal animosity, and partly on economic and social tensions. And then came the Islamicized Berbers, who had conquered Spain together with the Arabs, but were treated by the latter as inferiors, and pushed by the Arab upper class to the poorer peripheral areas of al-Andalus. As a result, they had been forced to settle primarily in the Ebro valley, in the area around Valencia, in the southern Meseta and in the Extremadura,[9] while the Arabs reserved for themselves the major towns and the fertile valleys, the Vegas and the Huertas. But neither did the Berbers constitute a homogeneous ethnic grouping; their tribal allegiances and their traditional way of life in their North African homeland (as nomads, semi-nomads or settled farmers) all ensured that differences remained.

As for the Christian inhabitants, they largely voluntarily converted to the religion of the conquerors,[10] learned the Arabic language, adopted Arab customs, and in some cases Arabicized their names. Sarah the Goth is a famous example of the way in which the Christian aristocracy quickly adapted: a granddaughter of Wittiza, she undertook the journey from Seville to the Umayyad court of Caliph Hishâm at Damascus, where she was received with honour. There she met the young 'Abd ar-Rahmân and also married a Muslim, with whom she returned to Andalusia and whom she bore two sons. After the death of her husband, she married a dignitary in the court of 'Abd ar-Rahmân, who had meanwhile seized power in Cordova. Him too she bore a son, whose descendants were numbered among the highest Arab nobility.[11]

The group of newly-converted Muslims appear in the sources as *Musâlimûn* or *Muwalladûn* (the former being used mostly for the converts themselves, the latter for their descendants). The minority who remained Christian, known as *Musta'ribûn*, or "the Arabicized ones", (known to European history as Mozarabs), enjoyed as *dhimmîs*, like the Jews, the protection of the state authorities, and in cities like Toledo, Cordova, Seville and Mérida formed relatively large communities. By comparison with these, we know rather little about Mozarabic communities in the countryside.[12] As for the Jews, they had actively supported the Arab invasion, and they went on living for a long time under official protection in the towns and cities, where they played an important economic role as merchants. Their everyday language seems to have been Arabic, but hardly any conversions to Islam have been attested.

While this disparity led the various groups in the population frequently to fight among themselves, they also formed mutual alliances directed against the Umayyad authorities. The former military system, based on universal military service for Muslims, had long since proved inadequate, and 'Abd ar-Rahmân set about creating, on the pattern of his Syrian forebears, a slave army consisting of North African and European "infidels".

The foundations of the administrative system had been laid right at the start of the Islamic conquest, and in all probability 'Abd ar-Rahmân did not change it. Around the heartland was a broad belt of territory where no adequate supervision from Cordova was possible; this region was divided not into provinces, but into three great "marches": the "Upper March" with its capital at Saragossa, dominated by the Banû Qâsî clan, who were of Gothic descent; the "Middle March", with its capital at Toledo, and

Mérida: Alcazaba "Conventual"
This Umayyad fortress has flanking towers connected to the main wall by an arch. They were probably a later addition to the perimeter wall, but still dating from Islamic times. The masonry of the wall has a bonding typical of Umayyad building technique.

Sâmarrâ: 9th century spiral minaret
Sâmarrâ, the Abbasid Caliphs' residence on the banks of the Tigris, 125 kilometres north of Baghdad, was founded in 836. The palace city housed not only the administrative centre of the Abbasid empire, but was also an enormous army camp. The construction of more and more new buildings caused a rapid increase in size, but in 892 the Caliphs moved back to Baghdad, and Sâmarrâ quickly fell into decay.

finally the "Lower March", based on Mérida, which included Portugal and the Extremadura. These marches were ruled not by a civilian governor, or *wâlî*, but by a *qâ'id*, or "margrave". The heartland around Cordova was divided into administrative districts (*kuwar*, singular: *kûra*), each headed by a governor (*wâlî* or *'âmil*) appointed by the central government, who ruled from a district capital or *qâ'ida*. 'Abd ar-Rahmân governed from Cordova with the help of a class of civil servants, who are hardly thought worthy of special mention by contemporary Arabic sources. The senior judge (*qâdî*) and the *hâjib*, who was Treasurer and Prime Minister at the same time, played important parts in the government; the designation "vizier" (*wazîr*), applied in the Orient to the Chief Minister, was merely an honorary title in al-Andalus, and did not refer to any office in the government.[13] The ruler surrounded himself with advisers, who formed an honoured and privileged body to whom the Emir turned for advice, but was, however, in no way responsible. Nevertheless this body did without doubt acquire some importance on a change in ruler, because the first and by far the most important oath of loyalty to the claimant to the throne was taken by courtiers and family members.

All in all, the court offices in Cordova seem to have been interchangeable and relatively undefined. Military, legal, police, fiscal and other administrative functions demanded no special training, and could thus pass from one person to another. The court officials were drawn from the Arab aristocracy, and were directly responsible to the Emir, who was the sole ruler, delegating none of his power to a caste of civil servants such as developed in the Abbasid empire. In this respect, the Andalusian state was closer to the former Umayyad Syria than to the contemporary Abbasid Caliphate in Baghdad.[14]

'Abd ar-Rahmân I's Successors

In spite of regular summer campaigns against the Christians, the reign of the devout Hishâm I passed off peacefully. It was in his time that the Mâlikî school of law was introduced in al-Andalus. This encouraged the growth of a highly conservative religio-legal upper class, which gained increasingly in influence, and guarded jealously against the penetration of alien religious tendencies into al-Andalus.

Under al-Hakam I, who had trouble enforcing his claim to the Emirate, insurrections broke out in many parts of the realm: in Saragossa, Huesca, Mérida, Lisbon, and above all in Toledo, where the rebellion of the *muwalladûn* was put down in a particularly bloody and treacherous fashion, which has gone down in history as the "Day of the Ditch" of evil memory: in 797 al-Hakam is said to have invited 5000 noblemen of Toledo to a banquet of conciliation in the Alcázar, where he had them murdered and their bodies thrown in the castle ditch.

Cordova itself witnessed the celebrated "Rebellion of the Suburb": the centre of discontent was the densely populated quarter on the southern side of the Roman bridge, opposite the mosque. It flared up time and again between 805 and 818, and was finally only extinguished in the blood of the citizens. Many of those expelled on this occasion fled to Morocco, where they took an active and meritorious part in the construction of the city of Fez, their contribution being remembered even today in the name *Madînat al-Andalusiyyîn*, or "Andalusians' Quarter".

His domestic difficulties left al-Hakam virtually no time for military campaigns against his Christian neighbours. It was during his reign that Barcelona was conquered by the Franks, whose expeditions extended as far as Huesca, Lérida and Tortosa.

Historians have always seen al-Hakam as a devout and conscientious ruler, submitting to the judgements of the *qâdî* even when it was not in his interest to do so. All in all, though, he seems to have been an altogether unpopular ruler; be that as it may, it was to his brutal energy that his son and heir, 'Abd ar-Rahmân II, owed the fact that it was a united country to which he succeeded as Emir.

The time of 'Abd ar-Rahmân II was marked by relative peace and prosperity. A few revolts in outlying regions (in Toledo and Mérida) did not seriously endanger his authority, any more than did incursions by the Normans along the Tajo and the Guadalquivir. The victory over the Normans, who were seen as a danger to all, enhanced the prestige of the Emir; moreover, it led not only to the fortification of Seville, but also to the construction of arsenals, and to a certain interest in naval warfare, which had, after all, traditionally been regarded by the Arabs with suspicion. Incidentally, Andalusian pirates had long been playing a role in the Me-

Cordova: water-wheel on the Guadalquivir
These large water-wheels with movable scoops and earthenware vessels for holding the water were a common feature in large areas of the Islamic world during the Middle Ages. Some of them are still in use.

diterranean region, quite independently of the central government – for example in the Aghlabidic conquest of Sicily (Fall of Palermo, 831), and in the Islamicization of Crete (825/26–960/61).

Vis-à-vis the petty principalities of North Africa, 'Abd ar-Rahmân II posed so to speak as their protector against powerful neighbours. Thus friendly relations are attested with the Rustumids of Tahert and the Sali-hids of the Riff, with their capital at Nakur. The fact that a Byzantine delegation arrived in Cordova to persuade al-Andalus to join in an invasion of Abbasid Iraq proves that the country had become a player on the world stage. The Emir's negative reply, while documenting the irreconcilable hatred felt by the Umayyads towards the Abbasid dynasty, at the same time demonstrates his wise appreciation of the art of the possible.

In spite of the political enmity between al-Andalus and the Abbasid Caliphate, cultural relations between the eastern and western branches of Islam were nonetheless intensive, and there was admiration in Cordova for the court of Baghdad and Sâmarrâ. The much-quoted Iraqi singer Ziryâb, a Persian freedman of the Abbasid Caliph al-Mahdî, who had come to Cordova from the court of Baghdad, was a veritable *arbiter elegantiarum* at the court of 'Abd ar-Rahmân II. He not only introduced new musical instruments and a new form of musical notation, but also new culinary recipes, new table manners, new hair styles, new fashions in dress, new fabrics, as well as the game of chess.[15] This period also witnessed the diffusion of other Persian customs in Andalusia, namely the celebration of the New Year and the Summer Solstice (a festival later subsumed in Spain under the Feast of St John the Baptist), and, above all, the game of polo.

To 'Abd ar-Rahmân II is ascribed the establishment of the first princely monopoly over the minting of coinage, as well as over the manufacture of luxury fabrics (following the example of Byzantium and Baghdad), and, in addition, the streamlining of the administrative machine.[16] It was during this period too that court protocol took on an oriental aspect, becoming more formal, more rigid and more sumptuous, leading to an increasing distance between prince and people. Slaves, among them numerous eunuchs, came to play an increasingly important role in court affairs.

Periods of Crisis (852–912)

The following sixty years constituted a period of dangerous crises for the Umayyad Emirate. On the occasion of the succession of Muhammad I, the Mozarabs and Muwalladûn, always ready to revolt, staged an insurrection. In the Upper Marches (Tudela and Saragossa), the independence campaign of Mûsâ ibn Mûsâ ibn al-Qâsî assumed dangerous proportions, while in the Lower Marches (Mérida, Badajoz) it was Ibn Marwân ibn al-Jillîqî (likewise a Muwallad) who liberated himself from the authority of Cordova. In Seville, Elvira and Almería, the leading families also sought to resist the claims of the Umayyad court. Most dangerous of all, and also the most celebrated, was the rebellion of 'Umar ibn Hafsûn in the heart of Andalusia. The inaccessible mountain districts to the south, between Ronda and Antequera, were inhabited by Berbers and Muwalladûn, in other words by socially and economically subjugated sections of society, who followed the events in the Marches with interest, and drew from them the courage to pursue their own campaign for independence. In 'Umar ibn Hafsûn they had at the same time a leader who was not only courageous and ambitious, but also up to the part.

'Umar ibn Hafsûn was a scion of a prosperous Muwallad family from the vicinity of Ronda. Having been guilty in his youth of an act of manslaughter, he was banished. His exile took him to Tâhert, in present-day Algeria, where he worked in an Andalusian tailor's workshop. Here he was recognized by another Andalusian, who prophesied a dazzling future for him. Thereupon (in 850 or thereabouts) 'Umar returned, and began to gather a band of adherents (mostly ruffians at first, we may assume), and to undermine the region's security. The rebels set up their headquarters in Bobastro, on an inaccessible mountain fastness.[17] In the year 883, Muhammad I sent the commander-in-chief of the army on an expedition against Bobastro; he succeeded in defeating Ibn Hafsûn and bringing him back to Cordova, where at first he served as an officer in the Emir's army, taking part in a summer campaign in the north. However, it was not long before he fled back to the mountains once more, from where he started his raiding activities again. He was supported by the Muwalladûn, the Mozarabs and the Berbers, in short, by all the disaffected groups. At first fortune smiled upon him, his power increased, and Bobastro grew into a proper town, with its own palace, church and mosque. Success made him all the more ambitious, and he evolved into a sort of sole ruler in the area between Cordova and the Mediterranean. He even instituted direct negotiations with the North African enemies of the Umayyads. He allied himself, albeit never for more than a short period at any one time, with the various rebel leaders in Andalusia, and occasionally even with the ruler in Cordova. All in all, his policy seems to have been dictated by the existing situation on the ground rather than by any long-term political goal or by any coherent ideology. For reasons unknown, he converted to Christianity in 899 along with his wife and children; politically, this was undoubtedly a mistake, as it caused many Muslims to desert him, thus weakening his position considerably. Even so, he managed to hold Bobastro until his death in 917, and it was only under 'Abd ar-Rahmân III that the revolt was finally suppressed, and Bobastro itself taken (927/29).

Typical of all these independence movements was the solidarity of Christians and Muslims. The leading families in the Marches, who all had strong ties of blood and affinity to their Christian neighbours, carried on wars in alliance with Christians or Muslims, and against Christians or Muslims, as circumstances dictated. Ibn Hafsûn's life-story is characterized by just such continually shifting alliances, in which religion can hardly ever have been a decisive factor. All this leads us to the conclusion that the chief motives for action in 9th-century Andalusia sprang not from religion, but from economic, political and social factors, or considerations of family interest.

The Architecture of the 8th and 9th Centuries

The Foundation of the Great Mosque at Cordova

It is difficult to ascribe any specific buildings to the period of the conquest. The first Arab and Berber tribes to arrive in Iberia seem to have contented themselves with what they found already standing, undoubtedly spending more time on military campaigns than on construction projects. Even so, the earliest Spanish mosques are said to have appeared in Saragossa and Elvira before the year 720.[18] Seville, the Arab conquerors' first capital, possessed a mosque whose *mihrâb* is documented in written sources.[19] Cordova too must have had its Friday mosque: the sources are explicit that it was here that 'Abd ar-Rahmân I had himself proclaimed Amîr al-Andalus in 756. Fortresses are also said to have been erected, but from today's perspective it is impossible to be precise about the 8th-century dating of any particular building. In Cordova, the massive Roman bridge across the Guadalquivir was renovated as early as 719/20, as were the city walls; however, both have undergone such frequent subsequent restoration that it is impossible to be precise here either.

The Friday mosque in Algeciras, the renovation and alteration of the Visigothic palace in Cordova, the erection of various smaller mosques in the capital, and the building of a *munya* or garden palace nearby – all these projects are attributed to 'Abd ar-Rahmân I in written sources, but none can be identified today.[20]

The oldest building which we really know to any extent is simultaneously a masterpiece, a high point of architectural achievement: namely the Great Mosque in Cordova, a building which sets the standard for all other sacred architecture in Andalusia. Over the centuries it has undergone numerous alterations, but every Islamic extension respected the spirit of the original building, so that it is possible to state without exaggeration that 'Abd ar-Rahmân I's personal taste has left its mark on Hispano-Moorish architecture as a whole.

'Abd ar-Rahmân I contented himself for a long period with the old Friday mosque (possibly a former Christian church), which occupied the site of what was to become the western section of the subsequent Great Mosque. It was not until he had moved into the renovated palace on the banks of the Guadalquivir that the Emir decided on a new building. It is said that he bought the rest of the church complex from the Christian congregation for the purpose;[21] it lay directly adjacent to the palace, and part of it had

Cordova: south side of the Great Mosque
In the foreground is the Guadalquivir with the (often restored) Roman bridge and the remains of a water-mill. From the outside the low mosque is totally dominated by the Cathedral, which was built on to, and into, the mosque in the 16th century.

39

already served as a mosque. It was here that the new Great Mosque was to be built. Among 'Abd ar-Rahmân's motives were doubtless not only artistic creativity but also the desire for a prestigious monument to proclaim the presence of the dynasty; on a more mundane level, the rapid growth in the city's population made the building of a new Friday mosque imperative.

The Friday mosque was the most important building in an Islamic city; every adult male believer was required to repair to it every Friday at noon for the service, when the ruler or his deputy would preach the sermon, whose contents were political as well as religious. The ruler's name, moreover, was mentioned in the Friday prayers, which thus took on some of the character of a political proclamation. So it is that the Friday mosque became the outward manifestation of the dynasty, the monumental self-presentation of a ruler at once both spiritual and temporal, who used the Friday service to maintain direct contact with his people. The imposing architectural ensemble of Friday mosque and emir's palace form one of the constants of the Islamic city from its origins in the Near East; the only remarkable circumstance in the present case is that apparently an analogous pair of buildings was already present on the same site in Cordova in Visigothic times.

'Abd ar-Rahmân I's mosque was completed in a single year between 785/86 and 786/87; the short construction period was only possible because numerous Roman and Visigothic remains were available for re-use *in situ*, and because booty from the successful Narbonne campaign had provided the necessary funds.[22] The building was square in plan and not particularly large, measuring some 74 metres along each side. It consisted of an open courtyard and a prayer hall; the east and west walls of the latter, which measured approximately 37 metres from front to back, were supported by four massive buttresses, of which the two southernmost, at the junction with the *qibla* wall, formed veritable corner towers. (We are no longer in a position to reconstruct the buttresses of the original south wall.) Of the four entrances to the mosque, one was on the *mihrâb* axis in the north wall of the courtyard, there was one each on the east and west sides of the courtyard, while the fourth was in the middle of the west front of the prayer hall. This last was known as the "Bâb al-Wuzâra'" or "Ministers' Gate", as it allowed the court officials direct access to the prayer hall from the palace opposite.

The prayer hall itself consisted of eleven naves (or a nave and ten aisles) perpendicular to the *qibla* wall, each consisting of twelve bays. The two outermost aisles were narrower than the rest, and the assumption is that they were divided off by grilles and reserved for the use of the womenfolk. The central nave by contrast was broader than any of the others, and thus the *mihrâb* gave the whole building its main axial orientation, right down to the north gate in the courtyard. This basilica plan quite certainly bears no direct relationship to the churches already present in the city, but is rather a restatement of one of the most important shrines of the Islamic world, namely the al-Aqsâ mosque in Jerusalem.

The two-tiered arcades in the prayer hall represent a unique and ingenious solution to the problem of how to create a lofty interior space in spite of the limited dimensions of the existing fabric of Roman and Visi-

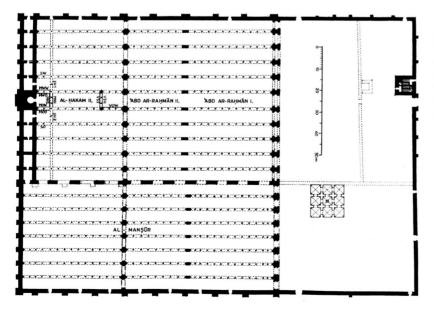

Cordova: Great Mosque, aerial view from the north-east

The contrast between the extensive mosque complex and the small houses round about is characteristic of all medieval Islamic cities, where squares and monumental secular architecture were unknown, and whose most important public building was the Friday mosque.

Cordova: reconstruction of the ground plan of the Mosque (Ewert)

Cordova: Great Mosque, Stephen's Gate
The former Gate of the Viziers is the oldest surviving gate in the whole complex. It goes back to
the original foundation, and the arrangement of
its decorative elements set the standard for all
subsequent gates.

gothic origin. The capital of every column is surmounted by a heavy impost, forming the base for a relatively massive pillar which extends the
column below, while supporting a further arcade, which in turn bears the
weight of the roof. The imposts also support the arches of the lower arcade, which fulfil the statically necessary function of tension beams found
in all the larger arcaded mosques. The lower arches are horseshoe-shaped,
while the upper, more massive ones are semicircular. Both sets of arches
consist of yellow stone voussoirs alternating with red brick. This alternation is common both in Umayyad Syria and in pre-Islamic Spain, and there
is thus no need to see in it – as is often done – an Umayyad import from
the Near East. The two-tiered arcade can be seen in a far more simple form
in Umayyad architecture in Syria, thus for example in the Great Mosque
in Damascus, in the al-Aqsâ mosque and in one of the palaces in 'Anjar.
Perhaps there, and in Cordova too, the idea was simply borrowed from
existing Roman aqueducts; be that as it may, the architect in Cordova
added a truly creative touch to the Roman model. As for the origin of the

horseshoe arch, the characteristic arch form of Andalusia, much has been said and written. While it was unusual in the Near East in pre-Umayyad times, it was not unknown; it appears in a very discreet form, also, in the Umayyad mosque in Damascus; by contrast, its appearance in the Visigothic architecture of Spain is quite frequent. Although the Germanic version is less sophisticated than that employed by the Arabs – being flatter, and less pinched at the bottom – there is still a perfectly good case for saying that local styles were developed here, without the need for assuming a Syrian import.[23]

The *mihrâb* of the original mosque has not been preserved; however, what is now known as the "Stephen's Gate" (the "Bâb al-Wuzâra'") dates in large measure from the first building phase. As the later *mihrâb*, like all the subsequent gates, borrowed and drew upon the vocabulary of forms evident in the Stephen's Gate, one may reasonably assume that the original *mihrâb* followed the same pattern. The tripartite vertical division into a gateway proper and two flanking façades, together with the two-storey arrangement, provide the basic thematic elements. The gateway itself has a flat top, surmounted by a horseshoe arch within an *alfiz*. The line of script accompanying the arch of the tympanum crosses the latter and emphasizes the horizontal effect of the lintel. The voussoirs of the arch alternate as in the prayer hall; their vegetal ornamentation was probably added during the restoration of 855/56, as the inscription on the tympanum makes reference to Muhammad I.

The niches of the blind arcade on the upper storey of the central zone, the areas between with their vegetal ornamentation, the projecting ledge above, resting on nine consoles with a kind of involute leaf pattern, the four-step battlements on the wall – these are all motifs which appear here for the first time, and henceforth have their place in the standard Hispano-Umayyad inventory of forms. The motifs associated with the lateral zones were also destined to become standard: thus the pommel-like roundels in the upper spandrel fields already point the way to Andalusian spandrel decoration of later periods; the battlement motif of the two incised rectan-

Jerusalem: the al-Aqsâ Mosque, dating from the early 8th century

The al-Aqsâ Mosque is one of the most important Umayyad mosques in the Near East; it served as a model for the Cordova mosque in many ways.

ABOVE:
View of the nave from the north

ADJACENT:
The façade and the narthex were added at a much later date, but the raised roof of the nave can be seen, as can the dome over the bay in front of the *mihrâb*, both of which features go back to the original Umayyad building.

gular areas, and above all the vegetal ornamentation creeping over the whole ensemble – both imports from the Near East of Umayyad and pre-Umayyad times – were to become part of the standard inventory of decorative motifs in Andalusian architecture from then on.

For all that, it should be noted that the vegetal ornamentation was not simply taken over from the Near East. There was already such a tradition in Spain itself, dating from Ibero-Roman and Visigothic days. The vegetal decor that we see here is specifically Spanish, and cannot be mistaken for anything from the Near East. In many respects it strongly resembles Visigothic forms, although generally superior in the matter of craftsmanship.

The walls are constructed of light-coloured ashlar blocks. The west wall of the prayer hall – medium-sized blocks in regular layers with occasional headers – is informative as to the building practices of the time. Bricks were used only for the red sections of the arches; wood had an important role, the nave and aisles originally being covered with painted wooden shingles, some of which have been discovered. The nave and aisles each have their own pitched roof, the lightweight frame being covered with tiles. In common with every other mosque of this period, 'Abd ar-Rahmân quite definitely had no minaret.

The personal taste of 'Abd ar-Rahmân I, the "Immigrant", was quite evidently steeped in the building traditions of the Near East. Was he himself the architect of his mosque, or did he send for a master-builder from Syria? This question is difficult to answer: According to the written sources his personal contribution was considerable, a view supported by Islamic tradition. Among the craftsmen employed on the project there were undoubtedly Syrians as well as native Iberians. While it is true that Syrian influences have always been emphasized, the part played by Visigothic and late Roman local traditions should not be underestimated. The incorporation of pre-Islamic Spanish columns and capitals in the dynasty's most prestigious building project is clear evidence of the Umayyads' admiration of this heritage, an admiration shared not only by 'Abd ar-Rahmân I but by his most celebrated successors too.

Damascus: the Great Mosque of the Umayyads, c. 715

ABOVE:
Marble grille
ADJACENT:
View of the mosque from the south-west

Few buildings dating from the period immediately following the foundation of the Great Mosque are known today. Hishâm I had improvements carried out to the bridge at Cordova, and he also had a shelter built on the roof of the Great Mosque, accessible by a staircase, from which the muezzin could issue the call to prayers five times each day.[24] The next ruler to interest himself in building projects was 'Abd ar-Rahmân II, whose reign was marked by a period of prosperity and a flurry of building activity: the foundation of the town of Murcia, the construction of the Alcázar in Mérida, the restoration and construction of city walls, aqueducts and palaces in Seville and more especially in Cordova, the erection of a new Friday mosque in Jaén, the extension of the existing Friday mosques in Seville and Cordova. The minaret of another mosque in Cordova, later St John's Church, also appears to date from this period. The mosque built in Pechina has not survived. The second half of the 9th century witnessed the building of the mosque in Tudela and the mountain fortress of Bobastro, the former by a rival of the Umayyads, Mûsâ ibn Mûsâ al-Qâsî, and the latter by an arch-enemy of the dynasty, Ibn Hafsûn.

The extension of the Friday mosque in Cordova under 'Abd ar-Rahmân II bears witness to the prosperity of the Umayyad capital, whose population had seen a substantial increase since the time of 'Abd ar-Rahmân I. The *qibla* wall was now moved eight bays to the south. Of the old *qibla* wall, ten pillars were left standing to take the thrust of the extended arcades. The prayer hall was now 64 metres from front to back as a result, and thus practically square. 'Abd ar-Rahmân II made no basic changes to his great-grandfather's building scheme: he too used such fabric of previous buildings as still remained, and continued the *leitmotif* of the central nave perpendicular to the *qibla* wall, set off by the decor and in particular by the capitals, just as 'Abd ar-Rahmân I had set out to do. Patrice Cressier[25] and Christian Ewert[26] have succeeded in showing that, from the very first building phase, the capitals played a major role in imposing a hierarchical structure on the individual elements of the prayer hall. Thus the central nave formed the unambiguous axis of symmetry for the distribution of capital types throughout the building right from the very beginning; in this scheme of things, however, it was not Roman remains that were preferred for the nave and the *qibla* wall, but rather Visigothic (at first) and then, under 'Abd ar-Rahmân II, Islamic copies of Roman and Corinthian patterns, the design of which, however, did not keep strictly to classical models.

The individuality of the architectural sculpture of the Emirate of Cordova in matters of style and craftsmanship is best seen in these capitals, and best of all in those still extant in the older parts of the Great Mosque, alongside numerous others whose provenance is not always clear. Many of them are remarkable for their technical quality and their zealous fidelity to the classical models which had been forced into the background during the Visigothic period. Other capitals from the days of the Emirs, while retaining the compositional structure of the Roman forebears, betray the far hastier techniques of the Visigoths in their surface treatment. Yet another, technically fairly heterogeneous group copies a particular, relatively

Cordova: Great Mosque, window grille
The window grille with its motif of interlocking circles is in the façade of the Stephen's Gate.

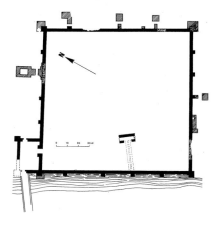

Mérida: river wall of the Conventual; ground plan (L. Torres Balbás)
The Arab fortress was built on top of Roman remains. In the foreground is the Guadiana.

infrequent Roman model featuring three acanthus crowns. All in all, the capitals of the Emirate period are distinctive for their uninterrupted vitality, their wealth of detail and their imaginativeness. In their technical quality and variety of forms they are far superior to Visigothic production. In view of the large debt which these capitals owe classical antiquity, many attempts have been made to discover possible Syrio-Umayyad traditions underlying them. However, although the Near East of the 8th century witnessed a return to older classical forms which seem to have fallen into oblivion in the centuries immediately preceding,[27] there is nothing in the field of capital art which is really comparable to that found in Andalusia.

Seville and Mérida

The Umayyad Great Mosque of Seville was perhaps enlarged under 'Abd ar-Rahmân II, and he may even have been responsible for its construction (as stated on a monumental inscription, dating from 830, now in the city's museum). Its site is now occupied by the Church of the Holy Saviour. Written sources indicate that it, like the Friday mosque in Cordova, con-

Roman cistern in the Alcázar in Mérida
The installations were maintained and used by
the Visigoths and the Muslims.

sisted of eleven naves running perpendicular to the *qibla* wall, the central one being higher than the others – this last feature again typical of Umayyad architecture in Syria. The naves were divided by arcades supported on columns cannibalized from ancient buildings. The building is said to have been almost 50 metres broad and considerably more from front to back. The present-day church tower incorporates only the lower portion of the former minaret, which was situated on the north side of the courtyard opposite the central nave; it was square in plan, measuring 5.88 metres along each side.[28] It consisted of a number of storeys, and was provided with twin windows. A spiral staircase led to the upper gallery. The mosque was seriously damaged by the Normans in 844, but restored; however, during the 12th century a new Great Mosque arose in the south of the city (the site of which is now occupied by the Cathedral).

The old and prosperous city of Mérida was a centre of regular unrest, due not least to its situation close to the frontier. In 828 matters came to a head with the outbreak of a revolt led by a Muwallad (Sulaymân ibn Martín) and a Berber (Mahmûd ibn 'Abd al-Jabbâr), which was given active support by Asturias and was only suppressed after years of protracted fighting. 'Abd ar-Rahmân II's response was to raze the city walls and erect a fortress (according to its inscription, a "hisn") at the head of the massive Roman bridge across the Guadiana; as a result, the city was effectively sealed.

The ground plan of this fortress – known since the Christian Reconquest as "el Conventual", as it was taken over by the Knights of Santiago – is rectangular in form, measuring 132 metres by 137. The riverside wall, with its buttresses, was built on the remains of the Roman city wall, and much Roman stonework was re-used in the fortress as a whole. The rectangular towers are built on to the outside of, and are only slightly higher than, the wall, and spaced at equal intervals along it. The gateway is not placed centrally in one of the façades, but at the west end of the north side, in a forecourt, a kind of barbican, which also encloses the bridgehead and the city gate. All in all, this structure follows the usual pattern of Byzantine fortresses in North Africa, with its regular ground plan, its rectangular external towers, its reinforced corner bastions and the narrow entrance between two towers.[29] Of the interior of the Arab palace very little remains; as early as the 12th century, contemporary sources[30] report it as being in a seriously dilapidated condition. Within the fortress there is a large cistern fed from the Guadiana; it is of Roman date, but probably continued in use under the Visigoths, while the Umayyads decorated it by using Visigothic marble slabs as door posts. Recent excavations have revealed, within the walls of the fortress, a Roman villa whose occupants were clearly wealthy, and it may be assumed that the Umayyads made good use of the remains.

Under the Romans and the Visigoths, Mérida was a city of extraordinary prosperity and importance. Even today, its Roman remains – temple, theatre, amphitheatre, circus, bridge and aqueduct – are extremely impressive. By contrast, the Islamic legacy in Mérida is of no particular note, although it does bear witness to the determination of the Umayyad rulers to enforce their authority on the ancient cities and to use their monuments for their own purposes as far as possible.

Bobastro rises proudly on a lonely hilltop high over the course of the River Guadalhorce, in what is an altogether impregnable position.[31] 'Umar ibn Hafsûn's building activities probably began during the 880s, and it is possible that the few ashlar blocks that are all that survive of the citadel date from this period.[32] The external walls of the rectangular fortress seem in part to grow out of the very rock. A few fortified towers, square in plan, are recognizable, and within the walls there are still the foundations of various buildings, all dominated by an imposing complex at the highest point of the plateau. The layers of ashlars are interspersed frequently, but at irregular intervals, with headers, so that they remind one of the masonry techniques which are the hallmark of the architecture of the Caliphate. However, this "Caliphate" technique, while widespread in the 10th century, is also documented at an earlier period, and thus cannot be regarded as a reliable dating criterion. Below the circumference walls, totally undatable cave dwellings have been chiselled out of the cliff. Lower down still, and again outside the fortified area, a church has been carved out of the cliff; this can be dated with some degree of assurance to the period between the conversion (899) and the death (917) of Ibn Hafsûn. With its nave and two aisles divided by arcades and pillars, its transept, its deep apse with a chapel and its two side chapels, it accords perfectly well with the usual type of Mozarabic church building;[33] what is extraordinary is the way it is built and the different floor levels of the various parts. The arches, which are of a pronounced horseshoe shape, together with the masonry technique of the citadel itself, demonstrate clearly enough how the influence of Cordova spread to the furthest corners of Andalusia.

Vitality And Richness of Form

No general assessment of the architecture of the Emirate period can deny its powerful vitality and its richness of form. The legacy of classical antiquity has seeped into it through several and various channels, without

Bobastro
The town occupied an imposing position on an isolated hilltop. The remains of the foundations of various buildings are still to be seen on the plateau, among them what appear to be a mosque and a palace. Below the circumference wall, cave dwellings have been carved into the cliff face.

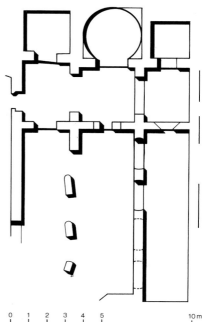

Bobastro: church; groundplan (C. de Mergelina) Outside the fortified area is a church which Ibn Hafsûn probably had hewn out of the cliff after his conversion to Christianity. With its nave and two aisles separated by arches supported on piers, its transept, its low chapel in the apse and its two side chapels, it accords very well with the usual Mozarabic church design. The method of construction, however, is unique. The very pronounced horseshoe shape of the arches bears witness to the spread of the influence of Cordova into the very remotest corners of Andalusia.

however becoming totally fused with it. We have no information about the organization of major building projects or about the commissioning of craftsmen; we do not know whether we should imagine Syrians and Iberians building and carving side by side, or whether particular tasks were allocated to particular homogeneous groups, family workshops, for example. The individuality of the ornamentation typical of this period does however indicate that, while no autonomous, unmistakable vocabulary of forms had yet taken shape, a characteristic stylistic purpose was nevertheless at work from the very start, seeking to put its own stamp on the various borrowings and adaptations. This stylistic purpose, which actually emanated only from one dynasty – the Spanish Umayyads – and one city – Cordova – was nevertheless intense enough to penetrate the strongholds of its creators' foes.

912-1031

A Golden Age: The Caliphate

'Abd ar-Rahmân III (912–961)

At the age of 21, 'Abd ar-Rahmân III became Emir of al-Andalus. Shortly after his birth, his father, Crown Prince Muhammad, had been murdered on the orders of *his* father, Emir 'Abd Allâh, who had used the same means to remove a number of would-be candidates for the throne, and finally designated his grandson as his heir in preference to any of his surviving sons. Like most of the Spanish Umayyads, 'Abd ar-Rahmân III, fair-haired and blue-eyed, had just as much European as Arab blood in his veins, his mother having been a Frankish or Basque prisoner-of-war, and his grand-mother a Basque princess.

Arab chronicles ascribe every imaginable physical, intellectual and moral quality to him: strength and skill, courage and decisiveness, intelligence and culture, kindness and magnanimity (although it must be said that the same sources tell of decisions of merciless cruelty, for example the death sentence passed on his son 'Abd Allâh). The depth of his devoutness is difficult to plumb, but there can be no doubt about his religious toleration.

The historian and vizier Ibn al-Khatib wrote of him: "It is said that when 'Abd ar-Rahmân took over the reins of government, al-Andalus was a glowing coal,* a spluttering fire;* with overt and covert resistance* seething between its borders.* Through his fortunate hand* and strong power, God pacified the country.* So it is that people compare the third 'Abd ar-Rahmân with the first: he tamed rebels (as they appeared);* he built castles, he planted cultures and immortalized his name.* He bled the unbelievers, until in al-Andalus no enemy was left, no rival raised his banner.* The peoples submitted to his law,* and accepted his peace.*"[34] (The line division of the original text is here indicated by a *.)

When 'Abd ar-Rahmân III took up his office, the country was in a difficult situation both at home and abroad. His first goal, and one which he pursued with unflagging vigour, was to restore internal unity. For this, he required some twenty years. It took years, too, to secure the country's external borders, but by around the year 960, the suzerainty of 'Abd ar-Rahmân was recognized by the princes of Asturias-León, Castile, Navarre and Barcelona, recognition being confirmed by regular payments of tribute. All the same, 'Abd ar-Rahmân made no attempt to conquer these independent Christian states to the north; the phase of the jihad and of territorial expansion was definitively over. In fact, the jihad had never been

a significant element in the propaganda of the Hispano-Umayyad rulers; struggle against the Christians was regarded as a political necessity, but never as one of the foundations of the structure of authority.

In North Africa, the Fatimid schismatics had been gaining more and more ground. In 909, 'Ubayd Allâh, the leader of the movement in Tunisia, had assumed the title of Caliph. His explicit claim to universal authority in the Islamic world, coupled with his worldwide and effective propaganda system, must undoubtedly have appeared to the Umayyad dynasty in Andalusia as a threatening development. Indeed, Ibn Hafsûn had quite obviously viewed the situation in these terms when he sought to create an alliance with the Fatimids in 909. A number of campaigns were required in order to preserve the Umayyads' North African sphere of influence, which extended approximately from Sijilmâsa to Algiers. 'Abd ar-Rahmân III sought on principle to exert influence indirectly rather than through direct military intervention. One of his last campaigns led to the capture of Ceuta (931) and Tangier (951), thus substantially strengthening the Umayyad position in North Africa. These two towns were both ruled directly from Cordova; with the remainder of its North African territories, 'Abd ar-Rahmân maintained a more or less reliable vassal relationship, about whose uncertain character, however, he was under no illusions.

The establishment of the Fatimid Caliphate was the decisive factor behind 'Abd ar-Rahmân III's resolve to assume the title of Caliph himself, in other words to have himself proclaimed the successor (*khalifa*) of the Prophet and commander-in-chief of the faithful (*amîr al-mu'minîn*). From the death of the Prophet until 909, this title had been universal in character, and, in theory at least, it had only ever been possible to have one rightful Caliph in the Islamic world at one time. It was not for religious motives that 'Abd ar-Rahmân assumed the title; he did not claim for his family the right to exclusive authority over the Islamic community, nor did his assumption of the title constitute a declaration of war against the Abbasid dynasty in Baghdad; his sole object was official confirmation of the power and importance of the Andalusian empire. At the same time he took up an oriental custom which the Abbasids had long since adopted, namely to assume the royal throne-name (*laqab*) of al-Nâsir li-Dîn Allâh, which translates approximately as "victorious fighter for the religion of God". For all that, the decision did not lead to any clearly defined ideology of authority with a specific programme of action: for instance, the reconquest of the Holy Cities (Mecca and Medina), without possession of which the whole idea of the Caliphate was in truth unthinkable, was never contemplated.

In various respects, court etiquette became more oriental and more formal during the latter years of 'Abd ar-Rahmân III's rule; it developed into a barrier, albeit a sumptuous one, between the subjects and a ruler who resided in an inaccessible palace surrounded by court lackeys, with no longer any direct contact with the people. But in this respect too, he was only following what had long been Abbasid practice in Baghdad.

PREVIOUS DOUBLE PAGE
Madînat al-Zahrâ': Salón Rico
The "Rich Hall" is one of the most splendid halls in the whole city, and is presumed to be 'Abd ar-Rahmân III's main reception hall. Monumental inscriptions indicate that it was built between 953 and 957. Like the "Great West Hall" it has a transverse passage in front of five longitudinal "naves", the two outer ones being divided off from the three inner. The polychromatic effect was achieved not only through the use of differently-coloured building materials, but also by painting. The Salón Rico has been largely reconstructed.

'Abd ar-Rahmân III's eldest son, al-Hakam II, had been designated heir to the throne at any early stage, but he was 46 before he finally came to power, and he was Caliph for only fifteen years. He is depicted as cultured and peaceable, as a generous lover of the arts (with a particular interest in the works of Antiquity), a noteworthy commissioner of new buildings, and at the same time a deeply religious man well versed in theology and law. "His name is uttered in one breath with strength and splendour,* with nobility and scholarship,* immortal works,* fine achievements his greatness*."[35] He continued the domestic and foreign policy of his father, albeit without the latter's energy, and he had the undisputed tendency to leave the affairs of state in the hands of his officials. Even so, he was able to repel a Norman attack by Almería, and subsequently enlarged his fleet. Arab historians are at pains to emphasize his building activities, and even today his name is linked to the construction of the new royal city of Madînat al-Zahrâ' and with the extension and beautification of the Great Mosque in Cordova.

Al-Hakam had just one son, born of a Basque mother when he was already of advanced age. This son, Hishâm, took the oath of loyalty from his father at the age of eleven, shortly before the latter's death. The child's investiture as Caliph met with resistance, and it was only with difficulty that his mother and her close associates managed to have him recognized. There was another Umayyad faction seeking to put a brother of al-Hakam's, al-Mughîra, on the throne; he was quickly incarcerated by his opponents, however, and murdered not long afterwards. The golden age of the dynasty was at an end, and with it the golden age of the city of Cordova.

The 'Âmirids

Hishâm was incompetent, effeminate and a pawn in the hands of his mother and his guardian Ibn Abî 'Âmir, who soon appropriated for himself the office of *hâjib*, the highest in the country. Ibn Abî 'Âmir was a scion of a land-owning family from the vicinity of Algeciras; he had the advantage of a thorough legal training, and his ambitions were far-reaching. In the sources he comes across as intelligent and energetic, and at the same time totally lacking in scruple. His close relationship with Hishâm's mother (it is said that they were lovers) and with the conservative legal profession in Cordova were the foundations of his rapid rise to power. In order to secure the favour of this influential community, Ibn Abî 'Âmir went so far as to have the books in al-Hakam II's library which they judged heretical (in particular the scientific works) publicly burned.

In 981 the *hâjib* transferred the seat of government from the Umayyad Alcázar to his own newly-built palace in al-Madîna al-Zâhira, thus demonstrating in no uncertain terms where power really lay. Of all the prerogatives of the Caliph, Hishâm was left merely with the right to have his name mentioned in Friday prayers and stamped on the coinage. Ibn Abî 'Amir also assumed a ceremonial name, al-Mansûr billâh, "Victorious through God", and it is under the name of "Almanzor" that he appears in Christian legend. In spite of his ambitions, Ibn Abî 'Âmir never usurped

Cordova: Great Mosque, Puerta St Catalina, detail
The 16th century relief coat-of-arms depicts 'Abd ar-Rahmân's minaret before it was converted into a church tower.

the title of Caliph. He managed to pass on his status in 1002 to his son 'Abd al-Malik, who, however, governed for only eight years. Under the first two Amirids, successful campaigns were conducted both against the Christians in Spain and in North Africa, and the prestige of Umayyad Andalusia seemed, at least from a distance, to be unimpaired. 'Abd al-Malik was succeeded by his incompetent younger brother 'Abd ar-Rahmân, who was totally out of touch with reality, starting his similarly brief career by demanding to succeed to the Caliphate. This third representative of the Amirids was murdered in 1008 after an unsuccessful military campaign.

There followed a long period of confusion and internecine war. Hishâm the Caliph was totally unable to enforce his authority, and was forced to abdicate in 1009, unleashing a struggle between numerous pretenders to the throne and plunging the Umayyad empire into bloody wars. At the same time local independence movements sprang up all over Andalusia once more; they had, after all, never really disappeared. Every major city suddenly witnessed the appearance of some aristocratic family which aimed either to sweep away the authority of the pseudo-caliph, or else to set their own candidate on the throne. In 1031 a group of citizens in Cordova decided there and then to do away with the caliphate altogether, and inaugurated a sort of government by municipal council, which of course only carried weight in the city itself and its immediate surroundings.

Thus was inaugurated what has gone down in history as the "rule of the petty kings" (*mulûk al-tawâ'if*), which lasted until the take-over by the North African Almoravid dynasty.

Andalusia at its Zenith

During the 10th century, Islamic Spain was, economically and intellectually, way ahead of the rest of Europe. Its wealth was based on an agriculture which, by means of artificial irrigation systems, exploited the country's potential to the full, on the region's natural resources, and on an unprecedented urban prosperity, where trade and crafts could flourish, so long as order and security prevailed.

The various sections of the population were at least to a certain extent fused into a single unit. The leading role was taken by the Arab nobility, whose language, religion and culture had, so to speak, achieved official status. As for the Muwalladûn, they were Iberians who in many cases (though by no means all) had dreamt up imaginary Arab genealogies for themselves. In view of the fact, however, that the Arabs often took Iberian wives, the two groups had in any case drawn closer together. The Muwalladûn had no corresponding Iberian values to set up against the "national pride" of the Arabs, but aimed rather at recognition and integration through assimilation. The anti-Arab Muwallad rebellions were not motivated by any nationalistic considerations; their motivation was, rather, economic and social.

The Christians, or Mozarabs, spoke – at least in the towns – not only proto-Spanish, but in most cases also Arabic, which was often better than their Latin. Their thought-patterns and way of life underwent lasting Arab influence. Thus the convinced Christian Alvaro of Cordova was already complaining in the 9th century that his co-believers preferred to read

Cordova: Great Mosque, detail of a side-porch dating from the time of al-Hakam II

Cordova: forest of columns in the Great Mosque

Arabic poems and romances rather than the works of the Church Fathers, and that they studied the Muslim theologians and philosophers, not to refute them, but in order to acquire a cultured Arabic style: "Oh, the pain and the sorrow! The Christians have even forgotten their own language, and in every thousand you will not find one who can write a letter in respectable Latin to a friend, while as soon as they have to write Arabic, there is no difficulty in finding a whole multitude who can express themselves with the greatest elegance in this language . . ."[36]. Around the middle of the 10th century, there appear to have conversions to Islam on a massive scale,[37] which would explain the lack of any Christian intellectual activity in the 11th century. As for the rural Mozarab communities, they hardly figure in the history of the period at all.[38] The Jewish community remained homogeneous and relatively independent, playing an active part in intellectual and cultural life and a major role above all in commerce, including trading with eunuchs, which other groups regarded as beneath them.

The *Saqâliba*, or "Slavs" had developed into a community of their own; they had originated as Europeans captured in the course of military campaigns, many of whom were castrated before entering the service of the court. Most *saqâliba*, however, were destined for military service, and not castrated. *Saqâliba* (singular: *siqlabî* or *saqlabî*) is the medieval Arabic word for the people of eastern Europe, the "Slavs"; however, the *saqâliba* of Cordova came from other parts of Europe, too, for example Germany, France, and Italy. They should not be confused with the black slaves, the *'abîd*.[39] The importation of the *saqâliba* had begun very early on; it is said that by the end of the 10th century there were 3750 in Cordova.[40] They were mostly young when they arrived at the court, with no roots in the country, and if they felt any ties at all, it was to the ruler. In fact they were often closer to him than to their own relations, and soon the key positions in the army and the civil service were exclusively theirs. Most of these Mamlûkes ("unfree")[41] were given their freedom after a certain period, they embraced Islam and settled in the towns where they had served. By virtue of their familiarity with the court, their influence was disproportionately large, even when they were not resident in the capital, and during the 11th century they played a major role in the struggle for the left-overs of the caliphate.

The organization of the Umayyad state was autocratic from the very beginning; the ruler was in charge both of foreign and of domestic policy, as well as being commander-in-chief of the army, and he was also the highest judicial authority. To this extent little had changed since the days of 'Abd ar-Rahmân I, apart from the fact that court etiquette had become more oppressive, and the distance between ruler and ruled greater. Along with the Caliph, the government departments – which of course were part of the court entourage – had moved to Madînat al-Zahrâ' in the middle of the 10th century, and here they stayed under al-Hakam II. Then they returned briefly to Cordova, before being transferred by Ibn Abî 'Âmir to al-Madîna al-Zâhira.

Al-Andalus now contained only two Marches, the "Middle" and the "Upper" – the "Lower" had by now been incorporated into the heartland – and twenty-one or so provinces. The administrative system was much as it had always been. Non-Muslims continued to live in their own, relatively independent communities, with their own jurisdiction, their own leader (*qûmis*, "count", from the Latin *comes*) who was responsible for the collection of taxes. Under 'Abd ar-Rahmân III gold coins were struck in al-Andalus for the first time.[42]

Already under 'Abd ar-Rahmân III, and to an increased extent under al-Mansûr, the army of free Muslims was being replaced by an army of non-Muslim mercenaries, either *saqâliba* or *'abîd*. Whole groups of Berbers also came to Andalusia from North Africa as mercenaries in the mid-10th century. The traditional Arab tribal army, organized into *junds*, had proved to be a breeding ground for discontent, because these relatively homogeneous, closed groups represented a latent threat of mutiny. Al-Mansûr mixed up the soldiers from the various *junds* during the period of their military service, and thus destroyed their tribal units. Later he went as far as to introduce the possibility of buying oneself out of military service, which resulted in the definitive replacement of a free Muslim army by an army of mercenaries and slaves. The title of Caliph, the court etiquette, the royal names, the slave army, the gold currency – these were all "orientalisms, copied from the Abbasids of Baghdad.

Cordova: Puerta de Sevilla
The form and the masonry of this gate on the old road to Seville suggest that it dates from Umayyad times.

The Architecture of the 10th Century

Madînat al-Zahrâ'

Monumental construction projects were for the Caliphs a means of demonstrating their power. 'Abd ar-Rahmân III's first such project was the extension of the Alcázar in Cordova, and the erection of a new palace inside it. In the summer, he would often reside in one of the country houses in the vicinity of the city which he had taken over from his predecessors. It is not clear whether he found the Alcázar too confined and the *munyas* too uncomfortable, or whether he simply deemed them unworthy of his dignity as Caliph: whatever the motive, in 936 he decided to build a new capital, Madînat al-Zahrâ', some five kilometres to the north-west of Cordova as the crow flies. The job of site foreman, so to speak, was entrusted to the Crown Prince, the later Caliph al-Hakam II. In 941 the mosque was consecrated, and a grandiose reception is documented for as early as 945. In 947, the government apparatus and the mint were transferred from Cordova to the new city, and building work continued after 'Abd ar-Rahmân's death in 961. Total construction time must have been about 40 years altogether, but no later than the beginning of the following century Madînat al-Zahrâ' was reduced to rubble by mutinous Berber troops. This tragically brief existence doubtless contributed to the flights of fancy of later chroniclers, leading them on to paint this ruin as a lost dream-world.

According to the written sources, 'Abd ar-Rahmân III named his new creation after his favorite wife, a certain Zahrâ'. A statue of this favourite is said – according to al-Maqqarî, an Arab historian of the 16th/17th century[43] – to have adorned the main gate of the city, and to have remained intact until it was destroyed by the Almahadic Caliph Ya'qûb al-Mansûr. Unfortunately, al-Maqqarî's sources are not always reliable, and a statue of the loved one above the city gate is inherently improbable. Nothing comparable is known from any part of the western Islamic world, and while statues above palace entrances are known from the Islamic Near East in the 8th century, women were never among those thus depicted.[44]

What is certainly true is that the city was created by 'Abd ar-Rahmân III out of nothing, and became the royal residence, the seat of government, and the dwelling place of the huge crowd of staff (20 000 is a figure often quoted) with which he surrounded himself. This was yet another way in which the Hispano-Umayyad Caliph followed the example of the Abba-

Madînat al-Zahrâ': view into the nave of the Great West Hall

61

sids, whose royal cities of Baghdad and Sâmarrâ were famous and much
admired. Like the Abbasid Caliphs in the Near East, the Andalusian Caliph also chose to create a proper distance between his court and the turbulent population of the old, and real, capital.

Construction costs are said to have swallowed up one-third of annual
state revenue, and 10 000 workers are said to have been employed on the
site. Apart from the foundations and paving stones, 6000 blocks are said
to have been cut every day, and a total of 4324 marble columns imported,
mostly from Tunisia, along with marble basins from Byzantium and Syria,
and twelve golden sculptures inlaid with pearls, also from Syria, for the
Caliph's bedroom.[45]

Some names associated with the project have come down to us, including
those of a certain Maslama bin 'Abd Allâh, the chief architect, an 'Alî bin
Jafar from Alexandria, who was primarily responsible for the transport of
construction materials, and 'Abd Allâh bin Yûnus and a Hasan bin Muhammad from Cordova, who are both mentioned as master builders.
However, none of these names can be linked with any identifiable figures
from the world of art and architecture: it must be assumed that al-Hakam
was not just the sponsor of the project, but also the leading architect.

All that remains of the former splendour is a ruin that stretches across
an arid slope of the Sierra de Córdova. Excavations were initiated in 1910
in the northern sector, and after lengthy interruptions are still not complete
today.[46] In recent years, Madînat al-Zahrâ' has become a major centre of

research and restoration.[47] In spite of the many discoveries on the part of the archaeologists, it is still difficult to correlate the written sources with the material reality.

The city covered a walled area measuring some 1500 by 750 metres. By reason of its hillside situation, it was built on three terraces one above the other, which were planned as three districts separated from each other by walls. The Caliph's residence dominated the whole site from its position on the northern, uppermost, terrace. The middle esplanade housed the government offices and the homes of senior court officials, while the lowest terrace was devoted to the common people and the army; here were situated the mosque, the markets, the baths and also gardens. These three terraces with their clearly demarcated functions are referred to in every ancient source, and al-Idrîsî, writing as late as 150 years after its destruction, described it as "an important city, built in tiers one above the other, so that the ground of the uppermost was at the level of the rooftops of the middle, and the ground of the middle at the level of the rooftops of the lowest. All three were surrounded by walls. The palace stood in the uppermost region . . . in the middle region were orchards and gardens, while the Friday mosque and private dwellings were situated on the lowest level."[48]

In reality, the demarcation of the individual sections cannot have been so clear, as there were marked differences of ground-level within each. Thus in the north-west of the middle esplanade there is a residential complex (2) at a level only 1.70 metres below that of the adjacent Caliph's palace (1) on the uppermost level, while itself ranging 7 to 11 metres above other buildings on the same terrace. This complex is bounded to the east by two houses with internal courtyard, separated by a ramp, the so-called "Twin Esplanade"[49] (3, 4), followed to the south by the "Colonnade Court" (10) and the "Prince's House" (11); to the south of the "Twin Esplanade" is a "Guardroom" (8) and the "House of the Vizier Ja'far" (9). Running almost along the axis of the North Gate is a solid north-south wall, which cuts into the more easterly of the two houses on the "Twin Esplanade" (4), and forms the main axis for the buildings to the east: the "House of the Army" (Dâr al-Jund), also known as the "Great West Hall" (5a), with its broad, low forecourt (5b), and to the north-east, a smaller dwelling house (6a), from which a ramp and arcade issue in a southerly direction (7). Further to the east there is a large courtyard which is still awaiting excavation (21), within which two buildings have been distinguished, the "Golden Hall" (22), a centrally-planned structure, and the "East Hall", a five-nave basilica (23) (cf. ill. p. 65). To the south of this central, really quite crowded group of buildings, somewhat displaced towards the west when compared with the "House of the Army" but also oriented in a north-south direction, lies the most important reception hall in the whole city, which the archaeologists have christened the "Salón Rico", or "Rich Hall" (12). It lies a good 11 metres below the level of all the other buildings on this terrace. On its eastern side it is bounded by the princely baths (13), while on its western side it is skirted by the "Lower Military Passage" (14). Further to the west on this middle terrace lay the dwelling houses of the court officials, which have not yet been excavated. Immediately in front of the "Salón Rico" is the "High Garden", in the

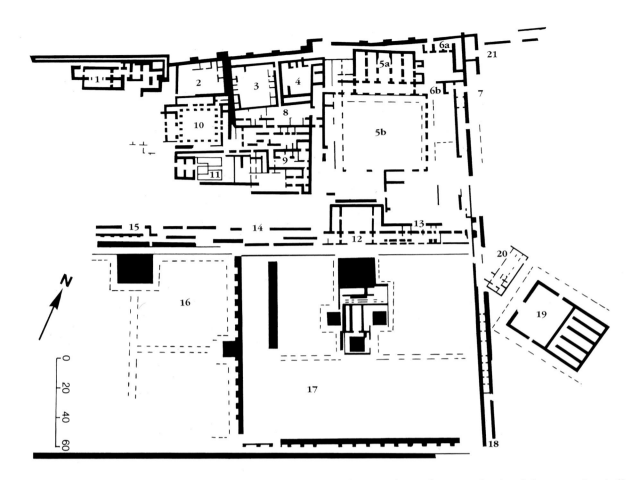

Madînat al-Zahrâ' (after S. López-Cuervo)
Ground plan of a number of building complexes in the north-west of the city.

middle of which, in other words on the central axis of the reception hall, there stood a pavilion surrounded by pools. This "High Garden" is surrounded by a solid wall, which also divides the middle from the lowest terrace. Below, to the south-west, that is to say on the lowest terrace, lies the "Low Garden", which, like the "High Garden", is divided into quarters by paths in the form of a cross. Adjacent to the east wall of the "High Garden" is a covered passage (18), which leads to the much lower mosque (19), which, though belonging to the domain of the lowest terrace, nevertheless dominates the latter by virtue of its position. Close to the mosque is another, relatively small, dwelling house (20).

The change of orientation apparent here, i.e. of the mosque vis-à-vis the buildings to its west and north, suggest a change of plan during construction, the mosque and the palace on the first tier having been completed first. The palace has not yet been fully excavated: it consists of a complex of a number of courtyards, a three-nave structure, a bath-house and a lavatory tiled in extravagant red marble.

The mosque was to a certain extent a little sister of the Great Mosque in Cordova (before the latter's rebuilding by al-Hakam II). Five naves (or a nave and four aisles) run perpendicular to the *qibla*; the central nave is broader than the aisles, and the inner aisles in turn are broader than the outer, which continue into the gallery of the courtyard. Parallel to the *qibla* is a strip of ground about 7 metres broad, raised somewhat by its paving of clay tiles, while the rest of the prayer hall has a bare earth floor, making it clear that the plan was determined by the T-scheme and the emphasis it gives to the nave and *qibla*. Behind the *qibla* there was a covered passage allowing the Caliph to enter the prayer hall without having to walk through the congregation. The minaret stands directly adjacent to the main entrance, which in its turn is directly opposite the *mihrâb*. The mosque employs the same basilical style of architecture as the reception halls.

Apart from the mosque, the lowest terrace has not yet been fully investigated by archaeologists. Even so, aerial photographs give some indication about what it contained. To the south, approximately in the middle, was the main gate ("Bâb al-Qubba" or "Gate of the Dome") (26), while a second gate, of which only the door-posts remain, was situated further to the north (probably that referred to in the written sources as the "Bâb al-Sudda", or "Gate of the Threshold"). To the east, not far from the mosque, were the market area (24) and the living quarters of the infantry (25); while to the west there were gardens, a game enclosure (27) and the living quarters of the cavalry (28).

The water supply to Madînat al-Zahrâ' was by means of a conduit that ran mostly underground, but in a number of places emerged as an aqueduct on horseshoe arches; it brought the water down from the mountains of the Sierra to the north, approaching the city at a right angle to the walls, where it emptied into a water-tower (in the north of the city); from here the water flowed into a marble basin and then over a ramp into lead pipes, which formed the main distribution system in the city below. There were also numerous collecting-tanks to catch and store rainwater, as the Sierra evidently did not provide enough water for the needs of the royal city, which must have been considerable, as the better-class houses which have been excavated so far were all equipped with a good water supply (including lavatories), and, moreover, there were numerous pools in the city itself. A number of chroniclers repeat one particular statistic, which must have impressed them: "12 000 loaves were required each day as food for the fish in the palace ponds."[50] This means that the "palace ponds" alone must have been of impressive size, and they only formed a part of the total.

The city was well fortified; its circumference wall – built of relatively small ashlar blocks – probably dates from the earliest building phase, as

Madînat al-Zahrâ': view of the Great West Hall
The arcade in the background forms the eastern border of the middle terrace.

Schematic plan of the entire complex
(after R. Castejón y Martinez de Arizala)

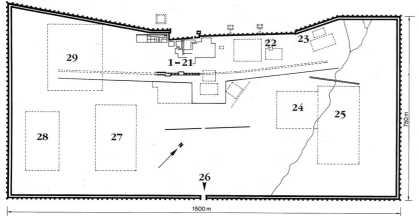

later phases worked with larger blocks. Only the northern section has been excavated. At this point it is 2.50 metres thick, and every 13 to 14 metres has a rectangular fortified tower built on to its external face. Along the inside runs a military passageway over 4 metres in breadth. Along the other three sides of the city, the defences seem to have taken the form of a double wall with a passageway in the middle, the whole having a thickness of some 15 metres.[51]

At least four gates are known: the main gate to the city in the middle of the southern wall (the "Bâb al-Qubba"); the "Bâb al-Shams" (or "Gate of the Sun") in the eastern wall; and the "Bâb al-Jibâl" (or "Gate of the Mountains") in the northern wall. In addition there was the "Bâb al-Sudda" ("Forbidden Gate" or "Gate of the Threshold") in the interior of the city to the north of the Bâb al-Qubba; it led to the Caliph's palace, and here those allowed entrance had to dismount and proceed further on foot to the government offices, which were built up the slope. Hitherto, only the north gate has been excavated. It is the nearest one to the Caliph's palace, and there is no doubt that it was re-built a number of times in order to strengthen its defences: to the original structure were added, in front, an extra guard-room and a wall turning away at right angles, as well as a defensive tower opposite the gateway.

Clues to dating are provided by the more or less contemporary reports, which have been preserved thanks to al-Maqqarî's compilation, and to a few monumental inscriptions: in the mosque, remains of an inscription have been found mentioning the date 941/42; according to written sources, it was built in 941 by 1000 workers in 48 days. Three dates have been found among the ornamentation of the "Salón Rico", indicating the years 953–57 as the period of its construction.

The Arab chroniclers describe a whole series of spectacular festivals and receptions for foreign embassies. In 949, a Byzantine delegation with generous gifts (including a Greek copy of Dioscorides' Treatise on Botany) was received in Cordova; thereafter, however, all such magnificent diplomatic receptions were held in Madînat al-Zahrâ'. We have detailed

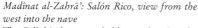

Madînat al-Zahrâ': Salón Rico, view from the west into the nave
The Caliph's throne probably stood against the rear wall.

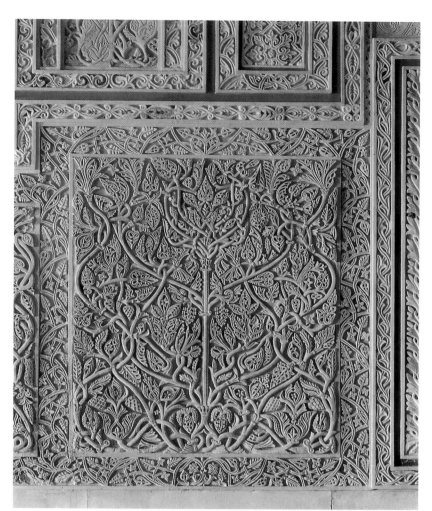

Madînat al-Zahrâ': marble panel in the Salón Rico

This and the panel illustrated opposite are very similar, probably deriving from the same workshop at an interval of about ten years. Both depict the ancient oriental "tree of life" motif; in both there is symmetry about the vertical axis, with a classical vegetal border. The relief design is carved vertically into the stone, resulting in a graphic, abstract quality. The internal patterns in the trunk, leaves and petals are cut with a similarly hard outline, a typical Hispano-Umayyad feature.

reports of many of these embassies, e. g. one despatched by the Holy Roman Emperor Otto the Great, who sent Johann von Gorze as ambassador to Andalusia in 956;[52] in 958 Sancho el Craso, who had been deprived of the throne of León, came to seek the help of the Caliph, his distant cousin; in 962, Ordoño IV of León appeared with the same problem; in 971 an ambassador sent by Count Borrell of Barcelona, who was also Bishop of Gerona, was received in Madînat al-Zahrâ'.[53] Shortly afterwards a number of missions from Castile, León, Salamanca and Pamplona were received, as well as from Provence and Tuscany. And even the "Sâhib Rûma", the "Ruler of Rome", is said by Ibn Khaldûn to have sent a delegation.[54] In 972 another Byzantine envoy arrived. More frequent were visits by Berber princes and other North African delegations; in 973 there was even a visit from an Arabian envoy.

Ibn Hayyân, whose father had been secretary to al-Mansûr, and who himself had held the post of Head of the Chancellery in Cordova during the 11th century, is regarded as the most reliable of the medieval chroniclers of Cordova, and it is to him we owe the following description of the

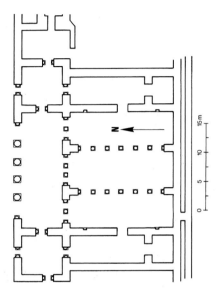

Madînat al-Zahrâ': Salón Rico; ground plan
(after R. Castejón y Martinez de Arizala)

reception accorded to Ordoño IV in 962. The Christian king, he writes, was accommodated together with his retinue in an Umayyad summer palace not far from Cordova. On the day of the audience he was accompanied by both Christian and Muslim dignitaries; the party rode between double ranks of soldiers to Madînat al-Zahrâ'; the embassy entered the city from the south through the main gate, then crossed the lowest esplanade until they came to the Bâb al-Sudda, where they were received by the Sâhib al-Madîna, a senior court official, all except Ordoño himself being obliged to dismount. The group then proceeded up to the middle terrace with its reception halls, their route being lined the whole way by a guard of honour. At the House of the Army, they stopped to rest, and then continued on foot up to the East Hall, where the Caliph was expecting them. The throne would have been no more than a low chair at the end of the nave, where the Caliph, probably in simple clothes, was sitting surrounded by richly-dressed dignitaries whose double ranks reached to the entrance of the hall. After the audience was over, Ordoño was taken to the House of the Vizier Ja'far, where he took refreshment and received a gown of honour, the traditional princely gift, along with jewelry and fabrics for his retinue. On the return journey he found not his own horse at the House of the Army, but a noble thoroughbred with a costly harness.

The importance of Madînat al-Zahrâ' in history of art is very great indeed. For one thing, the city represents a special Andalusian variety of the Near Eastern Islamic palace city, such as arose in the course of the same century in Tunisia (Sabra al-Mansûriyya) and in Egypt (al-Qâhira, which gave its name to Cairo). The hierarchical nature of the city and its dwelling houses, as reflected in the construction plan, the size of the whole complex and the artistic layout of the gardens, with their raised paths crossing in the middle, the close connection between reception hall, fountains and gardens, the animal enclosure and aviary, the complicated and in part well-protected passageways – these are all elements which can be found in the royal cities of the Abbasids. The purely basilical, many-naved reception halls (House of the Army, Salón Rico, East Hall) are apparently a peculiarity of Andalusia as far as Islamic royal architecture is concerned, because as early as the 8th century, the major role in the Near East was being taken by *iwan* and domed buildings. It is true that there are references in the literature to domed structures in Madînat al-Zahrâ', but the archaeological evidence indicates that they played a much less significant role than the basilicas. It is a matter of some note that the architecture of the secular reception halls was based on that of the mosques to a far greater extent than was the case in the Abbasid dominions.

The suites of rooms in the dwelling houses in Madînat al-Zahrâ' are arranged around a central courtyard, which in the more prosperous houses is usually square, otherwise trapezoidal or oblong. In the Prince's House the courtyard is replaced by a small garden with a pool; opening on to this *hortus conclusus* are ante-rooms with a central three-bay arcade, and the garden itself is bisected longitudinally by paths. A similar, albeit rather more grandiose arrangement is found in front of the Salón Rico.

The reception halls are richly ornamented, with much use of sandstone, marble and glass mosaics. Epigraphic, geometric and vegetal forms can be clearly distinguished; the decor has a pronounced carpet-like character.

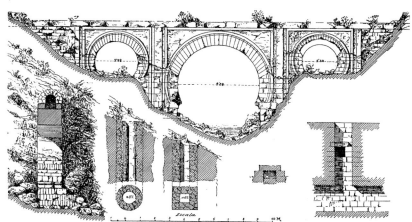

Madînat al-Zahrâ': aqueduct (M. Gómez-Moreno)

The life-blood of Madînat al-Zahrâ' was its water-supply; once this fell into neglect, the whole area became hopelessly arid. Formerly the water was brought as far as the city walls from the Sierra de Córdoba in the north, by way of pipes, which, while mostly underground, were supported in places on the horseshoe arches of aqueducts. Shafts were sunk into the underground channels to equalize the pressure.

Since Madinât al-Zahrâ' is in ruins, it is in the Great Mosque of Cordova that the most impressive documents of the architecture of the Caliphate are to be found today. Following its enlargement by 'Abd ar-Rahmân II (whose plans were completed under his successor Muhammad I, it being the latter's name which is mentioned in the caption above the Stephen's Gate, along with the date 855/56), no further alterations had been carried out, apart from the addition, by Emir 'Abd Allâh, of a covered passage from the palace to the facing west gate of the prayer hall (presumably the present-day Michael's Gate). The extended arcades which had resulted from 'Abd ar-Rahmân II's enlargement had caused the north wall of the prayer hall to bulge outwards; as a counter-measure, 'Abd ar-Rahmân III

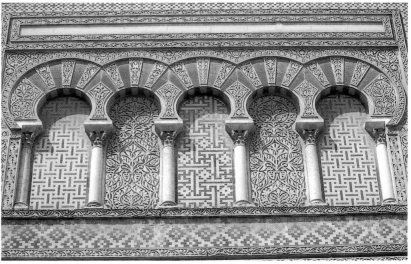

Details of one of the twelve later gates of the prayer hall

Cordova: Great Mosque, east porch, dating from the time of al-Mansûr

had this wall refurbished by the simple expedient of having a new façade placed in front of the old one on the courtyard front. There remains extant an inscription containing the names of the ruler, the supervisor and the master-builder, and the date 958.[55] Even earlier, according to written sources in 951/52, he had commissioned a minaret 100 cubits high to be built on the north side of the mosque, alongside the central entrance;[56] this minaret was provided with two parallel staircases, and during the 16th century it became the core of the present-day bell-tower, whose name "Alminar" harks back to the original structure. Archaeological investigations in recent years (by Félix Hernández Giménez) have revealed the original masonry with its large, regular ashlar blocks, and the two vaulted staircases separated from one another by a north-south wall.[57] The tower is square in plan, measuring 8,48 metres along each side. Two coats-of-arms in relief, dating from the mid-16th century, to be found on the Puerta de Santa Catalina, depict the minaret and the north porch of the mosque as they were before rebuilding. At ground level on either side was the entrance to one of the two staircases; above there were several storeys with two pairs of windows in each, then a dwarf gallery, and the castellated balustrade around the platform from which the muezzin issued the call to prayer;

Cordova: Great Mosque, Capilla de la Villaviciosa
This section with its impressive system of simple and interlocking multi-lobed arches is part of al-Hakam's extension. In the background the *mihrâb* can be seen.

Elevation of the east façade of the west arcade
(C. Ewert)

then followed a narrower turret, surmounted by a pavilion with four arched windows. The triangular gable visible on the coat-of-arms is probably a Christian addition. According to al-Maqqarî, the whole structure was surmounted by one silver and two golden apples on a metal rod, crowned by a small golden pomegranate. This minaret was not only built for the call to prayer, but also as a proud symbol of the Umayyads and their capital city. It is the most important Umayyad minaret known to us, and its influence on all subsequent minarets in the Islamic west is unmistakable. A far more modest minaret, dating from the year 930, has been preserved as the church tower of San Juan de los Caballeros in Cordova. This too already has two-tier arcades with horseshoe arches and voussoirs in two colours, and a dwarf gallery above.

As a result of the extension to the mosque carried out by 'Abd ar-Rahmân II, the courtyard had become too narrow in relation to the prayer hall, and as part of the same building phase as the works described above, 'Abd ar-Rahmân III extended it to the north so that it now measured a good 60 metres along this axis, and at the same time he provided it along three sides with a gallery six metres deep. On the basis perhaps of Byzantine models, this gallery was supported alternately by piers and columns.

Al-Hakam's masterpiece was the extension of the prayer hall. True, the

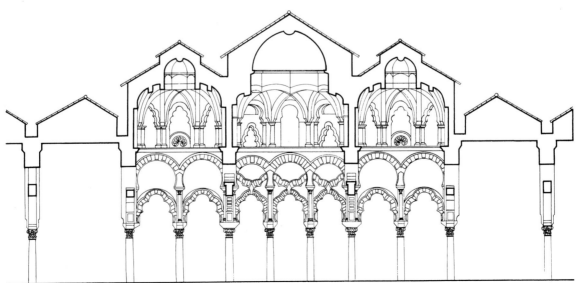

population of Cordova had grown, making it necessary to enlarge the mosque, but the fact that it was on 4th Ramadan 340 (17th October 961), the day after al-Hakam's coronation, that the corresponding order was given, thus making it one of the first official acts of his reign, suggests that he had long toyed with the plan in his mind and attached considerable importance to it. A senior dignitary was charged with the procurement of building materials, work began in July 962, and according to Ibn 'Idhârî was completed in the summer of 966. At first the new ruler had intended to change the orientation of the *qibla*, which had proved to be incorrect, but he changed his mind out of respect for the building of his predecessors.

Like 'Abd ar-Rahmân II, al-Hakam simply had the *qibla* wall demolished and then rebuilt twelve bays further south. This meant that the prayer hall was now almost 104 metres from front to back. In front of the former *qibla* wall cross-shaped pillars were left standing, which were connected by arches to form a kind of entrance façade to this "mosque within a mosque" (Félix Hernández Giménez). The new *mihrâb*, a deep niche heptagonal in plan and with a scalloped dome, is flanked on the east and the west by five square rooms respectively, the eastern ones being used as treasuries, while the western ones formed part of the covered passage to the palace, al-Hakam II having previously removed the passage installed by 'Abd Allâh. This southern tract is extremely unusual, and may serve the function of taking the compressive thrust of the domes; it has an upper storey of eleven rooms, whose purpose is unclear. The *maqsûra* probably extended to the two southernmost bays of the central nave and the two aisles to either side.[58]

The first three bays of the nave form a magnificent approach to al-Hakam II's prayer room, which is cordoned off from the surrounding area by an interesting system of simple and interlocking multi-lobed arches. This and the immense ribbed cupola contribute to the impressive spaciousness of this part of the building, which is known today as the "Capilla de Villaviciosa". From there, our gaze is directed through further interlocking

View into the area in front of the mihrâb
The aisle leading up to the *mihrâb* (until al-Mansûr's extension the central nave) had, ever since the mosque's foundation, been the broadest of the aisles. To this extent al-Hakam II changed nothing in the scheme of things worked out by his predecessors. The prayer hall had always been shrouded in gloomy darkness, with mystic overtones produced by al-Hakam's shimmering gold mosaics.

Maqsûra area of al-Hakam's extension: original ground plan (C. Ewert)

Cross-section (C. Ewert)

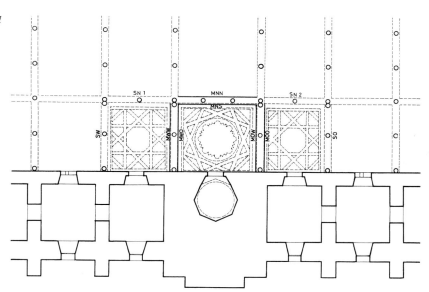

multi-lobed arches to the focus of the mosque, the *mihrâb*. The last two bays before the *qibla* wall are connected by arcades running crosswise to the aisles (and parallel to the *qibla*). In front of the three central bays, and the *mihrâb* bay in particular, they form a highly ingenious weave of arches, which resembles a piece of monumental lacework. These three bays have the same ribbed vault as the Capilla de Villaviciosa, only here their ground plan is square.

All four domes[59] appear from outside as relatively insignificant structures with small windows, each with its tiled pyramid roof. They are supported by a skeleton consisting of four pairs of parallel curved ribs embedded in springers of rectangular cross-section. These ribs span the space in the manner of centering or false-work scaffolding, in that they divide it into small, easy-to-span segments. The ribs never intersect at the apex; the master builders of Cordova were a long way from the technical skills of those who constructed the vaults of Gothic cathedrals, where the ribs conduct away the thrust in order to relieve the walls. The architects of Cordova had not yet grasped the potential of this technique (filling the spaces between the ribs, for example, with thick stonework, although a lighter weight would have been technically far more appropriate). For all its beauty, their work cannot be seen as the precursor of the Gothic.

There is some disagreement as to where the idea of the rib vault in Cordova came from. As was pointed out above, it has nothing to do with rib vaulting in the Gothic sense, quite apart from the fact that the latter also came later. One possible origin has been seen in the coffered ceilings of the Romans, but it really is a long way from there to the solution found in Cordova. The Armenian rib vault has often been cited as a model, but those examples which are datable and earlier than those in Cordova are illustrative of radial rib systems. It is not until later that we find Armenian vaults with rib support structures, which indeed are quite similar to those in Cordova.[60] Another candidate frequently adduced in this connexion is the Iranian vault; this, with its lightweight brickwork, does indeed display a formal resemblance to the rib systems found in Cordova, but in Iran the extremely light, plaster arches are erected in a sometimes radial, sometimes more complex pattern. The resulting ridges are filled with fired clay tiles, using an excellent quick-drying mortar. In fact the Iranian rib vaults are functionally no more than centering,[61] which can certainly not be said of those in Cordova, where they have a load-bearing function. Quite apart from that, it is hardly possible to speak of identity of technique, given the totally different materials employed: clay tiles and plaster in Iran, stone in Cordova. Furthermore, where the comparable rib vaults of Iran are datable at all, they stem from the late 11th century at the earliest, so that from the chronological point of view, such influence as there might have been could only have proceeded from Cordova. Such a conclusion would be quite absurd, however, as the Iranian rib structures of the Seljuk period, which resemble those of Cordova, are part of a self-contained tradition which is much older, whose beginnings in fact are shrouded in mystery. Then again, the domes of Cordova suggest no direct connexion with any more ancient building tradition in Spain either, and one possibility would be to assume a common, but unknown, source in the Near East for both

Area in front of mihrâb, view from east to west
The different perceptual possibilities of the interlocking multi-lobed arches bears witness to a decorative, ambiguous conception of architectural forms, representing an aesthetic sense foreign to that which informed the original foundation.

PAGE 78:
Dome over the bay in front of the mihrâb
All four domes in the Umayyad building appear from the outside as modest structures pierced by small windows and covered with tiled pyramidal roofs. All four are constructed using a skeleton consisting of four pairs of parallel ribs set in springers of rectangular cross-section. These ribs span the area in the manner of centering or falsework scaffolding, in that they divide it up into small, easy-to-fill sections.

PAGE 79:
Mihrâb façade
This, the culmination of the whole building, recapitulates the themes of the Stephen's Gate, at the same time enhancing them by the richness of the material, the innovativeness of the details and the quality of the execution. The inscriptions, in gilt mosaic on a blue background, mention the name of al-Hakam II and cite verses from the Koran.

*Mosaic details from the mihrâb façade and the
dome above the bay in front of the mihrâb*

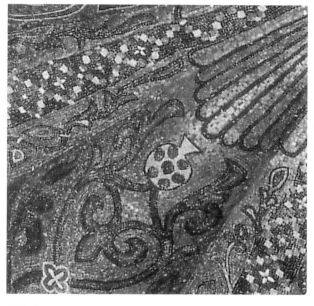
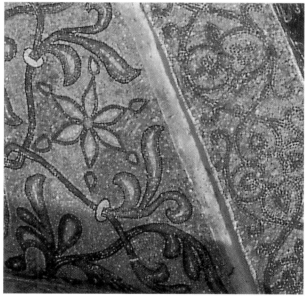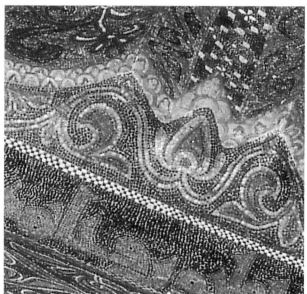

the Iranian and the Andalusian rib-vaulted domes.[62] Whatever the truth is, al-Hakam II's master builder was highly creative, and certainly in no way inferior to the original, late 8th-century, architect of the mosque.

The arcades which bear the weight of the domes are constructed of stone which was plastered over and painted before being set in place. Like the arcades of the original building, they are two-tier structures, the lower column supporting a rectangular pillar with an applied ornamental column. The arches of the upper tier are horseshoe-shaped, while the lower tier is made up of five-lobed arches. In many particularly significant places, this basic system is overlaid by further elements. The arches have smooth and ornamented facings alternately, a restatement and development of the original two-colour scheme. A characteristic sign of this liberation from the building traditions of classical antiquity is the introduction of unsupported arcades (that is to say, the springers of the middle tier of arches, where present, rest on the keystones of the lower tier); other signs of the same thing are suffort by columns without bases, and the increasing thickness of structural elements with increasing height.[63] The potential for various visual interpretations of the complex multi-lobed arches is also both conspicuous and new: the north arcade of the *mihrâb* bay has – unambiguously – three five-lobed arches in the lower tier, horseshoe arches in the upper, and an intermediate tier of trefoil arches; the west arcade, by contrast, by virtue of the facing of the voussoirs, suggests itself as an interlocking system of eleven-lobed arches, obscuring the three-tier structure. This decorative, ambiguous concept of architectural forms corresponds to a deeply-rooted Islamic aesthetic, and in the case of the Cordova mosque, represents a substantial development vis-à-vis the original building.

The climax of the mosque is the *mihrâb*, at the culmination of the main axis; its overwhelming effect is ingeniously anticipated and enhanced by the multi-lobed transverse arcades. The horseshoe-shaped niche is ensconced in a veritable façade, which takes up the themes of the Stephen's Gate once more, and composes variations upon them, albeit here with far greater wealth of detail. As in the gateway, here too we have a base zone, an arch with a surrounding *alfiz*, and a blind arcade above, all clearly demarcated. The base zone is faced with marble slabs; on either side of the *mihrâb* opening is a pair of dark-coloured marble columns which had been used in 'Abd ar-Rahmân II's *mihrâb*. The voussoirs of the horseshoe arch are faced with gold mosaics depicting arabesque patterns on differently-coloured backgrounds. The gilt spandrels display a motif of circles of various sizes, which in some form or other appears time and again in the art of Andalusia and the Maghreb. The arch and the spandrel are framed by a broad calligraphic border – gold Kufic characters on a dark blue background – itself within a sculptured marble border. The blind arcade of trefoil arches on marble columns plays upon the contrast between the pale marble and the glittering multi-coloured mosaics gold ground. The interior of the *mihrâb* is panelled at the base with smooth marble slabs, surmounted by a calligraphic frieze; above each slab is a trefoil arch on black marble columns which stand in sharp contrast to the alternately smooth and sculpted white voussoirs. A broad calligraphic frieze and another with a vine-leaf motif run along the base of the calloped vault. Inscriptions give

Ribbed vault of the Capilla de la Villaviciosa

83

the names of the ruler who commissioned the building, the name and title of the supervisor of building works, and the date of completion (November/December 965), along with the names of four craftsmen which have also been found in the Salón Rico in Madînat al-Zahrâ'.

The glowing gold-mosaic facing of the *mihrâb* façade and its two flanking, horseshoe-arch-surmounted doors, along with that of the central dome in front of the *mihrâb*, have a decidedly Byzantine character, an impression which is indeed confirmed by the written sources: Ibn 'Idhârî reports that the dome was completed in June 965, and that the mosaics were started immediately afterwards. Al-Hakam had previously asked the Byzantine Emperor Nicephoros II Phocas to send him a mosaicist capable of imitating the mosaics in the Great Mosque of Damascus. The Caliph's envoys had returned from Constantinople with the mosaicist as requested, and moreover with several sacks (amounting to some 1,600 kilograms) of gold mosaic cubes as a gift from the Emperor. The Caliph had then assigned the mosaicist a number of slaves as apprentices and assistants, who after a while had mastered the art so well that they surpassed their master, and were able to proceed on their own after the latter's departure. The story of the Byzantine connexion is found in other, earlier, authors, and the work of Henri Stern and Dorothea Duda[64] has made it clear beyond any doubt that Byzantine imports were involved.

It is said that the mosaics were not completed until late 970 or early 971, in other words a good five years after the structure itself. This period seems really quite long for an area of no more than about 200 square metres; however, progress may well have been delayed by the need to train the native craftsmen, and by their subsequent assumption of responsibility for the work. Henri Stern has established that the techniques employed in Cordova, while comparable with those used for the roughly contemporary mosaics in Hagia Sophia in Constantinople, are nonetheless of decidedly lower quality. Thus in Cordova the cubes were always laid flat, while the master mosaicists in Constantinople set theirs at an angle in particular places in order to exploit the light effects to the best advantage.[65] Thus, for example, the background of the mosaic of the Virgin Mary on the south gate of the narthex is convex in certain places (in the halo), while in others the light effects are enhanced by the use of silver cubes. The preliminary drawing in Constantinople was a complete picture in itself, while in Cordova it seems to have been no more than a rough sketch. On the other hand, more colours were employed in Cordova.[66] The mosaics of the west door were probably carried out by native craftsmen. And while the materials and techniques were thus of undisputed Byzantine origin, nonetheless we find in the inventory of forms features of a Hispano-Islamic style of ornamentation which had developed its own vocabulary since Madînat al-Zahrâ'.

For all the magnificence of his "mosque within a mosque", al-Hakam II remained faithful to the architectural principles of the original building. This respect for the existing structure was also a *leitmotiv* of the last great work on the building while it was still a mosque: al-Mansûr, the all-powerful minister who governed on behalf of Hishâm, embarked on a further substantial enlargement in 978/79[67], as the population of Cordova had seen yet another major increase as a result of the importation of

Berber mercenaries and their families. To the south, the building was bounded by the banks of the Guadalquivir; to the west lay the palace (on the site of the present-day Archbishop's Palace), so that only the east side was available for extensions, and it was here that eight new aisles were added along the whole length of the hall. The courtyard was also enlarged correspondingly. The broad nave leading up to the *mihrâb* now no longer formed the central axis, but the extension maintains an air of subordination and seems to make no attempt to compete with the splendour and prestige of al-Hakam's additions. Thus large sections of the former east wall were left in place, in order to clearly demarcate the main hall from the hall to the side; al-Hakam's south transverse arcade and the chambers to the south were not extended. Al-Mansûr's prayer hall was thus far simpler and two bays deeper than al-Hakam's. All this gave the Mosque the stately dimensions of 178 by 128 metres, making it the third-biggest in the Islamic world, exceeded only by the two Abbasid Great Mosques of Sâmarrâ.

Each of the three great rulers during the period of the Caliphate had left his own personal stamp on the Great Mosque of Cordova. The characteristic feature of 'Abd ar-Rahmân III's phase is the minaret, that of al-Hakam II consists in the domes, the interlocking multi-lobed arches and the Byzantine mosaics, while for al-Mansûr the characteristic feature is the size of the extension. Each contribution by a ruler can be seen as an image of his personality and of his concept of government. The tower is primarily

Decorative elements from the Great Mosque in Cordova (opposite and above left), and from the Alhambra in Granada (above right) (C. Uhde). The rich Hispano-Umayyad decorative flora included leaf and lotus forms, rosettes, semi-palmettes, trefoils, pine-cones and bunches of grapes; the individual elements always had rich internal decoration, and often pennate or perforated edging. The basic geometric organization is provided by outcurving branches. For all the stylization, the leaves and petals can still usually be distinguished from the branches and stalks. During the 12th century, smooth forms begin to take over, and the inventory becomes more stylized and repetitive. Broad cups, semi-palmettes and trefoil forms grow out of or into the stalks; the forked-leaf motif is everywhere, and vegetal growth is now based exclusively on geometrical principles.

a sign of prestige and domination, and only then a means of calling the faithful to prayer.[68] It is a proud symbol, visible from afar, of the legitimate power of the new Caliph. From the outside far less conspicuous, but incomparably more subtle, more creative and more profoundly conceived are the works of al-Hakam II, of whose famous collection of antiquities in Madînat al-Zahrâ' some remains have been preserved, and whose library is said to have comprised four hundred thousand volumes.[69] Al-Mansûr's extension, by contrast, testifies to thoroughness and efficiency, as well as to his characteristic mixture of far-reaching ambition and the politically shrewd humility which prevented him – outwardly – from competing with the Caliphs.

The volume of this mosque cannot be perceived as a whole; it is determined by the large number of long arcades, optically more or less divided by the double arches. Each nave or aisle can only be perceived singly as a homogeneous unit, albeit one whose beginning and end are blurred by the distance and whose sides are not solid. By contrast, the spatial sensation in the Umayyad basilicas of the Near East is striking precisely because of their self-contained immensity. The multiplication and the extreme length of the aisles in Cordova rob its hall of columns of the spatial impression characteristic of the basilica of late Antiquity or early Christendom. The prayer hall is shrouded in a murky half-light which is given a mystical note by the shimmering gold mosaics, and whose light effects are indeed reminiscent of classical Byzantine churches. The fragmentation of the spatial volume is a Cordovan characteristic nonetheless, and owes nothing to Byzantine models. It has its parallel in the blurring of architectural functions, exemplified by the fact that the load-bearing elements become thicker towards the top, that supports become part of the decor and *vice versa*. The organization of an enormous complex into small, clearly demarcated parts, the mutual interpenetration of function and ornament, the visual fragmentation of the self-contained volume – these are all unmistakable peculiarities of the Great Mosque of Cordova, taken up by all subsequent architecture in Andalusia and the Maghreb as a heritage to be exploited and developed.

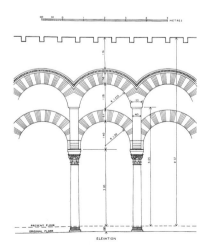

Elevation (K.A.C. Creswell) *and view of the forest of columns*

The two-tiered arrangement of arches in the prayer-hall represented a unique and brilliant solution on the part of 'Abd ar-Rahmân I's architect to the problem of creating a lofty interior space in spite of the limited dimensions of the individual supports. Above the capital of every column there is a massive impost supporting a yet more massive pier which extends the column below and supports the upper arch, which in turn supports the roof. The impost also supports the lower arches, which act as tension beams. These lower arches are horseshoe-shaped, while the upper, more massive arcade consists of semicircular arches. Both arcades consist of alternate red-brick and yellow-stone voussoirs.

86

Smaller Mosques

The most splendid architecture of the Caliphate period is to be found in and around Cordova. However, throughout Andalusia this period of wealth and internal tranquillity encouraged the construction of new buildings. Few have survived, but we do still have a number of impressive former mosques, for example San Cristo de la Luz in Toledo, San Juan in Almería, and most particularly, Almonaster la Real (in Huelva province), in its picturesque mountain setting; the Rábita de Guardamar del Segura, a sort of fortified monastery, is a sacred building and a residential complex at the same time.

The church of San Cristo de la Luz in Toledo was originally a mosque, which was extended by the addition of an apse in 1187.[70] Its Arabic name has not been preserved, but it is frequently recorded under the name of the nearby city gate, al-Bâb al-Mardûm. The foundation inscription, which has been preserved, gives the date of its construction as 999/1000, and also the name of the patron and the architect. It indicates that the mosque was privately endowed. It is a small brick building, square in plan, measuring approximately eight metres along each side. Its ingenious ornamentation in the brickwork suggests at first Mesopotamian inspiration. Closer inspection, however, reveals it to be a greatly reduced copy of al-Hakam's extension to the Great Mosque in Cordova. The two-storey façade and the internal arcades, the multi-lobed arches, the blind arcades of interlocking horseshoe-arches on the south-west front, and above all the nine ribbed

Seccion de la boveda n.º 1

Capitel de un partelar del 2.º cuerpo

Seccion de la boveda n.º 6

Seccion de la boveda n.º 2

Capiteles del cuerpo inferior

Seccion de la boveda n.º 4

Arcada lateral del 2.º cuerpo

Seccion de la boveda n.º 5

Seccion de la boveda n.º 3

Capiteles del cuerpo inferior

Seccion por la linea A B

Planta y proyecciones de las bovedas

vaults in the ceiling are direct "quotes" from the larger building. The prayer hall, divided into nine approximately square compartments by four massive, base-less columns, represents a centrally-planned structure without any orientation; the raised central dome corresponds to this ground plan, and the whole structure can thus be seen in its Near Eastern, Byzantine and Umayyad traditions. Nevertheless, its elavation does reveal an orientation: the arrangement of the openings of the arches in the intermediate storey is determined entirely by the *mihrâb* axes and by the priority of the three *qibla* bays, thus hinting at the T-plan which underlies the arrangement both at Cordova and at Madînat al-Zahrâ'. The arrangement of domes serves to indicate the same orientation scheme. This tiny, modest building reflects the intellectual situation of al-Andalus at the end of the Caliphate: while still in possession of its traditional heritage, it was at the same time on the threshold of a mannerist epoch – that of the *taifa* rulers of the 11th century (C. Ewert).

The little prayer room in the upper storey of the "Casa de la Tornerías", also in Toledo and dating from the end of the Caliphate, likewise has a nine-bay ground-plan (although the bays here are not square, but oblong); it is in fact a copy of the mosque of Bâb al-Mardûm.[71] Here, though, the ribbed domes are concentrated in the central compartment alone, which thus forms a "miniature building" with nine dwarf-like individual domes in the midst of the simply-vaulted surrounding bays. This nine-domed mosque goes even further than Bâb al-Mardûm in its reduction of the ribbed vaults to a small-scale decorative pattern; the way is no longer very long before we arrive at the total fragmentation of the rib skeleton and the introduction of the *muqarnas*.[72]

Almería was originally only the maritime suburb (al-Marîya, "watch-tower", around which the town of Almería grew up) of Pechina, which during the 9th century was a flourishing, largely independent maritime republic which did not return to Umayyad rule until 922. In the year 955 'Abd ar-Rahmân III had a wall built around Almería, thus turning it into a self-contained town which gradually pushed Pechina itself into a totally subordinate position. The Chief Mosque, today the Church of San Juan, certainly dates from this period. The original building probably consisted of a nave and two aisles,[73] before being enlarged twice during the 11th century. The *qibla* wall, a flimsy screen with an alternation of stretchers and headers over cement, is still preserved behind 17th-century arches. The *mihrâb* itself was given a plaster decoration in Almohadic times; today this is in a state of decay, revealing remains from the Caliphate period beneath: a smooth base zone, a frieze of blind arches with an umbrella dome above. As recently as 1987 remains of a seven-arch blind arcade were discovered 1.15 metres above the *alfiz* of the *mihrâb*, which leaves no room for doubt that the whole complex belongs in the Cordovan tradition.[74] In the stucco decor of these arcades, of which only four panels remain, vegetal forms are strongly in evidence; this too points to the art of the Caliphate as seen in Cordova and Madînat al-Zahrâ'. To be more precise, these seem to be exact quotations from motifs in the *mihrâb* vault and the entrance vault of al-Hakam's extension. The *mihrâb* in Almería is the only contemporary document which bears comparison with that in Cordova; it was directly influenced by the latter, but probably derives from a different workshop, as the details of its execution point to independent craftsmanship. This mosque points to the artistic dependence of Almería on Cordova, following upon its similar political dependence. The master builder at Almería was working consciously in the tradition of the capital, with which he was apparently quite familiar. The means at his disposal were not comparable with those at the Caliph's court, but they nonetheless enabled him to erect a monument which is both stately and in no way provincial.

Almonaster la Real (Arabic: al-Munastîr), today a somewhat remote place, was mentioned already by al-Bakrî as belonging to the *kûra* of Seville.[75] Its name (an Arabization of *monasterium*) points to an earlier settlement, as do the Roman and Visigothic remains incorporated into the fabric of the mosque. It is thus reasonable to assume that on the site of the Islamic mountain fortress with its circumference wall and its mosque, there were once Roman and Visigothic buildings. The mosque dates from the 10th century. It is an irregular structure of brick and rough stone, trapezoidal in plan; its shape was probably determined by the sloping ground on which it stands. The prayer hall consists of a nave and four aisles, the arcades of which, as at Cordova, are set at right angles to the *qibla*. The central nave is broader than the two inner aisles, which in turn

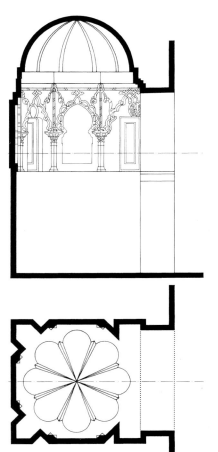

The mihrâb of the former Chief Mosque of Almería, plan and elevation (C. Ewert)
The *mihrâb* dates from the period of the Caliphate; under the early Almohads it was clad in stucco. It is the Almohad stucco panels which mainly attract the attention of the modern visitor. The masonry and the cupola are part of the original structure.

Almería: the mihrâb façade of the former Chief Mosque
The upper blind arcade of what is now the church of San Juan with its vegetal stucco panels above the horseshoe arch and the *alfiz* demonstrate that this *mihrâb* derives directly from that in the Great Mosque in Cordoba.

Ground-plan of the present-day church of San Juan (C. Ewert)

FOLLOWING DOUBLE PAGE:
Almonaster la Real
The present-day church can be recognized at a distance as a former mosque by the projecting *mihrâb* niche on the south side. The addition of an apse at the east end and a porch at the opposite end re-aligned the church, so to speak, in accordance with the requirements of the Christian religion. At the same time the minaret was converted into a church tower. Before the Islamic mountain fortress with its circumference wall and its mosque, there stood here a Visigothic settlement, itself on the site of a yet earlier Roman one.

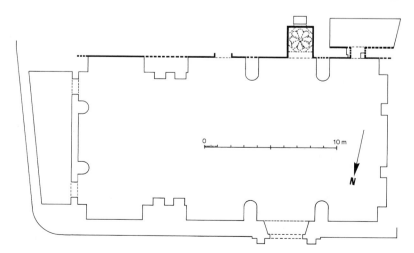

Almonaster la Real: interior of the prayerhall
In a highly simplified form, this rustic little building recapitulates some of the themes of the Great Mosque of Cordova. In the right of the picture is the *mihrâb*.

are broader than the two outer. The southern bays are wider than the others: thus we have a clear suggestion of a T-plan. The *mihrâb* has lost its facing; it is a deep, archaic-looking niche of brick and rough stone.[76] There is a tiny courtyard veritably hewn out of the rock face, representing an extension of the two east aisles; in the north-west corner is a disproportionately large pool. A rectangular minaret stands separate from the main building to the north, displaced to the west vis-à-vis the *mihrâb* axis. The mosque probably had just one entrance, in the north bay of the east aisle. What little light it had came from the courtyard, the doorway and three narrow window slits, of which two are immediately either side of the *mihrâb*. Sixteen undated graves have been discovered in the prayer hall.[77] During the Christian period the mosque was enlarged by the addition of an apse, with a sacristy alongside, and a porch on the west side, thus giving the building a new main axis corresponding to the new religion. The old gate was also rebuilt, together with the north side. The structure exudes a kind of rustic charm. Its archaic character could point to an early 9th-century date for its construction, but it might equally well be a provincial example of the architecture of the Caliphate. The hierarchical arrangement of the prayer hall would tend to support the latter view.

Every town possessed a chief mosque with a *mihrâb*, but apart from those mentioned above, few other examples from the Umayyad period are still extant. However, there is in Tarragona Cathedral a marble niche 1.26 metres high, whose inscription mentions the name of 'Abd ar-Rahmân III and the date 960.[78] Its plaited and arabesque borders are purely Caliphate in style, besides being of great charm in themselves. It is without a doubt the *mihrâb* of the chief mosque, which underwent a programme of renovation at that time.

The Rábita de Guardamar

The Rábita de Guardamar del Segura, 26 kilometres to the south of Alicante, situated in a pine copse in the middle of the dunes, is a relatively recently discovered complex of religious buildings of particular interest, the subject of excavation works since 1984, now largely complete.[79] As long ago as 1897 an inscription from the Guardamar area was published, whose precise provenance could not be established at the time. It refers to the completion of a mosque in the year 944.[80] This mosque was part of a *ribât*, in other words a fortified foundation somewhat monastic in nature, such as were frequently established in the frontier areas of Islam. Their purpose was to serve as a base for the Holy War, or else to offer a suitable ambience for religious retreat. The *ribât* at Guardamar was founded at the end of the 9th century and abandoned at the beginning of the 11th; this makes it the oldest known example in Spain.

Written sources document the existence of such *ribâts* in Andalusia during the 9th century; so much is known. This archaeological discovery thus confirms these sources. However, it was a surprise insofar as the *ribât* of Guardamar differs substantially from the usual western Islamic type. What we would have expected is a square or otherwise rectangular forti-

Ground plan of the complex
(R. Aznar Ruiz)

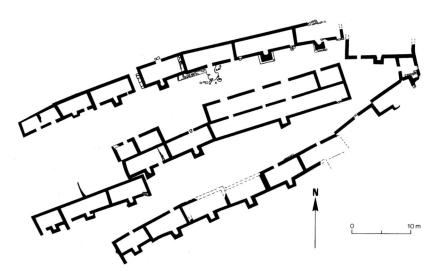

fied structure, such as we find in the ribât at Sousse or at Monastir in Tunisia, resembling the Umayyad desert castles of the Near East. Instead, what we have is an array of alleyways laid out in elliptical fashion between rows of mostly smallish cells, each with its own *mihrâb*; a long circumference wall surrounded the whole complex. The chief mosque, in which masonry remains dating from the 9th century have been found, is situated in the middle of the complex, and consists of two naves, or rather, halls. The foundation inscription from 944 was on the outside of the mihrâb of one of the prayer cells. The low buildings are of rammed clay on a masonry base. A very few remains of painted decoration are still visible. Excavations have brought to light ceramic material and numerous inscriptions. The water supply must have been spartan indeed: no plumbing of any kind has been found. These prayer and living cells are a special case, like the complex itself. They throw a new light on the typological diversity of the *ribât* phenomenon.

Fortresses and Bridges

The border regions of Andalusia were veritably sprinkled with fortresses in the 10th century, but even in the interior, there was a network of fortified garrisons, which kept the country under surveillance and thus guaranteed the authority of the central government, along with sentry posts, fortified inns, and castles where the people could seek refuge if needed. The precise function of these castles is not always clear; many were erected as the seats of the central power, while others by contrast were the expression of the local communities' desire for self-determination. Others yet again were the residences of more or less independent noble families. Many watch-towers in a centralized defence network may just as well have served as refuges for rural communities; their form does not always make their exact purpose clear.[81] A number of fortresses dating from this period have left impressive remains[82], thus for example Gormaz (dating from 965) not far from Soria, which was part of the fortification system of the

Baños de la Encina at the foot of the Sierra Morena
Baños de la Encina is one of the best-known and best-preserved fortresses of the Caliphate period. The inscription on its foundation stone gives a date of 986. It features the first fortification tower to have rooms one above the other.

northern frontier region. Less spectacular and almost unknown is Al-miserat in eastern Andalusia;[83] by contrast famous and often described is Tarifa, which played a major role in the defence system along the south coast. Baños de la Encina, to the north of Jaén, in the foothills of the Sierra Morena, is a particularly fine and imposing example from the fortification system of the interior; likewise the fortress of Alcaraz, from where the plains of the Mancha were guarded. In the Guadalimar valley there are remains of small fortresses placed at regular intervals. The rectangular circumference wall of El Vacar to the north of Cordova must have been for many soldiers and travellers alike the first stage along the road to Extremadura.[84]

Most Hispano-Islamic castle ruins have not been dated exactly, but it is likely that many of them go back to structures dating from the 10th century. Their positions are often spectacular, but the level of their defence technology hardly matched up to their robust appearance. Some are built of dressed stone, while others, particularly in the south of the country, are made of rammed clay; they have no barbicans, or even outer walls; the entrances are simple gates, the towers mostly rectangular, simply built on to the outside of the wall, and hardly any higher; mostly they are solid right up to the open parapet, and only rarely do they have rooms accessible by means of an indoor staircase. In some cases the flanking towers are absent, being replaced by kinks in the line of the wall (for example in Uclés, the foundations of whose walls probably date back to this time).[85] On the plains, the castles are mostly rectangular in plan, while in the mountains, this depends on the lie of the land. Andalusian fortification technology did not develop further until several centuries had passed.

The major Roman bridges were preserved into Visigothic and Umayyad times, thus for example the bridges over the Guadalquivir in Cordova, over the Guadiana in Mérida, over the Genil in Ecija, over the Henares in Guadalajara, and, famously, the Alcantara bridge in Toledo.[86] All these structures still retain the evidence of having passed through an Umayyad phase; restoration has been an ongoing process from the period of their construction until the present day, though, and individual measures are no longer precisely datable. The 10th century also saw the building of new bridges, but few of these have been preserved in their original form. The stone bridge known as the Puente de Pinos near Granada on the road to Cordova, with its three horseshoe arches and rounded breakwaters, is a notably picturesque, albeit now somewhat dilapidated example of bridge-building under the Caliphate.

Towns: the Example of Vascos

The fortifications of many towns still retain elements dating from the 10th century. In Toledo a part of the eastern section of the city wall containing re-used Roman and Visigothic remains probably dates from the time of the Umayyad Caliphs, and next to the Alcantara Bridge the remains of a city gate with what was once a straight passage between two towers can still be seen.[87] Some sections of the Cordova city wall also date back to the 10th century, including in all likelihood the Seville Gate. In addition to Roman remains, the Cáceres city wall may also contain some dating from the Umayyad period; most of the structure, though, is of Almohad origin.

In a deep gorge formed by a meander of the Rio Hiso in the west of the province of Toledo, not far from Navalmoralejo, lie the isolated ruins of a

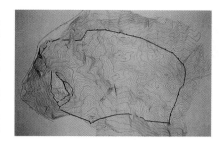

Vascos: map of the town wall and citadel; city wall with sally gate (R. Izquierdo Benito)

Toledo: Alcantara Bridge
The bridge, which dates from Roman times, has undergone frequent restoration. It was once the main access route to the city.

The Hammâm in Jaén

The Islamic hot bath has its roots in classical antiquity, and throughout the Islamic world is one of the essential components of urban living. The more or less centrally-placed changing and relaxation room is particularly important, and often, as here, has a domed ceiling and is surrounded by galleries. Hot water and steam play a far greater role in the *hammâm* than in the baths of antiquity, but unlike the latter, they have no proper *frigidarium*. Both classical and western Islamic baths were provided with underfloor heating, or hypocausts. In place of windows, the baths of western Islam have round or, as here, star-shaped apertures with ceramic cladding in the ceiling; these provide a necessary minimum of light.

10th century town now known by the name of Vascos, but whose original name is unknown.[88] It may be the town of Nafza, known from written sources, founded by the Berber tribe of the same name; it may even be the town, likewise known from written sources, in Toledo province, which Caliph al-Hakam II ordered to be rebuilt in 964 under the direction of one well-paid Ahmad ibn Nasr ibn Khâlid. Since 1975, excavation has been going on in Vascos, enabling us to form a picture of the general layout of the place, and a number of 10th and 11th century pottery fragments have also come to light. Vascos was an Umayyad military settlement intended for the protection of the middle section of the Tajo valley; it owed its prosperity presumably to mining, first and foremost of silver. Roman and Visigothic remains point to a yet earlier settlement. As a result of the Christian reconquest, the town gradually fell into disuse from the 12th century onwards.

The walls, two metres thick on average and still standing three metres high in places, consist of ashlar blocks with plenty of mortar. It has towers at intervals, and encloses an irregular quadrilateral of some eight hectares, with the *alcazaba* in the north. The west gate, with its horizontal lintel beneath a horsheshoe arch, and a straight passage between two towers, is still recognizable; there is a similar gateway on the south side. A number of smaller gates provide access to the river. Outside the wall, to the west, the remains of a public bathhouse and a private dwelling house have been discovered, while further to the west there was a large cemetery, with another – also outside the wall – to the south. Excavation work is not yet complete.

A number of 10th century bathhouses have also been preserved, at least in part, for example the one in the Caliph's Palace in Cordova. The *hammâm* in Jaén, probably dating from the 11th century, has undergone alterations at some intervening period.[89]

Here, as in later Andalusian *hammâms*, the hot rooms were heated in the Roman manner by means of hypocausts; however, they differ radically from the classical model not only in the small size of the individual rooms, but also in the absence of any *frigidarium* (i.e. cooling-off room) or gymnasium.

Ornamentation

Architectural ornamentation during the Caliphate showed a predilection for valuable materials such as glass mosaics and marble. Stucco[90] was also used, albeit somewhat discreetly in comparison with subsequent developments. Elements taken over from classical antiquity include ovolos and other mouldings, in which acanthus, vine-leaf and laurel motifs are to be met with time and again, along with arabesques and geometric patterns.[91] Alongside them we have Sassanian and other Near Eastern motifs, in particular in the form of rich composite palmettes of calyces, cornucopias and semi-palmettes, together with vine-leaves stylized to the point of unrecognizability and purely symmetrical arrangements of panels with tree-of-life motifs. The edges of the leaves of the semi-palmettes are mostly feathered, or else with a perforated border. The bunch-of-grapes motif, which occurs independently of the vine-leaf, has often hardened into a pine-cone.

ABOVE:
A pool in the hammâm in Jaén

BELOW:
A side room with vessels for drawing water

Capitals from the mihrâb entrance in the Great Mosque of Cordova
The capitals in al-Hakam II's *mihrâb* were removed from the old structure at the time of the extension of the mosque in 965 and carefully incorporated into the new building. They are so "classical" in appearance that on occasions they have been thought to be Roman remains.

Capital from the time of the Caliphate in the Louvre, currently in the Musée de l'Institut du Monde Arabe, Paris
Here the vegetal designs have dissolved into the geometric, evenly covering all the surfaces; even so, its model, the classical Corinthian capital, is still recognizable.

Leaf-stalks are almost always treated as decorative ribbons, often with one or more grooves or else a lozenge pattern; as abstract, rhythmical elements, they determine the whole decorative programme. Such themes, along with the tendency to leave no spaces void of decoration, were both widespread features of Umayyad art in the Near East, wherely Sassanian characteristics emerge more strongly. One specific feature of the architectural decor of the Andalusian Caliphate is the systematic interruption of vegetal ornamentation by deeply incised internal motifs. All in all, the vocabulary of forms is actually more restricted than in the 9th century, but this limited repertoire nonetheless gives rise to variations of great decorative effect.[92] Most of the sculptures were executed with a chisel, giving many of the panels and capitals a distinctly Byzantine flavour.

Since the 9th century, the capitals had moved further away from classical models. While a number of different types can still be distinguished, in general the output had become more standard. The basic form is still derived from composite or Corinthian capitals, but while in antique capitals the form was determined by the idea of vegetal growth and a progressive transition from the circular column to the rectangular impost, what we now see is an almost cylindrical lower section and an almost rectangular upper section without anything in between. This clear stereometric division between load and support was blurred during the first half of the Caliphate period by the luxuriant treatment of the surfaces. These capitals are mostly derivatives of the "fine-toothed acanthus capital" of Byzantine art, in which the abstraction of the vegetal motif is dominant, leaving room for geometrical patterns. Subsequent development of the capitals of the Caliphate period involves an enormous simplification. While they retain the same basic shape, they hark back to the smooth-leaved capitals of late antiquity, and treatment of the surfaces is reduced to a minimum. Al-Mansûr's extension to the Great Mosque of Cordova has exclusively this latter type, which had first made its appearance under al-Hakam, and which was to prove fundamental in the future development of Hispano-Maghreb capitals.

The epigraphic decoration is determined exclusively by the Kufic script. Inscriptions appear on the friezes of the *mihrâbs*, the gates and windows, and sometimes below the ceilings, as well as on imposts and plinths. They are very simple, insofar as the background has hardly any decoration, and the letters are, so to speak, self-sufficient. The substance of these inscriptions very often takes the form of a recital of dates, names and titles, suggesting that the artists were conscious of the value of their work. As with the vegetal decor, there is more affinity between 8th-century Umayyad inscriptions from Syria and 10th-century inscriptions from Andalusia than between the latter and contemporary Abbasid examples.

Numerous items of a high level of craftsmanship dating from the period of the Andalusian Caliphate are to be found in museums throughout the world. Fine gold ornaments of a distinctly Byzantine character, among them many pieces with glass bases, have been discovered in Madînat al-Zahrâ'.[93] The round or angular ivory caskets[94] with their rich figurative, vegetal, or epigraphic carvings are specifically Andalusian, in spite of their iconography, which is often reminiscent of Near Eastern models. Bronze fountain figures in the form of animals,[95] as well as charming pottery items with underglaze painting on a white background, often with highly lifelike animal motifs, are also typical of the art of the Caliphate period.[96] A very few textiles still extant bear witness to the celebrated activities of the Andalusian workshops: in Almería alone, which was famous for its silkworm breeding, there were, according to al-Idrîsî, no less than 800 looms in the 10th century. The cloth fragments that have been preserved are quite similar to Fatimid examples; silk and gold threads were woven into a linen base, the decor consisting of calligraphy, vegetal borders or human and animal figures incorporated into a medallion scheme.[97]

Figurative ornamentation was not used for architectural decor; what we do have are a number of large marble basins dating from the end of the 10th and the beginning of the 11th centuries. Alongside vegetal friezes, inscriptions and hunting scenes, they are noteworthy for large panels with hieratic-heraldic animal-fight motifs (eagles and lions taking goats).[98] Heraldic beasts are to be seen alongside natural ones on ivory-work pieces, too.[99]

As far as book-binding and book-illustration is concerned, unfortunately next to nothing is known; of al-Hakam's great library, just one manuscript has been discovered up till now.[100]

In spite of all the losses, the picture we can form of this prolific artistic output is overwhelming; the trials and errors of the 9th century were followed in the 10th by a confidence and competence that had a firm basis of technical ability and good-quality material to build upon. It is true that it is mostly the art of the court with which we are familiar, and it will have been from the court that the artistic impulses proceeded; nevertheless, more humble work has also been preserved, above all in the fields of metalwork and pottery. Like the mosque at Almonaster, they too convey the impression of creative vitality among the ordinary people of Andalusia and confirm the picture of general prosperity that we get from the historical sources.

ABOVE:
Ivory casket, the property of al-Mughîra, in the Louvre, Paris
This outstandingly well-preserved round box with lid was, as the inscription on it says, made in 968 for al-Mughîra, the brother and tragic successor of al-Hakam II. Its four eight-lobed medallions depict scenes characteristic of the iconography associated with the ruler in Umayyad Spain.

BELOW:
Ivory box, 966, in the Louvre, currently in the Musée de l'Institut du Monde Arabe, Paris

1031–1091

The Age of the Petty Kings

The history of Andalusia is basically the history of the tension that dominated the relationship between the central power and the innumerable peripheral and centrifugal forces that were immediately unleashed once the centre showed signs of weakness. The years between 1031 and 1091 are seen as the Age of the Petty Kings, or of the *Fitna* ("discord"); even so, it was neither the first nor the last such period.

Three ethnic "parties", (*tâ'ifa*, plural *tawâ'if*) – the Berbers, the Saqâliba and the Andalusians – faced each other in the early 11th century, but none was united within itself. The "Andalusian Party" included the Arabs and the Muwalladûn, who were subdivided into countless little groups, each with its own interests; the only common denominator was that each wanted to seize power for itself. The Berbers had come to Andalusia in the mid-10th century from various North African tribal groupings; they did not mix with the "Old Berbers" who had arrived between the beginning of the 8th century and the beginning of the 10th, and were by now fully integrated. The newcomers felt no loyalty either to Andalusia or to its ruler, but only to their own commanders.[101] For the Andalusian town-dwellers, the new Berber troops represented a feared and hated alien force. Curiously, though, they received no reinforcements from North Africa. Their weakness was due to the fact that they aroused the hostility not only of the Andalusian population, but also of each other. Like the Saqâliba, they had no roots in the country. The latter, too, were cut off from the land of their origin, and thus lacked any human reserves. The Andalusian slave aristocracy, unlike the Mamelukes in Egypt, who held power from the 13th century until the start of the 16th, had never grown into a homogeneous group; nor had they given any thought to new blood, nor had they ever founded a proper dynasty. By the end of the 11th century they had been absorbed into the general population.

In reality, then, the situation was not one of struggle between three ethnic parties, but rather of anarchy, where each was in principle involved in alliances with or against everyone else. "After the fall of the 'Âmirid dynasty, when the people no longer had an Imam, every town saw the rise of a leader who seized power, hired mercenaries, gathered a fortune and fortified his castle. These leaders fought each other for wealth, and each envied the other what he possessed." Thus the picture painted of the start of this period in the late 11th century, by Emir 'Abd Allâh al-Zîrî, one of the petty rulers in question.[102]

This text and others make it perfectly clear that the murder of the third 'Âmirid was followed throughout Andalusia by a seizure of power on the part of local strong men. These must have included, primarily at first, the local administrators appointed – or often simply confirmed in office – by the 'Âmirids themselves, thus for example Mundhir I al-Tujîbî in Saragossa and Abû Bakr bin Ya'îsh al-Qâdî in Toledo. Sometimes they were Berbers, for example al-Qâsim ibn Hammûd in Algeciras, 'Alî ibn Hammûd in Ceuta and Málaga, Zâwî ibn Zîrî al-Sinhâjî in Granada and Abû Muhammad Ismâ'îl ibn Dhî al-Nûn in Toledo. The Hûdids, who came to power in Saragossa in about 1040 were also Berbers. "Slavs" took over on the east coast, for example Mubarak and Muzaffar in Valencia, Mujâhid al-'Âmirî in Denia and on the Balearic Islands, Khayrân in Murcia and Almería, and Sâbûr in Badajoz. In Cordova and Seville, power was seized by leading patrician families (the Jauharids and the 'Abbâdids), while elsewhere the new rulers can only be described as robber barons.[103] The new political units were city-states in every case, many of them minute, their internal cohesion resting not on any cultural unity among their inhabitants, but purely on geographical considerations. On the periphery of Andalusia a number of these states, with a rich agricultural hinterland at their disposal, spread out to occupy a sizable area, thus for example Saragossa, Toledo and Badajoz. On the coast, by contrast, the units were small, managing to survive by virtue of their international maritime trade and their highly developed economic infrastructure.

All these statelets were monarchically governed; democratic or even oligarchic regimes were virtually unknown. Even so, the political fragmentation of Andalusia led to prominent local personalities playing a much more active political role than had previously been the case.[104] The Jewish communities also took part in cultural and economic life, and in Granada in particular their role was of extraordinary importance; here, a Jewish

Saragossa: Aljafería, east façade
The castle, which dates from the second half of the 11th century, owes its modern name to its builder, one of the most influential of the petty kings, Abû Ja'far Ahmad ibn Sulaymân, a member of the Banû Hûd clan. Its original name was *Dâr al-Surûr*, or House of Joy, and indeed, despite its well-fortified appearance, it was in fact a summer residence.

vizier, Samuel ben Naghrîla, found an opportunity to demonstrate his qualities of generalship as well as of civil administration over a period of almost twenty years.[105] The Christian minorities seem no longer to have played much of a role. Even so, it is clear that the threat from the Christian Reconquista never goaded the Muslims into persecuting the Christians at any time during the *taifa* period. During this period, Cordova's political role had shrunk to nothing, but it was apparently still an attractive place to be, as many dethroned rulers took up residence there. From the mid-11th century onwards, the 'Abbâdid family of Seville grew ever more powerful. The founder of the family's fortunes, the *qâdî* Muhammad bin 'Abbâd (1013–42), a prominent burgher, was succeeded by his son al-Mu'tadid and his grandson al-Mu'tamid. Seville went on to annex a good dozen of its neighbours, from Mertola in the west to Murcia in the east, and for a time ruled over Cordova too. All in all, Seville, Toledo and Saragossa outshone the other city-states both in the extent and the duration of their power.

Most of the more significant courts, whose rulers liked to adorn themselves with high-flown "names of honour", were distinguished by an active intellectual life; and for all their mutual enmity, intrigues and wars,

Málaga: Alcazaba
The fortress extends along a slope which climbs to the east. A wall connects it to Gibralfaro castle, which stands on the top of the same hill. Together, they form one of the strongest fortification systems in the whole of Islamic Spain. The double circumference wall of the Alcazaba was pro-bably built by one of the 11th-century Berber rulers to replace older Arab fortifications. Various towers were renovated during the 13th and 14th centuries.

these same ruling families nevertheless intermarried and invited each other to festivals and literary competitions. The "official style" of the 11th century is famous for its refinement; education and culture were in general highly valued, and the art of the period, insofar as we are familiar with it, is very sophisticated. The Andalusian cities of the 11th century also seem to have retained their bilingualism, Arabic and Romance both continuing to be spoken, a circumstance which led to poetic forms unknown elsewhere.[106] Patronage played an important role, for all these petty kings were eager to emulate the Caliphate in this regard. The proverbial generosity of the Arabs resulted not only in an inflation in the number of courtly panegyrists, and the erection of sophisticated prestige buildings, but also in inventions on the technological plane, for example the Toledan waterclock, which al-Zarqâl constructed for the local ruler. Poets, artists and scholars, motivated by promises of prestige and profit, seem not to have hesitated to move from one court to another to offer their sublime services. The most magnificent court by far was that of the 'Abbâdids of Seville.

This system did however result in an oppressive – and according to the Koran, unlawful – burden of taxation, and thus in the end to its own destabilization. On the other hand it is reasonable to assume that, after the removal of Hishâm and the disastrous internecine strife among the pretenders to the throne, the various cities and towns of Andalusia were quite ready to accept the authority of local leaders;[107] the dead-end into which the new power structure was leading would only gradually have become apparent.

The Christian rulers to the north, by contrast, had the situation summed up fairly quickly, and not only stopped paying tribute, but even went as far as to demand it from the Islamic petty rulers. Badajoz, Toledo and even Seville came to be dependent upon King Alfonso VI of León and Castile (1065–1109). The Islamic prince of al-Andalus, incidentally, had no religious scruples when it came to seeking aid from the Christians to help them in their struggle against their Muslim brothers: the necessary taxes were, it goes without saying, extremely unpopular among their own subjects. Rodrigo Díaz de Vivar, who has gone down in history as El Cid, is a telling example of the indifference of many *condottieri* towards either the Islamic or the Christian religion. He had been a courtier of Alfonso VI, with whom he quarrelled; he then sold his services as a mercenary leader to various princes both Christian and Muslim, among them the ruling family in Saragossa. He ended his career as the independent Christian ruler of the Islamic city of Valencia, which he had taken with quite remarkable brutality. "Cid" is derived from the Arabic title "Sayyid" via its dialect form "Sîd" ("master"). This adventurer has been highly praised by Christian historians, even though it really cannot be said that he reconquered for Christendom one square inch of Islamic territory.[108]

The Reconquista did proceed rapidly nonetheless, for during the 11th century Christian Spain managed to break free of its isolation from the rest of Europe. The Pope succeeded in imposing the Roman rite on the Spanish Church, and in return he took an active interest in the Reconquista. In addition, the influence of the Cluniac movement had also reached the Iberian peninsula. All the same, the question remains as to whether Alfonso VI really did want to reconquer Spain and Portugal for Christianity, or whether his real aim was not simply to enlarge and secure his kingdom. All in all, there was not much of a crusading spirit in Spain at that time. The titles known to have been used by Alfonso on a number of occasions – *Imperator constitutus super omnes Hispaniae nationes* and *Imbaratûr dhû al-millatayn* ("Ruler of the Two Nations")[109] – demonstrate that he saw no contradiction between being a Spaniard and being a Muslim.

In al-Andalus anarchy had reached totally unimaginable proportions. While the 'Abbâdids were the strongest among the petty kings, they were not able to enforce their authority on a general scale, and the dissatisfaction of the people, plagued as they were by tax-collectors, was growing all the time. The capture of Toledo in 1085 – her internal dissensions having practically placed the city in Alfonso VI's lap – was the signal for a gesture which was to be of great future significance: al-Mu'tamid of Seville – probably with the approval of the Ziridic Berber rulers – called on the powerful Berber dynasty of Morocco for help.[110] The African Almoravids under their ruler Yûsuf bin Tâshufîn probably had no intention at first to settle in Andalusia. After a spectacular victory over Alfonso VI at Zallâqa near Badajoz in 1086, they first returned to Morocco. But hardly had they left Spain, when the pristine disorder on the peninsula broke out once more.

Granada: capital from the Bañuelo in the Albaicín

Granada: Albaicín, 13th-century minaret, today part of the church of San Juan de los Reyes

Archez, Nasrid minaret
The minaret was subsequently converted into a church tower. The panels with the lozenge pattern are a legacy of the Almohads, while the blind arcade of interlocking arches is based on Cordovan Umayyad models.

Yûsuf was again called upon to help, landing in the spring of 1090, and this time not only had to survive numerous lengthy battles, but also had unexpected and tiresome problems with the petty Islamic rulers, who had secretly formed an alliance with the Christians against him. They were deceiving themselves, said one of them later (the Ziridic prince 'Abd Allâh, quoted above), "like shipwrecked sailors who drown each other."[111] Having created some semblance of order for a second time, Yûsuf decided to incorporate Andalusia into the Almoravid Empire.

The sources are explicit in reporting that Yûsuf came to this decision on the advice of Andalusian jurists, and that it thus did not represent a means of quenching his thirst for power. It is absolutely certain that the religious indifference of the commanders and petty kings was a thorn in the flesh of the Andalusian theologians and jurists, and that they regarded the puritanism of the Almoravids as a possible and desirable alternative. It is equally certain that the materially and morally exhausted people of Andalusia longed for an end to the chaos, and that the Almoravids must have been a welcome arrival, if for no other reason than that they promised a return to the taxes laid down in the Koran and thus the abolition of the heavy, and illegitimate, burdens imposed on them by the *taifa* princes. The latter, by contrast, were caught between the hammer of one powerful neighbour – Yûsuf – and the anvil of another – Alfonso; in the course of the Almoravid conquest, which lasted until the capture of Saragossa in 1110 (following Granada in 1090, Cordova and Seville in 1091, Badajoz in 1094 and Valencia in 1102; Toledo remained in Christian hands), Yûsuf summarily arrested many of these petty rulers and deported them to Aghmât at the foot of the High Atlas, the old capital, and to Marrakesh, the newly founded one.[112] The last Zirid ruler of Granada, 'Abd Allâh, whom we have mentioned a number of times, found in Aghmât that he had the time and the leisure to write his memoirs, a valuable contribution to the history of the period. As for al-Mu'tamid, the sensitive, cultured and in religious matters tolerant ruler of Seville who was originally responsible for summoning the Almoravids to Spain, he too ended his days as a captive in the mountain fortress of Aghmât, where he assuaged his enforced idleness and harsh conditions by composing timeless literary masterpieces. His epitaph, which he composed himself, read:

"May the morning and the evening rains drench you,
O alien grave; to you belongs now all that remains
of Mu'tamid, the marksman, swordsman, lance wielder,
the desert-spring, the balm of thirsty men.
Yes, so it is. A fate of heaven has
allocated me this place and set me this destination.
I did not know, before I came to lie here,
that mountains could shake to their foundations.
On your dead may God's blessing sink
without limit, and beyond number."[113]

The Architecture
of the Taifa Period

Fortresses and Castles

In spite of the economic, political and social problems that beset 11th-century Andalusia, her artistic energies were in no way diminished. The age of the grand commissions of the Caliphate was, it is true, gone for good; but in return, the number of princely patrons had increased. Cordova's heritage was fragmented, but in the process, penetrated deep into the hinterland. It was a development which gave rise to a number of local forms of expression, which have still to this day not been registered in detail. *Taifa* art as a general concept is familiar enough, but when we come down to particulars, it is difficult to identify all the various workshops.

It was a period of unrest, so not unnaturally a considerable number of fortresses were built or enlarged, especially in the interior of the country.[114] The towns and cities were given new circumference walls, and the old ones were improved. The age of the "open city" was past. The high rammed-clay wall with its massive rectangular and round towers that rears up over the Albaicín in Granada was built in the 11th century under the Zirids. Niebla, originally a Roman foundation, was fortified by a similar wall, still preserved, at the same time. The town of Játiva down on the plain was connected by a wall to a fortress situated on a rocky ridge. Almería, Denia, Orihuela, Balaguer and many other towns and cities all saw the erection of such connecting walls, many of which are still extant.

The walls now consist mostly of rammed clay; this was a technique that had already been used under the Caliphs, albeit without the corner reinforcements of stone which by now were standard (the only earlier example being the gate at Baños de la Encina). Many circumference walls are of rough stone, one reason why parts of the northern section of the Toledo city wall may be datable to this period. Neither the use of rough stone nor of rammed clay is clinching evidence of any African influence; true, both materials occur frequently in North Africa, but then again, both were used in Spain even before the arrival of the Umayyads. Many of these fortresses were erected on vantage points in the mountains, and their layout is dictated by the lie of the land; often instead of towers there are simply projections in the wall, as is the case for example in Rueda and Játiva.

Niebla was an important, heavily fortified trading centre on the road to southern Portugal. To this day it possesses an almost unbroken circumference wall, complete with innumerable towers and four gates, which

Saragossa: Aljafería, entrance to the prayer hall in the northern part of the palace

115

clearly indicate the progress of developments between the 10th and 11th centuries. While the earlier gates consisted of two archways on the same axis with a space in between, the later plan was to have an entrance on the ground floor of a tower, and to have a kink in the passageway; the exit opened parallel to the wall, under the protection of the tower. The city gate, potentially the weak link in the fortifications, was thus made a defensive feature in itself. In Niebla the gates were built of ashlar blocks, the walls by contrast largely of rammed clay. The horseshoe arches and the bonding of the stones recall buildings of the Caliphate.[115]

The Aljafería in Saragossa

Not much remains of the palaces of the *taifa* period. The best preserved and most beautiful example is the Aljafería in Saragossa. The Dhî al-Nûnids' palace in Toledo is represented by nothing more than a few decorative fragments in the museum,[116] and the same goes for that of the Hûdids in Balaguer. Of the castles and summer palaces in Valencia, all that is known is a single, badly-damaged capital.[117] In what were the grounds of probably the most sumptuous of these palaces, that of the 'Abbâdids in Seville, a garden has been uncovered beneath the Almohad palace. The 11th-century buildings of Khayrân's palace in Almería are no longer ident-

Saragossa: Aljafería, southern part of the palace
Flights of inexhaustible imagination transform the interlocking arch motif into ever more novel forms.

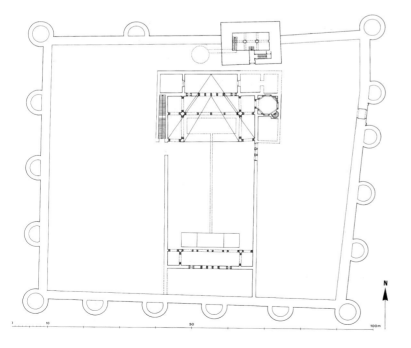

Aljafería: arcades leading to the entrance to the prayer hall in the northern part of the palace.

Reconstruction of the Islamic palace: ground plan (C. Ewert)

ifiable; in Málaga, though, the citadel still retains sections dating from the time of the Hammûdids.

"Dâr al-Surûr" ("House of Joy") was probably the original name of the summer palace of the Banû Hûd, built by Abû Ja'far Ahmad ibn Sulaymân al-Muqtadir billâh (1046/47–1081/82) during the second half of the 11th century on the banks of the Ebro to the west of his capital, Saragossa. It is now known as the Aljafería, which derives from *al-Ja'fariyya*, after the name of its founder.[118] He was the most powerful leader in the North March, and one of the most important *taifa* rulers. He liked to see himself as a poet, astronomer and mathematician, and he would receive artists and scholars in the Aljafería. The famous poet Ibn 'Ammâr, who had fallen into disfavour in Seville, also came to Saragossa before going on to Lérida, where Ahmad's brother was ruler. Shortly before he died, Ahmad divided his realm between his sons, who were unable to resist the onslaught of the Almoravids. In 1118, Saragossa fell to the Christians once more. The new rulers occupied the Islamic palace, making alterations according to their own taste, but these were minor. It was only in the 19th century that fundamental changes were made. 20th-century restorations have reinstated large sections of the Aljafería as the Hûdids knew it.[119]

The complex consists of a trapezoid surrounded by thick walls of cut stone, with round towers placed at intervals along them. The rectangular tower on the north side antedates the palace buildings, while the southwestern tower, originally round, has been subsequently clad with stone to make it square. The entrance is situated between two round towers in the

Saragossa: Aljafería, northern part of the palace, prayer hall, view of the mihrâb
The large *mihrâb* in the two-storey, octagonal, centrally-planned room keeps closely to the Cordova model. What is new is the mixture of linear forms employed in the lower-storey arches, flanking the *mihrâb:* rounded lobes are combined with angular forms, a motif that was to play a major role in later Hispano-Islamic architecture.

Saragossa: Aljafería, dome of the prayer hall, restored in the 19th century

northeast. The residential and reception wing is on the north-south axis in the middle of the quadrangle; it consists of two blocks along the shorter sides of a large rectangular courtyard, in which are situated pools reflecting the porticos and arcades; these pools are connected by a channel. The arcades on the long walls are a later addition; originally there seems to have been nothing here but ancillary rooms. The northern block contains the reception rooms: a rectangular hall, considerably longer than broad – the throne room – is flanked by two approximately square rooms, accessible only from the hall, not from the portico. The hall opens onto the portico in front through a two-tier, four-bay arcade with three central columns; two small side-doors flank the central arcade. This tripartite arrangement of hall and flanking alcoves is repeated in the portico, whereby the latter also acquires two bays, perpendicular to the axis of the hall, flanking the pool in the manner of two pavilion-like wings. The southern block repeats the general features of the northern, albeit in a somewhat simplified form.

On the east side of the north porch is the entrance to the mosque, a centrally-planned square space, with an inscribed octagon. It is a two-storeyed structure, whose entrance, like the *mihrâb* niche, is framed by a horseshoe arch. As in the architecture of the Caliphate, the modelling on the face of the arch runs eccentric to the intrados. The *mihrâb* keeps strictly to the pattern of that in the Great Mosque in Cordova on which it was modelled. A balustrade running round the room divides the latter into an upper and a lower storey, whose niches and blind niches are each provided with three columns, on which are supported multi-lobed arches. The original roofing has not been preserved.

The Umayyad connexions are clear enough: in contrast to Madînat al-Zahrâ', the site of the palace allowed an almost square ground plan, reminiscent of the desert palaces of Syria, and not unknown in the Maghreb either. This impression is reinforced by the round projecting towers, and the single straight entrance between two towers. The strict tripartite division has its model in the castle of Mshatta. The prayer hall with its central vault is probably a conscious reference to the Dome of the Rock. What is remarkable is the absence of any Abbasid features. The *mihrâb* façade and the conspicuously large, polygonal *mihrâb* niche are suggestive of al-Hakam II's *mihrâb* in Cordova. The group comprising the broad hall, flanking alcoves and portico has its direct model in Madînat al-Zahrâ', where the Salón Rico provides a highly attractive example of such an arrangement. In the Aljafería, though, "the motif of emphasizing the flanks . . . is dramatically enhanced" (C. Ewert). It is possible that there was also a conscious allusion to pre-Umayyad models: the centrally-planned room with galleries, a feature of Late Classical and Byzantine architecture, and one of the models for the Dome of the Rock, is closer in spirit to the Aljafería mosque than the Dome of the Rock itself; it may have reached Saragossa via Carolingian and post-Carolingian architecture.

The most remarkable feature of the Aljafería is to be seen in the systems of interlocking arches which here reach a dazzling degree of complexity. They seem to have liberated themselves from any mundane supporting function and to have evolved into abstract braided patterns whose dimensions and proportions range from broad arcades to miniature decorative elements on the capitals. The variety of arch forms is well-nigh inexhaustible: round, multi-lobed, and traditional round horseshoe arches are joined here for the first time by pointed horseshoe and mixed-linear arches. As they interlock and crisscross each other, an endless variety of network patterns are formed. Along the shorter sides of the courtyard, the layers of arches compensate for lack of depth in the ground plan, producing a visual architecture resembling a theatrical backdrop, not without illusionist effects. This theatricality gives expression in its way to the situation of the *taifa* rulers, whose exaggerated claims to power had no real basis in their actual political strength.

Aljafería: Columns supporting arches, detail

The palace in Balaguer, the Sudda, was probably closely related to the Aljafería.[120] This picturesque hamlet was, in the 11th century, an important town in the Upper March, part of the territory of the Banû Hûd, and the seat of government of a brother of Ahmad al-Muqtadir's, Yûsuf al-Muzaffar, until he was driven out by Ahmad in about 1080. After years of toing and froing, the town finally fell to the Christians in 1103.

Balaguer

Balaguer has an early Islamic fortress, probably dating from the 9th century, whose wall, along with its towers, is still largely intact. The cut-stone wall, with a combination of stretchers and headers (simple, double and triple) in no particular rhythm, is comparable with that of the fortress of

Balaguer: details of the stucco ornamentation
LEFT:
Harpy within a leafy tendril
BELOW:
Vegetal motif (C. Ewert)

Merida. This early Islamic structure was used by Yûsuf al-Muzaffar as the circumference wall for the palace which he had built shortly after coming to power in 1046/47; of the buildings of the palace itself, nothing has been preserved. A few decorative fragments do allow us a certain insight into the artistic activities at this particular court, however. The stucco work, which was originally painted, features interwoven geometric tracery designs as ornamental backgrounds, as frieze motifs or in conjunction with vegetal patterns. Fine stucco composite palmettes are occasionally reminiscent – in their dense coverage, exuberant volutes and decorative elements built up from concave and convex curves – of the first Sâmarrâ style. The pinnate leaves, by contrast, are specifically Andalusian, and the kerfs in Balaguer are concave; the oblique kerfs so typical of Sâmarrâ are totally absent here. A fragment of a tree of life with harpies and birds is worthy of special mention, because this oriental motif represents a fairly unique example of its kind in the architectural decoration of the period, and is otherwise known only in Andalusian ivory carvings. The rather

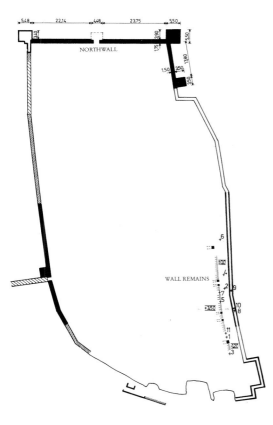

Balaguer with its citadel, view from the south-east

Balaguer was an important border town in Islamic Spain. Its circumference wall probably dates from the 9th century. During the *taifa* period the palace was built, of which almost nothing remains apart from some excellent stucco items. They may derive from the same workshop as the stucco work in Saragossa, to which they bear a striking resemblance.

Plan of the circumference wall (C. Ewert)

sparse remains which have been preserved in Balaguer testify to the activities of a stucco workshop whose technique was simple, but whose inventory of forms was extremely wide-ranging. The relationship to the stucco work in Aljafería is so close that one can safely assume that the same workshops were involved in both. The intellectual and artistic exchange between the courts of the two brothers, in spite of their mutual hostility, seems to have been lively, as indeed it is reported by Ibn 'Ammâr in his biography.

Other Palaces and Works of Art

According to the written sources, Almería enjoyed a period of prosperity in the 11th century;[121] "the Gateway to the East, the Key to Profit, the City in the Land of Silver, on the Sand of Gold and on the Emerald Shore"[122] had been made the capital of his petty state by Khairan, the one-time slave of the 'Âmirids and ruler of Murcia. He undertook considerable extensions to the city on its northern and eastern sides, besides enriching it with a number of buildings. The shipyard was working to capacity during this period, and the dockyards were a major entrepôt. The water supply, still a problem even today, also witnessed some improvement. Khairân seems to have been responsible for fortifying the castle. After a number of battles, power in Almería passed to the Arab, Abû Yahyâ Muhammad ibn Ma'n ibn Sumâdih al-Mu'tasim. He fortified the Alcazaba and within it built a palace surrounded by gardens with ornamental fountains, the al-Sumâdihiyya, of which one can form a picture today only on the basis of the contemporary descriptions which have been handed down. The walls of rammed clay, which connect the city with the Alcazaba and are still partly extant today, date largely from the 11th century, probably from the time of Khairân.

The Alcazaba in Málaga, which was built over during the Nasrid period,

Málaga: Alcazaba, Nasrid pavilion in the middle of the residential wing

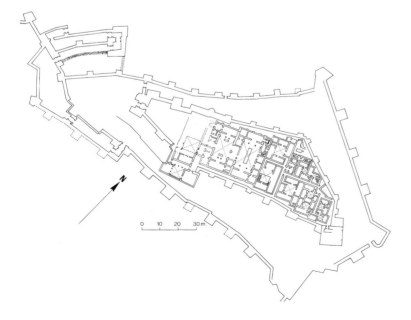

Málaga: Alcazaba, one of the heavily fortified gates of the citadel

Ground plan of the fortifications
(M. Gómez-Moreno)

0   10   20   30 m

Málaga: Alcazaba, south section of the west courtyard of the palace, dating from the 11th century

still preserves a group of rooms belonging to the 11th-century palace;[123] an open pavilion facing the sea, with interlocking arches, and a three-bay arcade to the portico. The slender columns support almost circular horseshoe arches. The patterning of the facings of the arches with smooth and decorated voussoirs, albeit here confined to the tops of the horseshoes, the eccentric placement of the rear mouldings and the decorated initial sections of the arches are all a legacy of the Caliphatera; here, it must be said, the decor is more monotonous and in lower relief.

The Zirids' palace in Granada, al-Qasaba al-qadîma, was situated on the slope of the Albaicín going down to the River Darro; all that is left of it are a vaulted, four-bay well and some remains of the walls.[124] Not much is known, either, about the 11th-century structures on the Alhambra; it has been thought that this was the site of the palace, known from literary sources, of the Zirids' Jewish minister, Yehoseph ibn Naghrîla; there is no archaeological evidence to support this, however.[125] All that is known for certain is that on the site of the Alcazaba there was a fortress, of which remains are still extant in the Vela tower and perhaps also in the Torres Bermejas (which, however, are largely 12th century in date). Until the 11th century, Granada was merely a relatively minor town in the shadow of Elvira (at the foot of the Sierra de Elvira); a minaret (today the church tower of San José) and a bridge over the Genil probably date back to the 10th century. During the *taifa* period, Granada was an administrative centre, and had a higher and longer circumference wall built around it, leading from the Albaicín down to the Darro, and on the Alhambra side up to the aforementioned fortress. In the Albaicín a fine bath from this period is still extant, the "Bañuelo" which strongly resembles the contemporary *hammâm* in Baza.[126] In the immediate vicinity one can still discern the remains of the *qâdî*'s bridge, which was built across the Darro in the mid-11th century. Granada's Zirid Chief Mosque has had to make way for the cathedral. Its ground plan, six naves running parallel to the *qibla* and a courtyard surrounded by deep galleries, is known only from a drawing dating from 1704.

Al-Qasr al-mubârak, the famous palace of al-Mu'tamid the 'Abbâdid, stood close to the Guadalquivir in Seville.[127] It was not the 'Abbâdids' only castle, but it was the most important; in addition, at least two nearby summer residences and another, older, city palace are known from written sources.[128] The Qasr al-Mubârak was built immediately next to the more or less well preserved Dâr al-Imâra, the former governor's palace, with the deliberate aim of outshining the latter and thus demonstrating the power of the 'Abbâdids. Poems with extravagant descriptions of this palace were composed; some verses by Ibn Hamdîs suggest that the main domed hall was decorated with figurative images.[129] It is at least possible that the present-day "Ambassadors' Hall" dating from Pedro's time was built on the site of this domed hall. The Almoravids probably did not bother to maintain this palace; under the Almohads it was certainly still in use, even though sections of its outer wall were demolished during this period, and the stones re-used in the foundations of the Almohad Chief Mosque.

Insofar as there are any remains that can be confidently attributed to the 'Abbâdid period, they are few. A garden has been discovered by Rafael Manzano, with sunken beds, the remains of an irrigation system, pools,

Fish-shaped basin from the Alcazaba in Málaga

and probably fragments of a portico on one of its short sides.[130] It belonged to the north range of the old palace; today, it is part of an administrative complex to the south, outside the present-day Alcázar, the site having been used for the Almohad palace, the "Crucero". The principles of this garden architecture lived on in Morocco for centuries; a cross is formed by raised paths above the tops of the orange trees; in the quarters of the cross there are rectangular pools alongside flower beds, and in the middle a round pool and a little pavilion.[131] Another of al-Mu'tamid's gardens with sunken beds more than three metres below the general level, has been uncovered in the Alcázar itself. It too was surrounded by arcaded walls which also housed the water supply channels. The size of this latter garden is considerable.

Thanks to its walls and its citadel, Játiva, a famous paper-manufacturing centre, was an extraordinarily well-fortified town, whose rulers, in particular the 'Âmirid slave Khairât and his immediate successor, were at times able to put up an effective defence against their powerful neighbours, above all the rulers of Valencia. The town has now all but lost its walls, and the citadel has been built over so many times that it is hardly possible today

Granada: Bañuelo, an Islamic thermal bath dating from the taifa period in the Albaicín
ABOVE:
Barrel-vaulted *caldarium* with bathing area separated by an arcade.
ADJACENT:
The central hall, with a pool in the middle, functioned both as a changing room and a relaxation room, as well, in practice, as a *frigidarium*; from here there was direct access to the *sudatorium*. A surprising feature here is the large number of re-used capitals dating from Roman, Visigothic and Umayyad times.

to identify the 11th-century elements in it. The museum in Játiva still has a marble fountain and a richly-ornamented stucco arcade, but this latter is more likely to date from the Almoravid period.[132] The iconography of the marble fountain is astonishing: the ancient oriental motif of princely pleasures, namely men eating, drinking and making music, alongside duelling scenes, is juxtaposed with a wrestling match, a stickdancer, and, totally unexpectedly, a woman giving suck to an infant. The heraldic beasts – eagles taking gazelles, lions fighting, and goats charging each other – are derived from the iconography of the Caliphate. The figures are in high relief, and the execution is not concerned with details; the folds in the garments are reduced to an abstract play of lines reminiscent of the reliefs of Palmyra or certain Syrio-Umayyad draperies. It must be said, however, that the same play of folds is found in Andalusian miniature painting.[133] The whole impression is one of almost rustic charm, bearing witness to a creative vitality on the part of the fountain's sculptor. It is greatly superior to the usual run of *taifa* sculpture, most of whose known examples appear to us to be excessively refined.

In view of this fountain, one cannot help wondering whether *taifa* art really was as homogeneous as it appears to us today. While the craftsmen in the various centres undoubtedly dreamed of the splendours of the Caliphate, they nevertheless exploited local possibilities to create works with a specifically regional flavour, or at the very least bearing the mark of the workshop responsible.

However that may be, *taifa* art added new, fertile elements to the heritage of the Caliphate, thus for example the pointed arch and the mixed-linear arch, which provided the inspiration for the infinite variety of tracery patterns which from now on were to enjoy ever greater popularity. Even in Cordova, ornamentation and load-bearing function had never been clearly separated, especially where vertically interlocking arches were concerned. This tendency was now developed further, extending additionally to non-vertical elements. The way from the cut-stone rib-vaulted domes of Cordova to the plaster rib-vaulted domes of the 12th century and the later *muqarnas* domes had a staging-post in the *taifa* period.

Marble basin from Játiva, Detail
The basin is aproximately 1.50 metres long. Its outer sides bear a design in low relief depicting various figurative subjects.

During the 11th century walls became simpler and cruder; rammed clay and rough stone replaced the cut stone of the Caliphate with its decorative bonding; the palaces themselves became more cramped, and ornamentation was forced into more confined areas.

As far as vegetal ornamentation was concerned, this came more and more exclusively to be dominated by asymmetrical, pinnate semi-palmettes and a whole variety of forms based on buds and pine-cones; the leaf-stalks, now very thin, provided the material for geometric patterns. Pomegranates were used less often, while vine and acanthus leaves had virtually disappeared. Individual elements in the designs were smaller, finer and more abstract, and a progessive geometricization of the vegetal patterns can be discerned. Ornamentation moved further and further away from the naturalistic forms of classical antiquity; in its place there appeared the mathematically conceived vegetal pattern we know as the arabesque.

Undeniably, *taifa* art is indeed characterized by mannered and in a sense even decadent features; even so, its role is more than just an intermediate stage between the Caliphate and the later Berber dynasties, and its own creative share in the total picture of Andalusian art cannot be estimated too highly. It not only set its mark on Andalusian and Maghreb art for the next few centuries, but lived on still further in the Mudéjar centres in the north and east of Spain.

Seville: Crucero
The Crucero is a 12th-century garden, laid out on top of an existing 11th-century garden; it was part of al-Mu'tamid's famous palace, the Qasr al-mubârak. This garden, with its raised paths forming a cross, its sunken beds, its pool, and its arcaded galleries along the short sides, already displays all the characteristic features of later Hispano-Islamic garden design, which was to live on in Morocco for centuries.

131

1091–1248

The Period of Berber Domination

The name "Almoravid" is derived from *al-Murâbitûn* ("people of the Ribât"), a term associated with the Holy War. From the Senegal basin in the western Sahara, a nomadic Berber tribe, the Lamtûna, a member of the Sanhâja group, emerged towards the middle of the 11th century to undertake a wave of conquests in the north, in the name of religious renewal.[134] Mystical and religious ideas were the moving force which breathed spiritual life into the fighting qualities of this tribal army, which soon became the leader of a far-reaching tribal coalition, and before long had conquered the whole of Morocco and western Algeria. The persuasiveness of a religious reformer, Abd Allâh bin Yâsîn al-Jazûlî, combined with the energy and stamina of one of his converts, the Berber leader Yahyâ ibn 'Umar, to create a new distribution of power, in which tribal feuds and love affairs, or at least marital affairs[135] (Almoravid society may have been matriarchal in structure) played a decisive role, leading to the foundation of the Almoravid empire under Yûsuf bin Tâshufîn.[136] The Almoravid campaigns in Andalusia have already been mentioned in connexion with the end of the *taifa* period.

To the Andalusians, the upper classes above all, these dark-skinned, illiterate Berbers were fanatical barbarians. Barbarians or no, they were quickly and lastingly impressed by the splendour and the sophistication of Andalusian culture, for which their crude energy was no match.

If one is to believe Andalusian sources, the Almoravid period was one of cultural regression, in which the ruling class no longer had any appreciation of secular learning or the fine arts, the tone being set by bigoted jurists and theologians. This view is certainly too one-sided, since many works of art of the period show that while the Berbers covered Andalusian culture in a blanket of religious fanaticism, they did not suffocate it. The Almoravids ushered in a period of new, intensive religious feeling; this development, which incidentally was paralleled in the Christian areas of Spain, led to outbreaks of intolerance towards the Christian and Jewish minorities. During this period, countless Christians were deported to North Africa.[137]

The year 1118 saw the recapture of Saragossa by Alfonso I of Aragon; in 1133, Alfonso VII of Castile penetrated deep into southern Andalusia, and in 1144/45 insurrections on the part of the Islamic population led to the overthrow of the Almoravids. In Morocco the dynasty had been encountering opposition for some time already, and was rapidly approaching its end. Until a new Berber dynasty seized power in Andalusia in 1170 or thereabouts, the region was ruled by petty kings once more, often referred to as the Almoravid *taifas*.

The Almohads: Berbers from the High Atlas

The Almohad empire also had its roots in a North-west African religious revival centred on Berber tribes. But while the Almoravids were nomads from the Sahara, the Almohad doctrine was spread by their traditional enemies, the sedentary Masmûda Berbers of the High Atlas. The latest religious reformer, Ibn Tûmart, had come into contact with new philosophical and religious movements while on a trip to the Orient in the early 12th century.[138] His teachings are distinguished from those of the Almoravids, which had been restricted to a rigorous Malikism, by their greater originality.[139] The name "Almohad" is derived from *al-Muwahhidûn* ("those who affirm the unity of God"); Ibn Tûmart's struggle was directed against the "anthropomorphists" and the "polytheists", and thus against the widespread tendency to supply God with human attributes. For the Almohads, God was pure spirit, eternal and infinite and so absolutely sublime that even such attributes as goodness and mercy appear blasphemous if taken literally, so that where they appear in the scriptures, they must be understood figuratively. For all this, Ibn Tûmart was not so much a philosopher as a preacher of virtue and a revolutionary who addressed the masses, if need be in the Berber language. Under the Almohads the Koran was translated from Arabic into Berber, something that was by no means a matter of course at this time.

With the help of a disciple and pupil, 'Abd al-Mu'min, Ibn Tûmart succeeded in stirring up the population of large areas of Morocco against the decaying Almoravid regime in Marrakesh. First of all Tinmal, a small town in the Atlas Mountains about ninety kilometres south of Marrakesh, was enlarged and made the capital; it was here that Ibn Tûmart, the *mahdi*, died in 1130. Three years later, 'Abd al-Mu'min, an outstanding administrator and general, was proclaimed "Commander of the Faithful". In 1147, Marrakesh fell to the Almohads, who at first concerned themselves primarily with the conquest of North Africa, including Tunisia; Andalusia was only subjugated following their invasion in 1161. Abû Yâ'qûb Yûsuf (1163–84), the son and successor of 'Abd al-Mu'min, made Andalusia a province of the Almohad empire. Seville, however, was only taken in 1172, following the death of the local ruler, Ibn Mardanîsh. Abû Ya'qûb Yûsuf resumed the tradition of summer campaigns into Christian areas. He had been Governor of Cordova before he succeeded to the Caliphate, and seems to have been deeply impressed by the achievements of al-Hakam II. Like his Umayyad predecessor, he collected books and surrounded himself with scholars, among them Ibn Zuhr (Avenzoar), Ibn Tufail and Ibn Ruschd (Averroës). Alongside Marrakesh, Seville was where he most liked to reside, and he was generous in providing the city with new buildings. The reign of his son Abû Yûsuf Ya'qûb "al-Mansûr" (1184–99) was the most magnificent of the whole

Seville: city wall
Some sections of the well-fortified Almohad structure, along with its towers and outer wall, are still standing, in spite of the fact that it is only built of rammed clay.

Seville: old view of the city
The picture shows the Almohad Torre del Oro
with the Cathedral in the background, the latter
having been built on the site of the Almohad
Friday mosque. The Guadalquivir (from the
Arabic *al-Wâdî al-kabîr*, "the great river") has
played a major role in the life of the city since
time immemorial.

FOLLOWING DOUBLE PAGE:
Cordova: Calahorra
On the left bank of the Guadalquivir, exactly opposite the Great Mosque, a bridgehead fortification tower was built, probably under the Almohads. The present-day structure does not date from Umayyad times, showing as it does a far more advanced concept of defensive architecture.

dynasty. He too, like his predecessor, was a major patron of architecture. He achieved a series of spectacular military successes both in North Africa and on the Iberian Peninsula. The victory at Alárcos, between Cordova and Toledo, over Alfonso VIII of Castile in 1195 was one of the last Islamic victories in Spain, and while it undoubtedly added to the prestige of the Almohads, it did nothing to extend the actual power of the Muslims vis-à-vis the Christians. In total contrast, in July 1212 he provoked a devastating counter-attack by the Christians at Las Navas de Tolosa, where León, Castile, Navarre and Aragon managed to join forces for a short while.

Abû Yûsuf Ya'qûb was succeeded by his son Muhammad "al-Nâsir" ("the Victorious" – this in spite of Las Navas de Tolosa), and he in turn in 1213 by his son Abû Ya'qûb Yûsuf II, who was fifteen years old at the time, and incapable of putting a halt to the disintegration of the empire. After his death in 1224, family feuds accelerated the end of the dynasty, plunging Andalusia into a new civil war, in which local potentates and *condottieri* vied for power. The Reconquista, now expressly understood as a crusade, made rapid progress. James I of Aragon, and above all Ferdinand III of Castile (from 1217) and León (from 1230) pushed without difficulty into the very heart of Andalusia. Memorable dates are the fall of Cordova (1236), of Valencia (1238) and of Seville (1248). Jérez de la Frontera managed to hold out until 1261, Niebla until 1262 and Murcia until 1266. The Kingdom of Granada alone remained in Islamic hands – until 1492.

Among the local rulers who rebelled against the Almohads and succeeded in resisting the Christian advance for some while, the Banû Hûd in Murcia and the Banû Mardanîsh in Valencia are worthy of special mention. Muhammad ibn Yûsuf ibn Hûd, a mercenary leader who claimed descent from the ancient Hûdid dynasty of Saragossa, managed between 1228 and 1230 to expand the area under his authority from Murcia to Denia, Játiva, Granada, Almería, Málaga and on to Cordova and Seville, and then even as far as Ceuta. Valencia alone preserved her independence under Zayyân ibn Sa'd ibn Mardanîsh. It is true that Hûdid power collapsed almost as suddenly as it had arisen; ibn Hûd himself was killed by one of his adherents in Almería in 1237.[140]

The sudden end of Almohad power in Andalusia can be explained by the unpopularity not only of the Almohad dogma, but also of the markedly Berber character of the ruling family. For all that, the Almohad period witnessed the construction of extraordinarily beautiful and remarkable buildings, above all in Seville and the south-west.

Almoravid and Almohad Architecture

Almoravid Remains in North Africa and Andalusia

In Morocco and western Algeria Almoravid rule was responsible for significant and unique works of architecture; in Andalusia there is no evidence of anything comparable. At first the Berber armies would most likely have simply plundered and destroyed, and most of the *taifa* palaces suffered the same fate as that of al-Mu'tamid in Seville.

In North Africa the Almoravids appeared first as the founders of towns and fortresses, and soon as the builders of mosques and palaces too. The fortresses of Beni Touada, Amergo and Tashgimout in Morocco are typical examples. The two former, which are older, are built largely of rough stone, and their general style is archaic. Amergo has round towers, a barbican and a kind of keep; all three elements point to Christian Spanish sources. Its entrance arch is reminiscent of the Puerta de la Bisagra in Toledo. Tashgimout was built around 1125; its rammed clay walls and rough stone foundations, and its towers with vaulted halls one above another, clearly indicate the legacy of Andalusia,[141] but the high niches with their ribbed half-domes which decorate the entrance have their immediate origin in the central Maghreb, in the Qal'a of the Banû Hammâd. The Almoravids' most famous foundation was their new capital, Marrakesh, which was to give its name to the whole country (Marrûkush, via Spanish Marruecos, is the origin of our word Morocco); its foundations were laid in 1070.[142] In Marrakesh a palace was built, the Dâr al-Hajar, or "Stone House", of which three courtyards are known as a result of excavation. This palace also included the small open pavilion, still extant today, which was built for 'Alî ibn Yûsuf (1106–42), the son of an Andalusian mother. Its umbrella dome is a copy of the dome in front of the *mihrâb* in the Great Mosque in Cordova. It rises above a system of ribs consisting of mixed-linear interlocking arche, which in its turn represents a mannered miniaturization of the ribs in the Cordova structure. The copings are richly decorated with carved stucco work; the building is totally within the tradition of *taifa* architecture in Andalusia.

Excavations in Chichaoua (in the west of Marrakesh) have revealed remains of sugar-cane plantations and an estate of well-kept dwelling houses; fragments of their decoration – stucco and mural painting – while still within the *taifa* tradition, do nevertheless seem somewhat more robust; elements from the central Maghreb are unmistakable, and many details

Jérez de la Frontera: Alcázar, Santa María la Real
A wide vault rises above an octagonal prayer hall inscribed within a square. The fabric of this former mosque, which dates from the Almohad period, is largely of brick; its austere simplicity is highly impressive.

141

Kairuân, Tunisia: Sîdî Oqba Mosque
This, the most important religious building in the Maghreb, was founded at the time of the Islamic conquest. Its present appearance dates largely from the 9th century. It was here that the T-plan appeared in such a clear form for the first time in the entire Islamic world.

ABOVE:
Prayer hall, view from the west; to the right the mihrâb is visible

ADJACENT:
Courtyard front of the prayer hall

point already in the direction of Almoravid aesthetic taste.[143] A well-preserved bath in Nedroma provides an example of the public *hammâms* to be found in Almoravid towns.[144] Its main hall, a relaxation and changing room, has an impressive monumental dome; the more modest hot bath was, like its classical counterparts, heated by means of hypocausts and hot-air ducts within the walls. The architectural achievement of this bath-house is its central domed hall, which has no known antecedents either in the western Maghreb or in Andalusia. The Dyers' Bath in Tlemcen dates from approximately the same period, and its architecture is comparable.

Of the Almoravid palaces in Fez and Tlemcen, next to nothing is left. By way of compensation, a number of North African Great Mosques bear witness not only to the religious enthusiasm of their patrons, but also to the expertise of their builders. The Great Mosques of Algiers, Nedroma and Tlemcen are Almoravid structures, while the Qarawayyîn Mosque in Fez owes much to the dynasty. Almoravid Friday mosques have no standard ground plan: while the mosques in Algiers, Nedroma and Tlemcen take over the nave scheme with one or more transverse arcades – in other words that found both in Cordova and in Qairawân – the Qarawayyîn Mosque has transverse naves, following the pattern of the Umayyad mosque in Damascus. The Qarawayyîn Mosque was not newly built during this period, however, but was rather an extension of a 9th-century building, which could explain its archaic design. In addition to the forms of arch met with in Andalusia, we also have dentate arches. As in Cordova, the *mihrâb* axis is emphasized by the use of domes. The dome in front of the *mihrâb* in Tlemcen, dating from approximately 1136, consists of a richly ornamented, pierced stucco cladding on masonry ribs; here for the first time in this region of the Islamic West we see the *muqarnas* motif. It should thereby be mentioned that *muqarnar* had already appeared – albeit in a very different form – in the decorative scheme of the Qal'a of the Banû

Tlemcen, Algeria: courtyard of the Great Mosque
The Almoravid mosque dates from the 11th-century, and was enlarged in the 13th.

143

Hammad in the 11th century. Masonry ribbing and *muqarnas* testify to a hitherto unknown acceptance and incorporation of Iranian techniques and forms in the architecture of western Islam. In the upper zone of the *mihrâb* façade there is a barred window through which light shines into the vault. The refined forms of the carved stucco of the dome, which are further enlivened by the play of light from the window, create an illusion of weightlessness. Between 1135 and 1142 the Qarawayyîn Mosque was rebuilt: its somewhat excessive vegetal, geometric and epigraphic stucco decor seems to have been taken over more or less directly from *taifa* models, while the ground plan, many of the increasingly complex arch forms and the *muqarnas* domes all reflect inspirations that were quite independent of Andalusia. Dogmatic considerations meant that none of these mosques has a minaret. The call to prayer rang out from the rooftops or simply from the door of the mosque.

Andalusia, cultivated and densely populated, did not lend herself to being ruled in the same way as North Africa, and the Almoravids founded no cities or fortresses on the Iberian peninsula. Although the destruction wrought subsequently by the Almohads and the Christians must not be underestimated in this connexion, it is still nevertheless true that there was never any specifically Almoravid-Andalusian architecture in Spain; from the purely material point of view, the Almoravids did not have the opportunity to commission any major building projects: Yûsuf ibn Tâshufîn accompanied three military campaigns to Spain; 'Ali ibn Yûsuf came on four; and Tâshufîn ibn 'Alî never came at all. In compensation, a number of local rulers who had either managed to come to a more diplomatic arrangement with the Almoravids than had al-Mu'tamid, or else had been able to resist them, exercised a certain degree of patronage; thus al-Musta'in, the Hûdid in Saragossa, and the rulers of Valencia and Murcia; in Niebla, Mertola and the Portuguese town of Silves, power was for a while in the hands of dis-

RIGHT:
Alcalá de Guadaira
The ground plan of the fortress is determined by the lie of the land. The circumference wall has mainly rectangular towers of various breadths, along with a walkway protected by a castellated balustrade. As always in Islamic Spain, it does not overhang the wall. Little remains of an outer wall which also had defensive towers.

LEFT:
Salé, Morocco: Great Mosque
The mosque is an Almohad foundation dating from the 12th century.

ciples of the mystic leader Abû l-Qâsim ibn Qasî, a pronounced opponent of the Almoravid movement. Rather than Almoravid architecture, then, one should speak of a *taifa* architecture in Spain during the Almoravid period. Even of this, however, little remains. During the period of the decline of the Almoravids, the Portuguese city of Mertola played an important role in the politico-religious insurrectionary movement headed by Ibn Qasî, but the building of its Chief Mosque is probably to be dated no earlier than the beginning of the Almohad period, i.e. after 1157.[145] The *mihrâb* of the former Chief Mosque of Almería also preserves remains of stucco ornamentation which date from this period.

Murcia and Monteagudo

The Castillejo of Monteagudo near Murcia is considered by some authorities to date from the Almoravid period;[146] according to the results of recent research, however, it was constructed under Muhammad ibn Mardanîsh (1147–72).[147] This ruler, known to the Christians as "King Lope", was descended from a Muwallad family: "violent in temper, robust in constitution, steadfast in courage and fighting spirit",[148] he was able, following the confusion of the battles between the *taifa* rulers and the Almoravids, who had never really imposed their authority on eastern Andalusia, to impose his own on Valencia and Murcia. His realm extended for a time as far as Jaén and Almería, Cádiz and Granada. Under his rule, Murcia, his capital, became a major political, economic and cultural centre. The city lies in exceptionally fertile country, intensively cultivated thanks to large-scale artificial irrigation. It is conspicuous for the number of its castles. The first impression is one of a tight network of fortresses,[149] Aledo, Mula, Orihuela

Monteagudo
Above, the Castillar, a Roman foundation; below, the Castillejo, an Arab country residence.

Ground plan of the Castillejo (M. Gómez-Moreno)

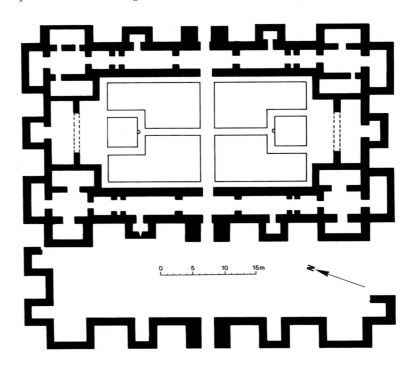

and the Castillejo of Monteagudo being unmistakably military complexes. In many other cases, though, what we see are *munyas*, in other words, former country residences of citizens of Murcia; the numerous remains of walls still extant today probably had a demarcatory rather than a defensive function. The Castillejo of Monteagudo, 400 metres to the north-east of the Monteagudo foothills, may well have been one such *munya*. A rectangular structure measuring 61 metres by 38, it has rammed-clay circumference walls with rectangular towers, three on the short sides and five on the long; the only entrance still extant is in the middle of the long, north-east side; in the corresponding place on the opposite side there was probably another entrance or else a balcony. There are the remains of another wall about 14 metres in front of the north-west wall. The interior of the palace complex is characterized by a central garden, which is divided into four equal quarters by a cross formed by raised paths; on each of its short sides is a pavilion, a motif which would turn up again in the Nasrid Alhambra, from where it spread its influence as far afield as Morocco. The long sides have passages, the short sides each have a reception room built into the central tower, with projecting porches. The other towers, with the exception of the gate-towers, also project beyond the line of the walls. Remains of paintings and stucco have been found in the ruins. The vegetal elements carved in the stucco, in particular the pinnate leaves, asymmetrical semi-palmettes and

Tabernas
This strategically important fortress controlled the road from Almería to Murcia, and at the same time guarded access to the Sierra de los Filabres.

leaf-stalks, are still in the *taifa* tradition, while the geometric painted ornamentation is characterized more by elements originating in the Maghreb. The palace raises a whole series of questions; neither its function nor its dates are known for sure. But however that may be, it is certainly a significant and interesting example of the architectural achievement of a local ruler who had remained independent of Berber domination. In addition, the Castillejo, like the Aljafería, represents a link between Madînat al-Zahrâ' and the palaces of the Alhambra.

Crafts

From this period a number of artistically-woven silk fabrics have been preserved, with heraldic animal motifs in medallions. They may come from Murcia, which was famous for its silk manufacture. The tradition of richly-carved ivory caskets and boxes seems to have been lost after the mid-11th century; those attributed to the late 11th and 12th centuries are rare, most originating from Cuenca, where there was a workshop which had probably previously operated in Cordova. The design of these pieces testifies to artistic impoverishment, even exhaustion.[150] A bronze mortar in the Villanueva y Geltru Museum in Barcelona, a silver casket among the San Isidoro treasure from León, and various carved wooden panels with inscriptions and friezes (for example in the Frederico Marés Museum in Barcelona) could possibly date from this turbulent period.[151] A very fine tombstone made in 1103 for the Sanhaja princess Badr can be seen in the Archaeological Museum in Málaga.

One magnificent achievement is the *minbar* in the Kutubiyya Mosque in Marrakesh, which was commissioned by the Almoravid rulers for the

Marrakesh, Morocco: Ben Yûsuf's Madrasa
A *madrasa* was a college of theology and jurisprudence. This one is a Marînîd foundation, dating from the 14th century.

ABOVE:
The main gate, restored in this century

ADJACENT:
Detail of a wall-panel with 18th-century faïence mosaics and faïence engraving, demonstrating the continuing fidelity to old models.

Friday mosque in their capital city, and made in Cordova between 1125 and 1130. The enemies and successors of the Almoravids, the Almohads, while destroying the mosque itself, nevertheless spared the *minbar*, in order to incorporate it into their own mosque. This pulpit, almost four metres tall, is decorated with inlay work. The stringboards of the *minbar* are covered with an interwoven network pattern, incorporating a chequer-board lozenge design with ivory and hardwood inlay work, thereby introducing a discreet polychrome element. The polygonal fields are decorated with rich arabesque ornamentation, comprising pennate asymmetric semi-palmettes, pine-cones, palmettes and buds. The wealth of motifs and the various carving methods suggest an important studio, to which the *minbar* of the Qarawayyîn Mosque in Fez may perhaps also be ascribed. This latter is somewhat smaller, and bears the date 1144; otherwise it is really quite similar to that in the Kutubiyya. Both are probably based on the model of al-Hakam II's *minbar* – now lost – and confirm that the arts of woodcarving and inlay work had not been forgotten in the Spain of the Almoravids.[152]

In every fair-sized town the pottery workshops probably went on producing items for daily use without significant interruption.[153] Lustre ware was probably being produced from as early as the 10th century, although it may be assumed that, as a luxury product, commissions suffered during

Bronze lion, c. 1200, in the Louvre, Paris
This lion was discovered in the Province of Valencia, but it is not known how it came to be there. The inscription consists of nothing but a blessing. It was probably intended for a foun-tain, because in addition to its wide open mouth, the figure has another opening on the underside.

FOLLOWING DOUBLE PAGE:
Earthenware crockery for daily use, in the Archaeological Research Centre, Murcia
Finds from the well-shaft of the "Arab house" in the San Nicolás district of Murcia: a coal-scuttle, cooking utensils, drinking vessels, plates and bowls, two-handled jugs ond oil-lamps, all dating from the first half of the 13th century.

149

Peacock silk, woven in Spain during the 12th century, Musée de Cluny
The original purpose of the fabric is unknown. It is convincing tangible confirmation of the literary texts that from the 11th century onwards sing the praises of Andalusia's weavers.

Fragment of the cloak of Don Felipe, Musée de Cluny
13th century silk, probably from Almería

the endless wars of the Almoravid period. Even so, there are in Murcia gold lustre fragments dating from the time of Ibn Mardanîsh.[154] The technique blue-and-white cobalt-oxide ware was presumably imported from the East under the Almoravids, although its heyday only came later, under the Almohads.[155]

The Almoravid period is by no means a blank space in the rich spectrum of Andalusian art, but we cannot form any complete or coherent picture of it. The Almoravid architecture of the Maghreb is deeply influenced by the Andalusian *taifa* period: the cultural gradient in the western Mediterranean ran without any shadow of a doubt from north to south, at least as far as architecture and the visual arts are concerned. And by the time the Almoravid architecture of the Maghreb had reached its zenith, and was in its turn in a position to exercise an influence of its own, the decline of the dynasty had long since set in, leaving the harvest to be gathered by their successors.

New Directions: in Religion and in Aesthetics

Along with their new religious beliefs, the Almohads brought a new aesthetic. At first these sedentary Berbers from the High Atlas were no less ascetic and inimical to the arts than their predecessors, their anti-Almoravid propaganda being based not only on religious, but also, and especially, on moral arguments. They reproached the Almoravids with their luxury and their softness, holding their palaces and their lifestyle in contempt. Their religious creed called first and foremost for a return to absolute simplicity. For all that, they underwent a change of tastes and attitudes even more quickly and more thoroughly than the Almoravids themselves, and the Almohad period was to go down in the history of art, and especially in the history of architecture, as one of the most significant in western Islam, being far more fruitful than that of the Almoravids or the *taifa* rulers.

The political capital of the Almohad empire was Marrakesh; Tinmal continued to be a venerated shrine. The centre of Almohad power was, and continued to be, Morocco. And Almohad architecture cannot be understood in its Spanish context alone any more than can that of the Almoravids.

Of Almohad architecture likewise it is chiefly the mosques that have survived, the oldest being that in the town of Taza founded in 1135. The first Kutubiyya in Marrakesh was probably built in around 1147, the Memorial Mosque in Tinmel around 1153, the second Kutubiyya in around 1158,[156] the Almohad Friday mosque in Seville shortly after 1172, that of Salé at about the same time, that in Rabat in about 1196/97, that of the Qasaba in Marrakesh also at about the same time, while the Andalusian mosque in Fez was enlarged between 1203 and 1207. In addition, countless smaller prayer halls were erected throughout this huge empire.

The typical Almohad Great Mosque is characterized by a nave and aisles perpendicular to the *qibla*, the nave being distinguished by its pronounced breadth. The nave and aisles open into a transverse *qibla* nave, a "transept". This T-plan, which goes back via the Cordova of the Caliphate, via Qairawân and Sâmarrâ all the way to Medina, is now given clear architectural

Marrakesh, Morocco: minaret of the Kutubiyya
The oldest of the Almohad minarets, the hallmark of Marrakesh and the direct ancestor of the Giralda in Seville.

153

prominence. In Tinmal and Marrakesh the bays where the nave and aisles merge with the *qibla* transept are given prominence by means of *muqarnas* vaults; the second Kutubiyya even has two additional bays of this kind. The motif of several cupolas over the transept was possibly derived from the Fatimid al-Hâkim Mosque in Cairo; in the Almohad scheme of things, however, it is more austere and more purposefully exploited, as each of these cupolas binds one nave or bay to the transept. The aisles are extended to form galleries which surround the courtyard, and thus incorporate the latter as a kind of outside spatial element into the prayerhall itself. This tendency to formally integrate the courtyard and the prayerhall can be seen even more clearly in the Qasaba Mosque in Marrakesh and in the mosque in Rabat. From the very beginning, Almohad sacred architecture was based on clearly drawn, generous plans, which were carried out strictly to the last detail. It is the harmony between groundplan, typological concept, geometric foundations and ornamentation that makes these mosques into remarkable masterpieces. The first builder's office seems to have been established at Marrakesh; it was from here that construction work at Tinmal was supervised,[157] and from here that the influence of Almohad ideas on architecture spread to Andalusia and Tunisia.

Even the planning of whole towns was subordinated to the chief mosque. Thus Taza is unambiguously oriented towards the *qibla* of its chief mosque, and the same principle can be seen at work in Salé, Rabat and the Qasaba in Marrakesh.[158] The scale and boldness of these architectural projects exceed anything seen up till then in western Islam.

The Maghreb has no Almohad palaces still extant; the secular architecture of the period is known to us only through a few impressive city gates, which, with their almost overpowering façades and sequences of mutually-offset spatial components – domed halls or courtyards –, went far beyond what was actually needed for defensive purposes, and provided an appropriate setting for receptions and judicial pronouncements.

The architectural ornamentation also reflects new ideas: a uniform geometric dimensional scheme was obligatory for ground plan, elevation and ornamentation alike, in spite of the difference in proportions.[159] As a result, the ornamentation was more austere, less playful, although by no means

Seville: the Alcázar of Pedro the Cruel, entrance façade
It is probable that craftsmen from Granada were engaged on this project. The Arabic inscription has a religious meaning.

Seville: view of the Alcázar from the Giralda
The 'Abbadîd palace of al-Mu'tamid and later the Almohad palace of Abû Ya'qûb occupied more or less the same site as the subsequent Alcázar of Pedro the Cruel, which without doubt took over many features from the earlier structures.

Seville: the Giralda
The former minaret of the Almohad Friday mosque, now converted into the Cathedral bell-tower, is the hallmark of the city. The original structure, one of the most splendid of the Almohad towers, has been preserved up to the top of the blind arcades.

more monotonous than under the *taifa* and Almoravid rulers. The difference between the stucco decoration of the Alfería, for example, or 'Alî ibn Yûsuf's pavilion, and the mosque in Tinmal is striking; the new style is limpid and broad, able to take in large empty spaces and create generously proportioned total compositions.

The stucco technique had been in common use since the *taifa* period; it now underwent further development, especially in the capitals at Tinmal and in the Kutubiyya, as well as in the *muqarnas* domes. Carefully fired bricks were used both for the structure and for the decoration, and now formed large panels with interwoven lozenge designs. Cut stone, which hardly occurs at all in 11th-century work, was now used once again, and carved for use on the façades of monumental gates. New both in Morocco and in Spain was the use of ornamental glazed bricks, which appeared for the first time in western Islam in the exterior ornamentation of the minaret

155

of the Kutubiyya, deriving without any doubt from origins in oriental Islam via the central Maghreb. Painting too was among the standard decorative techniques: carved stucco had been given a cover of paint since time immemorial, but now plain white surfaces were painted with geometric patterns, as was the case for example in the Castillejo of Monteagudo and in Chichaoua.

Seville, the Capital, and her Friday Mosque

Seville was the Almohads' Andalusian capital; the minaret of the Almohad Chief Mosque, the Giralda, still stands even today as the symbol of their former power, and has become the city's hallmark. This tower was erected between 1172 and 1198; the lantern with which it is crowned today was added in the 16th century. Its name derives from the statue which surmounts it, which turns in the wind like a weather-vane ("giraldilla"). The fabric consists of large ashlar blocks for the foundations, 'Abbâdid remains for the next section, and above all carefully-fired bricks. Coloured glazed bricks, or *azulejos*, were used, as in the Kutubiyya, for the ornamentation.[160] The minaret, once over 70 metres tall, rises from a square ground plan, measuring 14.85 metres along each side. It consists of a central core of seven vaulted rooms one above the other, around which a ramp in thirty-four sections lead up to the platform (and to the Christian extension). The façades are divided into three zones: the lowest is smooth, the upper two are decorated with a lozenge motif. Vertically there is also a tripartite division: a central zone with windows being flanked on either side by recessed panels bearing a blind arcade surmounted by a lozenge pattern in relief. The top section (of the original minaret) is formed by a blind arcade of multi-lobed dentate interlocking arches.

A relief of the Giralda in its original form has been preserved; it shows that this last-mentioned blind arcade was formerly surmounted by a castellated platform, on which was a slender turret with twin arches at its base; this turret also had panels with a lozenge pattern, and a castellated balustrade around its concluding dome, which was itself surmounted by three gilded globes one above the other.

The tower is taller and more slender than 'Abd ar-Rahmân III's minaret in Cordova. Its proportions are reminiscent of minarets in the central Maghreb, such as that of the Qal'a of the Banû Hammâd in Algeria. The topmost blind arcade, however, with its interlocking arches, and the twin windows, are a recapitulation of motifs from the Caliphate period, showing that the new patrons did not look down upon the ancient heritage, but on the contrary, exploited it for their own ambitious prestige projects.[161]

The walls of the cathedral's inner courtyard also contain a few Islamic remains, whereas the original prayerhall has been totally rebuilt.[162] The original Almohad Friday mosque was built in around 1171 by Abû Ya'qûb; it had a nave and sixteen aisles, each of thirteen bays; the nave and aisles ended in a transept the breadth of one bay. The nave and the outermost aisles were broader than the remaining aisles, and the bays they had in common with the transept probably had domed ceilings. The courtyard

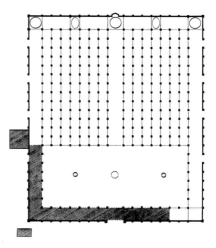

Seville: schematic ground plan of the Almohad Chief Mosque (after H. Terrasse)

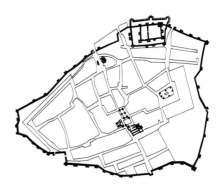

Niebla: city wall; ground plan of the city wall and the Alcázar (A. Marín Fidalgo)
The hilltop town is surrounded by a three-kilometre circumference wall. The remains of an old castle also date from Moorish times.

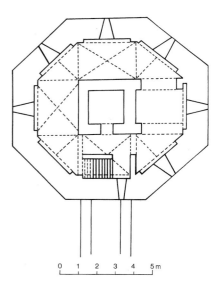

was ringed by a colonnaded walkway, the main entrance being in the middle of the north side. The ground plan is in general typically Almohad, although the length of the arcades is probably copied from Cordova.

Near Bollulos de la Mitación, to the west of Seville, there is a small Almohad mosque which has been converted into a church: the Ermita de Cuatrohabitan. It has a prayerhall with a nave and two aisles, the two arcades consisting of five simple arches each surrounded by an *alfiz*. The entrance is where the *mihrâb* used to be. At the north end is the minaret; like the Giralda it is square (each side however measuring only 3.28 metres) and built of brick. Each of the four façades of the tower is different: one is smooth, while the others have three recessed panels one above the other, each with two window slits; in the two lower panels, this slit is framed by a twin arcade. The whole minaret is a modest, yet harmonious, replica of the Giralda. The building is not dated and was probably erected between 1198 and 1248.

Other Almohad Mosques in the South-Western Province

The present-day church of Santa María de la Granada in Niebla, whose building history is still shrouded in some uncertainty, has in its courtyard the remains of multi-lobed pointed arches supported on columns, a reliable indicator of an Almohad phase, which probably also included the construction of the original minaret (now rebuilt and serving as the church tower). The main building has a nave and two aisles, and the *mihrâb* is still extant. The church of San Martín in Niebla, now largely in ruins, has a brick arcade still standing, which may once have formed part of an Almohad mosque.[163]

The mosque in the north corner of the Alcázar of Jérez de la Frontera, the present-day Capilla de Santa María la Real,[164] is of a totally different

Ground plan (L. Torres Balbás)

Niebla: one of the 11th century city gates

Niebla: remains of a (probably Almohad) mosque, today the church of San Martín

Niebla: Santa María de la Granada
The church has a complicated building history; there is no doubt however that it includes an Almohad phase.

type, one that appears very surprising at first sight. The prayer hall is square in plan, measuring not quite 10 metres along each side; it is surmounted by a broad octagonal dome. On its north-west side, three arches open on to a little courtyard with a U-shaped path around it. The courtyard has a minaret built into its north corner, while in the middle there is a pool; in the north corner there is a deep well, whose ceramic rim is still extant. The building is almost entirely of brick. The domed hall, contradictory though it may seem, is oriented in a particular direction: the *mihrâb* is a deep niche, square in plan with a (restored) domed ceiling, which is repeated in miniature at the corners of the *qibla* wall; the triangular spandrels behind the large diagonal corner arcades, on which the main dome is supported, each have a miniature dome on the *mihrâb* side, on the opposite courtyard side by contrast only simple half groin vaults.

Jérez de la Frontera: Alcázar

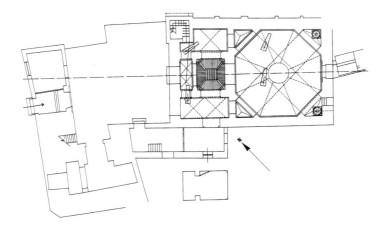

Ground plan of the mosque in the Alcázar
(A. Jiménez Martín)

Jérez de la Frontera: Santa María la Real, the former minaret in the Alcázar

Almohad mosques have as a rule a nave and at least two aisles; the mosque in the Alcázar at Jérez de la Frontera seems to be so much of an exception that attempts have been made to interpret it too as having been originally of this form. However, it was not a Friday mosque, but rather a palace "chapel", like the mosque in the Alfería. In both, the plan is an octagon inscribed within a square. The architect of the Alcázar mosque, however, did not simply take over the earlier tradition of a centrally-planned hall for a castle chapel; the three little domes on the *qibla* side act as pointers, and they are the result of a consistent application of the central plan to the ideological demands of a new age. The extraordinarily limpid and harmonious structure was erected at the end of the 12th century, when Hispano-Almohad architecture was in its heyday.

Palaces and Fortresses

Seville: old view of the park in the Alcázar

Of the Almohad palaces of Andalusia, only in Seville are any traces still extant; these remains are however insufficient to enable us to reconstruct the whole complex.[165] Within the present-day Alcázar there are doubtless numerous cuartos and patios which go back to Almohad times; the complex however has been destroyed, rebuilt and altered so often, that dating of individual elements is difficult. Most of the buildings date in their present form from the time of Pedro the Cruel, who in the third quarter of the 14th century commissioned craftsmen from Nasrid Granada to furnish a palace to his own taste. Arabic inscriptions in praise of Allah are thus no proof of Islamic patronage. However the Almohad complex had already been altered in the 13th and early 14th centuries, and moreover, it has still not been established with any precision what the Almohads themselves retained of Mu'tamid's 'Abbâdid palace. In addition, new features were added in the 15th and above all in the 16th century as well, albeit in most cases clearly recognizable as such. Almohad beyond doubt is the Patio del Yeso, a long, rectangular garden with beds and a channel in the middle. The buildings are of brick, and there is a seven-arch portico on one of the long sides. A centrally-placed, tall pointed arch has the typical multi-lobed profile, with both deeply pointed and shallow lobes; the spandrels are covered with the usual network of criss-cross arches. Flanking this central arch on each side are three smaller arches, surmounted by an open trellis-work of interlocking arches. On one of the short sides, a similarly stuccoed three-bay arcade provides access to a domed hall, which was however altered by the Christian rulers when they moved into the Alcázar. A *muqarnas* dome with stucco ribs in the Patio de las Banderas may also be of Almohad origin.[166] The Crucero, mentioned above, is a garden with raised paths crossing in the middle, along with pools and sunken beds, which was laid out on top of an existing 'Abbâdid garden. In the middle, where the paths cross, is a pool with masonry sides, the walls still showing traces of decorative paintwork. The brick walls of the sunken beds, in which among other things orange trees grew,[167] are also decorated with fine paintings, using the vocabulary of forms already seen on the stucco work. Perhaps the intention was to provide some winter colour.[168]

The hall on the long side of the Patio del Yeso has a motif which thenceforth was to appear again and again in western Islamic architecture: the doors of the state rooms are surmounted by windows with artistic stucco bars, so that even when the doors are closed, the room is both ventilated and discreetly illuminated. In the Alcázar are many capitals deriving from the Madînat al-Zahrâ' of the Caliphs; they probably found their way into the Christian building via the Almohads; they were a popular element even in Almohad mosques.[169]

One thing is clear from the few material traces of Almohad palaces still extant:[170] the austerity so highly praised by Ibn Tûmart, and actually practised in religious architecture, was not even aimed at here. Rich architectural ornamentation, fountains and scented ornamental shrubs all come together in the *hortus conclusus* to create a sophisticated refinement of the pleasures of life, and in this, the Patio del Yeso is not far behind the gardens of the Alhambra. The park which still today extends behind the Alcázar is

ABOVE AND BELOW:
Seville: Alcázar, Patio del Yeso
The Almohad features of the Patio del Yeso have been largely preserved. The threefold rhythmic façade with its lozenge panels – consisting of interlocking leaf-arches – is one of the very rare examples of Almohad palace architecture.

163

probably also of Almohad origin. Almohad Marrakesh was already famous for its extensive parks with their generously proportioned artificial ponds and lakes, some of which are still there today.

The Almohad period was the last time an attempt was made to consolidate Islamic rule in Spain. Fortresses and fortifications of all kinds were built or restored, not only in the frontier areas, but throughout the country – on the one hand to reinforce resistance to the Reconquista, on the other to maintain a firm administrative hold on an Andalusia which was generally hostile to Berber rule. Every sizable town had its walls rebuilt or reinforced, town fortifications were repaired and new castles were founded. The new capital, Seville, the old capital, Cordova, along with Badajoz, Cáceres, Trujillo and Montanchez in Extremadura, and further to the south Écija, Jérez de la Frontera and Gibraltar – all were re-fortified. Alcalá da Guadaira dates from this period. In the east, the areas around Valencia, Alicante and Murcia were fortified anew in the late 12th and early 13th centuries,[171] and numerous picturesque hilltops crowned with the remains of walls still bear witness to this last military confrontation between Christendom and Islam in south-eastern Andalusia.

Barbicans with towers were now erected in front of the high main walls of cities such as Cordova and Seville. These towers may be round, polygonal,[172] or, in most cases, rectangular. They are larger than those of the Caliphate period, and loom higher over the walls. The base is always massive, but at the level of the walkways along the battlements guardrooms are built into the walls, with a castellated terrace above. One innovation of this period is the *albarrane* tower: these were flanking towers, standing some distance from the main wall, and linked to it by a connecting wall. These *albarrane* towers have a solid base, over which there are guardrooms, often on more than one storey, with a castellated terrace at the top. The walls were made of rammed clay, often with imitation bonding painted on; while the towers and gatehouses were built of brick and stone. In more remote districts, however, traditional techniques continued to be used, for example large slates and earth in the Sierra de los Filabros.[173] Even today it is only in exceptional cases possible to assign an exact date to all the Andalusian *burûdj*, *husûn*, *qusûr*, *qilâ*, *qulay'ât*, *qaryât*, and *qasabât*,[174] these countless, highly-varied fortification systems, which covered the country in a close-meshed network, serving the needs of administration, defence, attack, and storage.

The Calahorra in Cordova and the Torre del Oro in Seville rise out of the general run of such structures. They are not merely structures designed to demonstrate the power of the builders, but well-thought-out and well-executed bridgehead fortification towers. The Torre del Oro, a dodecagonal tower with a central hexagonal staircase, and originally three storeys tall, was a corner-tower of the city wall; a similar tower must once have stood on the opposite bank of the Guadalquivir, making it possible to span a chain between the two towers and thus protect the entrance to the harbour. The Torre del Oro takes its name from the shimmering gilt lustre tiles with which it was once clad.

South-eastern Andalusia had never really submitted to either the Almoravids or the Almohads, her aim always being independence. It is thus perfectly justified to speak not only of an Almoravid but also of an Almo-

Seville: Alcázar, entrance to the Sala de la Justicia
This design of the inner courtyard façades is quite clearly inspired by the Almohad Patio del Yeso, although it no longer attains the latter's harmonious balance and more concise rhythm.

Seville: modern pavilion in the park of the Alcázar
The decor of this pavilion demonstrtes the continued vitality of the old Moorish forms.

OPPOSITE AND FOLLOWING PAGE:
Details of faïence mosaics in the Alcázar

168

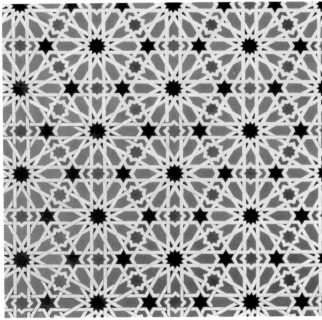

OPPOSITE:

Seville: Torre del Oro

It is assumed that this dodecagonal tower once had its counterpart on the opposite bank of the Guadalquivir, and that a chain thrown between them was used as a means of blocking the harbour entrance. However that may be, the existing tower is not just a remarkable bridgehead fortification, but at the same time a symbol of Almohad power.

Ground plan of the former fortress complex
(J. Navarro Palazón)

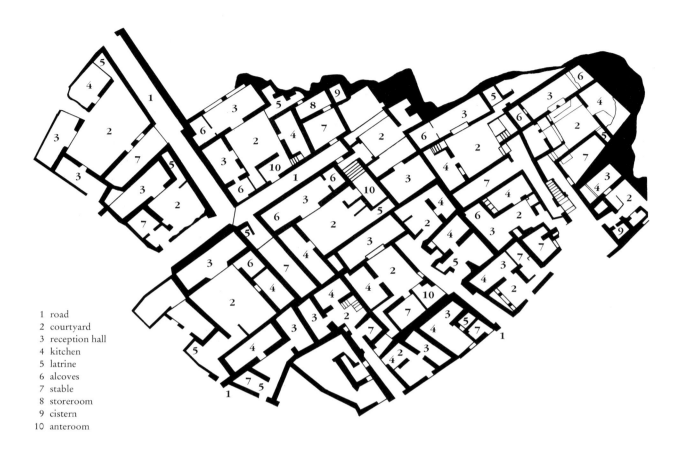

1 road
2 courtyard
3 reception hall
4 kitchen
5 latrine
6 alcoves
7 stable
8 storeroom
9 cistern
10 anteroom

Cieza: ruins of the old Islamic town of Siyâsa
The town, abandoned after the Christian reconquest, once guarded the Segura valley. Excavations have been under way for a number of years.

had *taifa* period in Valencia or Murcia. As far as the history of art is concerned, the question thus arises of whether these centrifugal forces led to a specific artistic form of expression, or a specific style. Excavations carried out in recent years in Murcia and its surrounding region are beginning to provide an answer in the affirmative.[175] They have brought to light very revealing, in many cases unique, finds, for example in the present-day monastery of Santa Clara, a richly ornamented palace dating from the 12th and 13th centuries, where a stucco *muqarnas* ceiling is worthy of particular mention. Other such finds include ceramic pieces from a well shaft in the San Nicolás quarter, and the *esgrafiada* ceramics found throughout the district: manganese-black, unglazed items, with engraved ornamentation, whose technique was probably inspired by the wish to imitate metalwork. Among the ceramic remains, the vase-stands in the form of a house deserve special attention; hitherto they were known only from the Orient, and they crop up here as a curious parallel phenomenon.

Murcia Province: Cieza

Modern Cieza, to the north of Murcia, is situated on the plain of the River Segura, to the east of a *despoblado*, an "abandoned place", in this case an Islamic town by the name of Siyâsa, which, after its incorporation into the Kingdom of Castile in 1243, was gradually deserted by its inhabitants, apparently without any violence or destruction, and never re-settled. Siyâsa, a staging post on the axis from Cartagena to Toledo, was founded on high ground at some unknown time (remains of Roman pottery have been found there).[176] A walled town, it has a fortress in its north-west corner, and a cemetery outside the walls to the south. Excavations have been carried out so far in its eastern quarter, where, separated by alleyways, dwellinghouses of a greater or lesser degree of affluence have been found, complete with interior courtyard, living and reception rooms, kitchen, latrines and wells. The mosque has not yet been discovered. Archaeological findings and written sources indicate that the town was flourishing during the 12th and early 13th centuries. The ornamentation of the houses was obviously mainly confined to the patio and the oblong main hall. It consists of artistically carved and painted stucco items, which can be classified into three groups: post-Caliphate with a clear echo of Umayyad designs; a second, with some affinity to the Patio del Yeso; and a third, which on account of its particular finesse has been described by Julio Navarro Palazón as proto-Nasrid.

Influences on the Christian North

In cities and towns which had long since been reconquered by the Christians, such as Toledo, or in centres which were never in Islamic hands, such as Burgos, one can nevertheless encounter genuine Almohad stucco decoration, proving that the inexorable progress of the Reconquista did not deter Christian rulers from enthusing about the artistic talents of their defeated enemies and commissioning work from their studios. The stucco capitals and the wall decoration in the former synagogue in Toledo (now Santa María la Blanca)[177] or the Capilla de la Asunción in the convent of Las Huelgas are purely Almohad. Las Huelgas was founded in 1187 by Alfonso VIII for his wife Eleanor, daughter of King Henry II of England. The Capilla de la Asunción was probably not completed until the early 13th century; its main dome with stucco ribs, the three smaller stucco

Convent of Las Huelgas near Burgos: wooden ceiling in the Capilla de Santiago
This Cistercian convent was founded in the late 12th century by King Alfonso VIII, and was always directly subordinate to the crown. In the main cloister and in two chapels there are many details of architectural decoration which bear witness to the admiration felt by the Christian elite at the time of the reconquest for Moorish art. This colourful wooden dome with its pattern of stars, along with the stucco cladding in the vaulting of the cloister of San Fernando, are examples of mudéjar work, dating in all probability from the late 13th century. While largely in the "Moorish style", they are not necessarily the work of Muslim craftsmen.

muqarnas cupolas, the shape of the spandrels, and above all the leaf arches, the hanging-pine-cone vaults, the multi-lobed arches with broken lobes, and the vegetal motifs with which the spaces are filled – smooth semi-palmettes and buds – all these are among the highest achievements of Almohad decorative art. The ceiling stucco work in the main cloister of the convent probably date from the same period; while executed in all likelihood by mudéjar master craftsmen, the inventory of forms unambiguously betrays its indebtedness to Almohad motifs.[178] In this private chapel, the Hispano-Islamic legacy begins its long influence on Hispano-Christian art.

There had been Berbers in Islamic Spain from the very beginning, but like the Turks under the early Islamic dynasties of the Near East, they occupied a subordinate social position for a long period. When at last, centuries later, Berber dynasties came to power, they encountered bitter resistance on the part of the old Arab upper classes. In spite of this, the contacts were fruitful for both sides. While Andalusia was the benefactor, where architecture was concerned, during the Almoravid period, it was the beneficiary under the Almohads, who had been the recipients of the Almoravid legacy. Seldom were buildings used more consciously as a demonstration of a will to power than under the Almohad caliphs; for all their self-assurance and strength, they sought continually to legitimize their position by reference to the splendour of the Cordova Caliphate.

Stucco cladding in the cloister of San Fernando

The arms of Castile

FOLLOWING DOUBLE PAGE:
Convent of Las Huelgas near Burgos: Capilla de la Asunción
The stucco decoration of the domes and arcades is probably the work of Almohad craftsmen.

1237–1492

The Rule of the Nasrids

Muhammad ibn Yûsuf ibn Nasr, the founder of the Nasrid dynasty, belonged to the Arab Banû l-Ahmar family. As the Almohad empire fell into decay, he succeeded in seizing power first in Arjona, near Jaén, in 1232, then the following year in Jaén itself, before taking Seville for a month in 1234; in 1237 he occupied Granada, a Zirid foundation dating from the 11th century,[179] and finally incorporated first Almería and then Málaga into his new Sultanate in 1238. When Jaén fell to Ferdinand III in 1246, Muhammad I withdrew to Granada and acknowledged Ferdinand's suzerainty, in other words he paid regular tribute and took part in Christian campaigns, for example against Seville. In return he was permitted to continue ruling over an area whose southern border stretched from Tarifa to about 60 kilometres east of Almería, and whose northern frontier passed close by Jaén. These borders should not be regarded as unchanging, because they shifted during the history of the Sultanate as circumstances, and especially military circumstances, dictated. The country corresponded at first to the modern provinces of Granada, Málaga and Almería. The conquest of this mountainous terrain, whose rugged coastline provided numerous safe havens for reinforcements from Africa to come ashore, probably seemed too much bother for the Castilians, especially as Muhammad I had shown himself to be a reliable vassal.

During this final Sultanate on the Iberian peninsula, Baladiyyûn, Shâmiyyûn, Muwalladûn and Berbers had long since fused into a homogeneous Arab-Islamic population, which was distinguished, according to Ibn al-Khatîb, an historian and vizier from Granada, by "medium height, pale skin, black hair, even features, lively disposition and a talent for teaching . . ."[180]

The mozarabic congregations had largely dissipated, most of their members having fled to Christian Spain during the persecution of the Christians by the Almoravids and Almohads. Even so, there were still Christians in Granada: in the Sultan's personal bodyguard, and among the traders and merchants, who are known to have included Catalans, Florentines, Venetians and, in particular, Genoans. In addition there were a considerable number of prisoners, who having been captured in raids or by piracy, were forced to perform hard labour, and were occasionally bought free. As for the Jewish community, it had enjoyed considerable power under the Zirids, which was however broken by the pogrom of 1066. Under the Almohads the Jews were persecuted throughout Andalusia, as they were later under the Christian rulers too. By contrast, the Nasrid Sultans readily gave shelter to Jewish refugees. They participated in the cultural and economic life of Granada as doctors, interpreters, craftsmen and merchants; as traders they acted as middlemen between the large foreign merchant houses and the local population.[181] A further element in Granada was represented by Muslim refugees from areas captured from the Christians: the heights of Albaicín were settled by East Andalusians. Granada's foreign policy was exhausted in continual manoeuvring between powerful neighbours, namely the various Christian princes and the Berber rulers of North Africa, who for their part were constantly entering into new alliances.

Since the downfall of the Almohads, a new dynasty had ruled in Morocco. During the 12th and 13th centuries, the Marînids had wandered around eastern Morocco before conquering Taza, Fez, Meknes and Salé in the mid-13th century, and Marrakesh twenty years later. Their claim to power had no religious basis whatever, which may explain why they sought all the more to legitimize it through the jihâd. However, their six Spanish campaigns between 1275 and 1291 led to no lasting results, and the Marînid jihad policy was ended once and for all by their crushing defeat at the Battle of the Rio Saldo in 1340. Nevertheless the Marînids were able to assert their presence for some time in Algeciras, Tarifa and Ronda, which last belonged mostly either to the Nasrids or the Marînids, but in practice remained largely independent until it was taken by Ferdinand in 1485.

Nasrid domestic policy was often addressed towards rebellious local chieftains, who for their part sought support either from the Christian princes or from their Moroccan neighbours. Granada enjoyed her real age of splendour in the 14th century under Sultans Yûsuf I (1333–54) and Muhammad V (1354–59 and 1362–91). Her intermittently good relations with both Castile and Morocco enabled her to overcome internal unrest. All in all, the 14th century was a period of economic prosperity; intensive agriculture, highly developed crafts and far-ranging trading contacts pro-

Ronda: Cathedral
The present-day cathedral still preserves the remains of the stucco decoration of a late 13th-century *mihrâb*.

Ronda: Puente San Miguel
The town, perched on a rocky plateau, is divided into two by a steep gorge (the "Tajo") which plunges down to the Gualdalevin: to the south, the old Moorish town, and to the north, the modern town. The three bridges over the Tajo are spectacular.

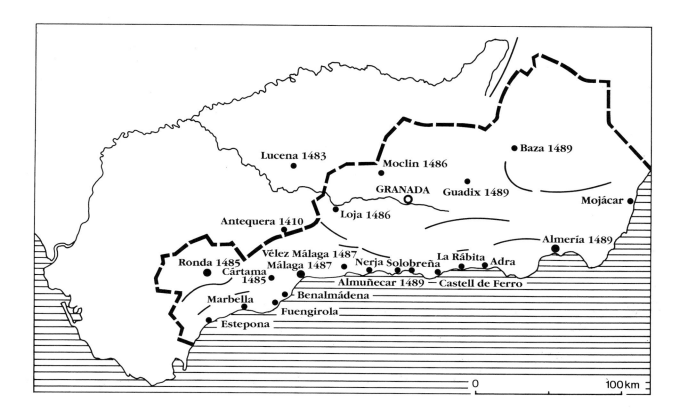

Map of the Nasrid Sultanate of Granada
(R. Arié)

vided a solid base for the justly famed flowering of Granada. It was this period too that witnessed the building of the Alhambra and of Granada's most beautiful palaces.

Arguments over the succession, in which every claimant to the throne pursued his own interests, were responsible for weakening Granada in the same measure as the threat from the Christians was growing. The unification of Castile and Aragón by the marriage of Ferdinand and Isabella in 1469 sealed the fate of the Sultanate. Antequera had already fallen in 1410, Gibraltar and Archidona no later than 1464, Málaga surrendered in 1487, Almería in 1489. The last Nasrid, Abû 'Abd Allâh Muhammad XII, known to the Spaniards as Boabdil, left the Alhambra in January 1492.

The political history of Spanish Islam thus came to an end, but its artistic legacy was to endure for centuries, not only in North Africa, where Nasrid Granada remains the dominant artistic influence, but also in Christian Spain, where mudéjar art enjoyed widespread prestige. However, the fall of Granada marked the start of a period of religious intolerance, which reached a nadir of horror with the Inquisition and led to the Expulsion Edicts of 1609 to 1614, which put an end to the story of Islam in Spain.

The Architecture of the Nasrids

The Alhambra: from Fortress to Palace City

"The City of Granada finds her equal
  not in Cairo, nor Damascus, nor Iraq.
She is the Bride unveiled,
  while the others are just the dowry."
Or:
"This city on which God's mercy shines is the balcony over the broad Vega; from here the streams can be seen like silver threads between bushes and emerald meadows. The zephir of her *najd*, the sight of her *hauz*, caress the senses and the understanding; her praises do not sing enough of a wonderland."
  Or again:
"God bless it, the wonderful time spent in the Alhambra.
As the night passed, you went to keep your tryst.
The ground appeared to you as silver, but how soon
the morning sun wrapped the Sabîka in her golden cloak."[182]

These quotations are taken from the work of an exile from Granada, and can thus hardly be regarded as objective. And yet even today Granada is a delicious oasis in a bleak mountain landscape. Its development as a major city began in the 11th century, but on the Sabîka hill itself there stood nothing but an insignificant fortress. But it was here that the Nasrids built the Alhambra (from *al-qal'a al-hamrâ'*, or "red citadel"), with its shimmering red, castellated rammed-clay ramparts above the city lying in a semi-circle at its feet, Granada, to which it was connected by a wall. The Alhambra was a palace city from the outset, from where the burghers' city of Granada and the sultanate of the same name were ruled. In this respect it is in a direct line of descent from Madînat al-Zahrâ' and the Almohad *qasaba* of Marrakesh, and is far larger and more complex than the citadels and palaces of the *taifa* rulers. And yet its pronounced fortress-like character and its strategically impregnable position stamp it unmistakably as a palace city of the late Middle Ages. In the history of architecture it represents a synthesis of the palaces of early Islam and the far more advanced defensive fortresses that arose subsequently in consequence of centuries of threat.

The Alhambra occupies a site measuring 720 metres by 220 on an outcrop of the Sierra Nevada, which to the west rises steeply into the Madîna,

Granada: Alhambra
View from the Generalife of the Torre de las Damas and the Partal complex, the Peinador de la Reina and the Comares tower. The Alhambra is a heavily-fortified citadel as well as a luxurious prestige palace, besides containing living quarters on a more intimate scale.

183

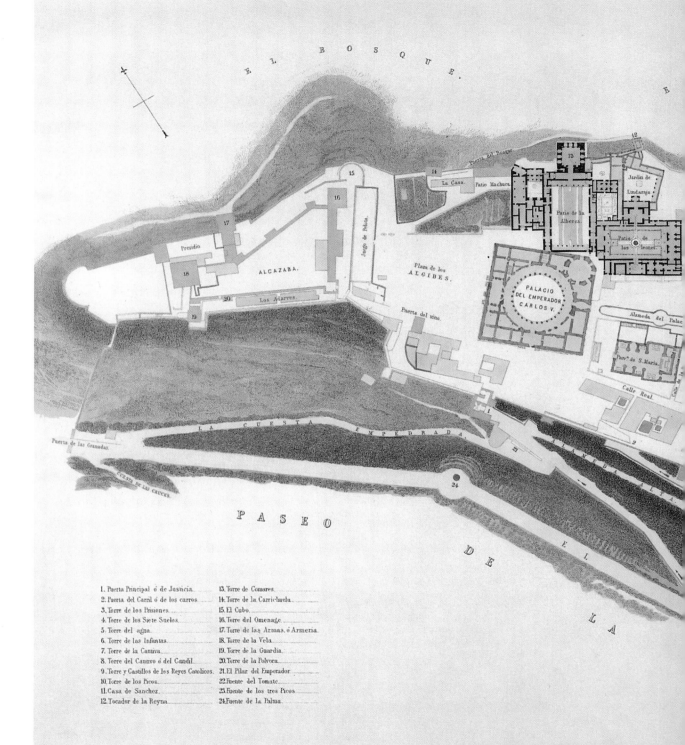

1. Puerta Principal ó de Justicia.
2. Puerta del Carril ó de los carros.
3. Torre de los Prisiones.
4. Torre de los Siete Suelos.
5. Torre del agua.
6. Torre de las Infantas.
7. Torre de la Cautiva.
8. Torre del Cautivo ó del Candil.
9. Torre y Castillos de los Reyes Catolicos.
10. Torre de los Picos.
11. Casa de Sanchez.
12. Tocador de la Reyna.
13. Torre de Comares.
14. Torre de la Carrichuela.
15. El Cubo.
16. Torre del Omenage.
17. Torre de las Armas, ó Armeria.
18. Torre de la Vela.
19. Torre de la Guardia.
20. Torre de la Polvora.
21. El Pilar del Emperador.
22. Fuente del Tomate.
23. Fuente de los tres Picos.
24. Fuente de la Palma.

B O S Q U E.

Camino de Generalife

Puerta de hierro

LA HUERTA DE S. FRANCISCO.

Calle de San Francisco.

Plaza de S. Francisco.

Convento
de
S. Francisco

A L H A M B R A   A L T A.

ALAMEDA ALTA

S A L O N

ALHAMBRA.

PASEO   DE   GENERALIFE.

PREVIOUS DOUBLE PAGE:
Plan of the Alhambra, after Owen Jones, 1842

BELOW:
Plan of the Comares palace and the Lion Court palace, after Owen Jones, 1842

In spite of its early date, the drawing is fairly accurate, albeit with certain errors in the names of rooms etc. in the western section. Thus "La Mezquita" should actually be "Mexuar", while the obliquely placed, small room at its northern end is in fact a prayer room, which the author clearly had not appreciated as he has turned the *mihrâb* niche into a doorway. The "Patio de la Mezquita" is known today as the "Cuarto Dorado", the main access to the Comares palace.

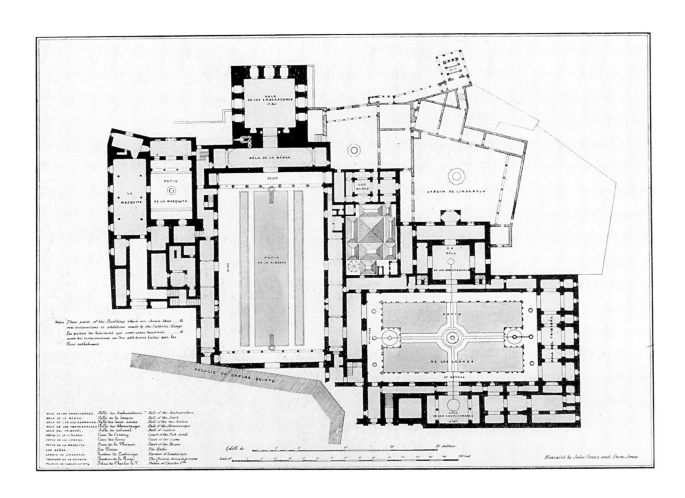

like a "huge ship anchored between the mountain and the plain" (L. Torres Balbás). It thus looms over the deep gorge of the Darro on its north flank, and the Vega and the broad valley of the Genil on its southern side.

The walls with their twenty-three towers and four gates once enclosed, alongside seven palaces, dwelling houses for a whole range of social classes, as well as offices of all kinds, the Royal Mint, public and private mosques, workshops, garrisons, prisons, public and private baths, the Royal Necropolis, gardens, a defensive structure (the Torres Bermejas), a summer residence (the Generalife), along with an 11th-century fortress erected by the Zirids on the western summit of the hill, the remains of which are still present in the Vela Tower. The Alhambra included an "upper city" in the south-east, and a "lower city" in the north-west; the two were connected by two longitudinal axes, which crossed the whole site, the present-day Calle Real and Calle Real Baja. The simpler buildings have disappeared in

Alhambra: aerial view from the north-west
"Like a giant ship anchored between mountain and plain" the Alhambra stretches along an outcrop of the Sierra Nevada above the fertile Vega. Architecture and nature undergo a unique visual symbiosis in the Alhambra. With his massive palace, King Charles I of Spain, the Emperor Charles V, put an indelible stamp on the Nasrid palace city.

187

Alhambra: Partal palace
The palace is a kind of ante-room to the Torre de las Damas behind it, from which there is a magnificent view. The Partal, which has apparently never had a patio, was probably one of the buildings erected by Muhammad III, which would make it the oldest palace in the Alhambra still extant.

the course of the centuries; only the most beautiful palaces have been consciously preserved, so that the present picture is seriously misleading: like all other Islamic palace cities, the Alhambra too had its shops and workshops, its poor and its rich.

The Sultanate of Granada was the last refuge for Spanish Muslims on the Iberian peninsula, and the Alhambra was their pride and joy. The Catholic Kings took it over, destroying nothing in the process, and made themselves at home there, with the obvious desire to preserve the palaces as far as humanly possible. Even Charles I of Spain (i.e. the Emperor Charles V), whose massive addition does not really harmonize with the aesthetics of the existing Nasrid structures, only intended it as a kind of imperial gateway to the actual palace, that of the Nasrids; and while he had the latter furnished for his own purposes, he did not do anything destructive. During the 17th and 18th centuries, no one bothered much about the conservation of the Islamic buildings, and it was only in the context of the Napoleonic Wars and above all the Romantic movement that the interest of Europe in the palace city of the Nasrids really awoke. Scholarly research began more than a century ago, and is still proceeding.[183] While a fair amount is known about the general building history of the Alhambra,

Carved and painted wooden ceiling in the Partal gallery

many details are shrouded in mystery even to this day, and excavations continue to produce regular surprises.

Muhammad I viewed the Zirid Alcazaba shortly after occupying Granada, and as a first step ordered the construction of a water-supply system and of a long circumference wall. His son and heir, Muhammad II, completed the construction of the external wall. His reign appears also to have witnessed the building of the "Ladies' Tower" and the "Battlement Tower" on the north side of the fortress. Muhammad III (1302–09) had a Friday mosque built (on the site now occupied by the church of Santa María), and next to it a public bathhouse. The outer façade of the Wine Gate also dates from his reign, and recent research also ascribes the Partal Palace to him, which would make it the oldest surviving palace in the whole complex. Although the small mosque attached to it includes inscriptions with the name of Yûsuf I, the structure probably does go back to Muhammad III. From the beginning of the 14th century at the latest, the Alhambra was a palace city independent of the city below. Its chief patrons were, however, Yûsuf I and above all Muhammad V, who were responsible for the buildings, many of them still standing, which made the Alhambra world famous, even though this did involve demolishing existing struc-

Granada: Alhambra
View from the Generalife, looking west towards the palace city. The circumference wall with its towers, looming above the steep slope, is a reminder of the former vulnerability of the complex, a situation which it is easy to forget in view of the grace and splendour of the interior.

ADJACENT:
Alhambra: Mexuar
The "conference room" of the Arab rulers, it served as a Christian chapel for centuries, during which period it was substantially remodelled.

RIGHT:
Alhambra: Torre de las Infantas
Like the Torre de la Cautiva, this tower too was turned into a "summer house" with patio and galleries.

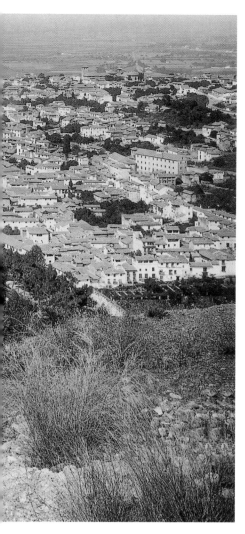

Granada: Inner façade of the Puerta del Vino
This gate, to which one of the main roads from the palace city led, probably dates from the time of Muhammad III; the decoration on this side however was replaced under Muhammad V. The discreet colour effects are due to brick, painted stucco and blue and white faïence work.

Alhambra: Torre de la Cautiva, wall decoration in faïence mosaic and carved stucco
Koranic inscriptions adorn not just the prayer rooms, but also the reception halls and living quarters. Here, in clear cursive script on a pale background, one of the most important verses to challenge Christian doctrine is reproduced: "In the name of the merciful God. Say: He is God, alone, God, through and through. He has neither begotten, nor is He begotten. And none is His equal."

Alhambra: Dome of the Sala de las Dos Hermanas

The tiny niches and niche fragments in the *muqarnas* domes of this "Hall of the Two Sisters" are arranged according to a geometric scheme based on a central star. The vaults, which seem to hover above the ring of light provided by the windows, have a purely decorative function. They were hung ready-made in the wooden roof-truss, and fastened to it by means of beams invisible from below.

Alhambra: Cuarto Dorado, south wall

The main façade of the Comares palace was erected under Muhammad V. The right-hand door gave access to the Sultan's private suite, while that on the left led to a passage with a number of sharp turns, which in turn led to the Comares palace. The wall, raised above the court by three marble steps, is one of the most impressive examples of Nasrid architecture. The decor – faïence, stucco and wood – covers the whole surface. The varying details of the patterns, based on geometric, vegetal and epigraphic motifs, are incorporated within clear geometric forms such as rectangular panels, borders, spandrels and friezes. The whole represents the culmination of an aesthetic sensibility which had a horror of harsh accents, garish colours, improvisation and disorder, and sought instead to create austere, subtle harmonies.

192

The wall decoration follows a precise scheme: below, a faïence mosaic with geometric motifs topped by a kind of castellated frieze in two-colours faïence; above are stucco panels. The spandrel motifs are primarily vegetal, while the soffits are decorated chiefly with geometric patterns. The decorative motif of the *alfiz* is largely epigraphic.

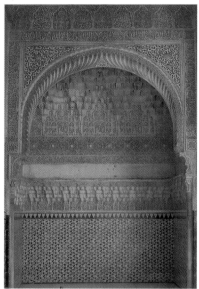

tures on the site. The gates "de las Armas", "de la Justicia" and "de Siete Suelos", the towers "del Candil", "de la Cautiva", "de Machuca" and "de Comares" were all either built or, more probably, rebuilt during the reign of Yûsuf I. None of these additions, however, necessitated any repositioning of the walls. Presumably the Mexuar (from *mashwar*, "conference room") and the Cuarto Dorado date from the same period, although the magnificent south façade of the latter, which is also the entrance façade of the Comares palace, bears inscriptions in the name of Muhammad V. The mighty Comares Tower[184] contains the "Ambassadors' Hall", Yûsuf's throne-room and thus one of the crowning glories of the Alhambra. In front of it, the "Sala de la Barca" (from *baraka*, "blessing"), an entrance hall, opens on to the portico which forms the north side of the Myrtle Court; also known as the "Alberca Court" (from *al-birka*, "pool"), most of it is taken up by a long myrtle-lined pool, measuring 34.7 metres by 7.5, in which the façades around the court are reflected. On the east side is Yûsuf's bathhouse.[185] This in turn is connected to Muhammad's palace, which stands perpendicular to the Myrtle Court complex; in the middle of the palace is the Lion Court. The direct link was commissioned by the Catholic Kings, who occupied these palaces. In the middle of the Lion Court is a fountain guarded by twelve stone lions; on each of the shorter sides is a pavilion with fountains within; running from the middle of each side to the central fountain is a paved path with a channel down the middle. The plinth with the twelve lions was obviously not made for the fountain basin which it now supports; it is in fact often attributed to the 11th century. However, the lions are so similar to those of the Partal that it can be safely dated to the second half of the 14th century.[186] The courtyard is surrounded on all four sides by colonnaded galleries; the beds in the courtyard were formerly sunken. The four sides are formed by stalactite-vaulted state-rooms: west, the long hall "de los Mocárabes", a kind of vestibule

Alhambra: wooden ceiling of the Comares Hall
This masterpiece of monumental marquetry, dating from the early 14th century, served for centuries as the model for Moorish and mudéjar ceilings in state rooms. The star decor, arranged in seven levels, consists of more than 8,000 polygonal wooden panels. It can be understood not just as a stylized representation of the starry heavens, but in addition as an allusion to the seven heavens of Islamic eschatological literature. The dominant central cupola functions here as an image of the throne of God, overlooking all creation.

with a more recent Renaissance ceiling; east, the much sub-divided "Kings' Hall", the most important in the whole complex; in the south and north there are two apartments, the first of which is grouped around the tripart-ite "Hall of the Abencerrajes" with its central pool, and the second cent-ring upon the square "Hall of the Two Sisters"; this latter leads to a wide room with a central alcove, the "Mirador de Daraxa" (from *dâr 'Â'isha*, or "house of 'Â'isha"). Today the view from here is on to a romantic court-yard laid out by Christian kings, but formerly it looked out over the Darro and the Albaicín. The friary of St Francis, now known as the Paradór, rises up above an Islamic palace. The remains of another important complex above the Partal garden were once part of the palace of Yûsuf III (1408–17); its tower once loomed over a patio with a long rectangular pool, together with side-courts, a bathhouse, a monumental entrance and various build-ings not yet identified.

The Royal Necropolis, the Rauda, has largely fallen victim to Charles I's palace; it was probably laid out in the early 14th century.[187]

There is a path from the "Puerta de Hierro", through the "Torre de los Picos" to the Generalife, a private summer palace built along the main water conduit on the slope above the Alhambra proper. A number of dif-

Alhambra: the Alberca or Myrtle Court
The north end of the court is taken up by the Comares tower with the Sala de la Barca and its portico in front. The Comares tower is one of the most massive in the whole of the Alhambra; its interior is occupied largely by the Sala de Comares, the "Ambassadors' Hall", which served as Yûsuf I's official reception hall.

Alhambra: view of the Lion Court

The Lion Court palace, a work dating from the heyday of the Nasrid sultanate, was built by Muhammad V during the second half of the 14th century. The Lion Court itself forms the heart of a self-contained palace, which is in turn composed of a number of self-contained living-quarters. In this sense, it corresponds closely to the classical Andalusian patio; however, the patio theme is subjected here to extraordinarily subtle variations. The oblong court, formerly a garden, is surrounded by a cloister-like colonnaded gallery, of the sort previously reserved for particular façades, but never used for enclosing whole courtyards or gardens, in other words, open-air spaces. The short sides of the oblong have projecting pavilions with fountains, from where channels lead to the central fountain with its lions. The latter have often been criticised for their awkwardness, allegedly incompatible with the art of Muhammad IV. However, it is almost beyond doubt that they are contemporaneous with the basin, and that the fountain was in the garden from the outset. The graceful columns surrounding the courtyard are arranged singly, doubly or in threes. These compositions, seemingly arbitrary at first sight, obey a subtle rhythm, in which various axial systems interlock, giving the patio a harmonious visual perspective.

FOLLOWING DOUBLE PAGE:

Lion Court: details

Vertical motifs are predominant, thanks to the columns. This vertical impression is assuaged, however, by the shaft rings, the abacuses, the impost blocks, the *muqarnas*, and the lozenge panels. A striking feature is the fragmentation of the decor, whose determining principle is the multiplication of variations of small and very small elements. Geometric, vegetal and calligraphic motifs merge into one another; originally vegetal motifs are only vaguely related to their natural models.

DOUBLE PAGE 200/201:

Alhambra: painting on leather in the cupola of the middle alcove in the King's Hall

The picture depicts a gathering of ten Islamic dignitaries. It has been asserted on occasion that they represent the rulers of the Nasrid dynasty, but this is hardly possible. All three alcoves have paintings on leather like this; it is generally assumed that they were commissioned from Christian artists by Muhammad V. The painters may well have belonged to the circle of the Avignon school.

ferent kinds of garden are arranged around the oblong "Patio de la Acequia" (from *al-sâqiya*, or "channel"). The *hortus conclusus* theme has here
been exploited and enhanced in a variety of ways, and set off to maximum
effect by the architecture, in particular by the effective use of the different
levels. One unique stepped waterfall – more accurately, a flight of steps
flanked by water ramps – was already arousing the admiration of travellers
in the 16th century.[188] As in the Alhambra proper, the view from within
was consciously incorporated into the overall planning of the Generalife,
where, moreover, nature is ubiquitous, playing the major role in the interior, too.

The Generalife, whose name probably derives from *jannat al-'arîf* ("The
Artist's Garden"), is presumed to date from the first third of the 14th
century, there being one inscription in the name of Ismâ'îl I. It has been
radically altered since the Christian conquest. A fire in 1958 allowed thorough archaeological investigations to take place, and the complex was
largely reconstructed in its original form.[189] A prayerhall and a bathhouse
were discovered in the process, indicating that the Generalife could have
functioned as a self-contained summer residence. The "Patio de la Acequia" resembles the Lion Court in its crossed paths; its present-day fountains are modern, but remains of earthenware pipes prove that fountains
were always present.

Further up the slope, to the north, are the ruins of a similar *munya*,
known as "Dâr al-'Arûsa" (or "House of the Bride").

ABOVE:
The roof of the Pavilion of the Abencerrajes

OPPOSITE:
*Alhambra: muqarnas dome in the Hall of the
Abencerrajes*
The contrast between the rich and highly sophisticated interior decoration and the simple ex-
teriors which characterises the buildings of
western Islam is a regular source of surprise, attaining in the Alhambra a climax which is almost insurpassable.

Alhambra: Sala de los Reyes, or Hall of the Kings
Also known as the Sala de la Justicia, this hall occupies the eastern end of the Lion Court. The *muqarnas* arches give the room an extraordinary visual depth.

Principal Architectural Themes of the Alhambra

There are some striking peculiarities in the intimate palace architecture of the Nasrids; for example, the characteristic connexion of reception halls with fountains and gardens; the unmistakably hierarchical grouping of the rooms; the strange fortress-cum-summer palace theme; and the complexity of the communication systems.

Even in Madînat al-Zahrâ', pools were already playing a major role; furthermore, at least one had been laid out in front of a reception pavilion (the Salón Rico) with the intention that its reflections should enhance the beauty of the surrounding buildings. Various *taifa* palaces worked on this theme, polishing it up, until by the time of the Alhambra and the Generalife it had achieved a hitherto undreamed-of height of perfection and differentiation. The pools here are mostly rectangular (as in the Acequia and Alberca), but also U-shaped (as in the south of the Partal), but never

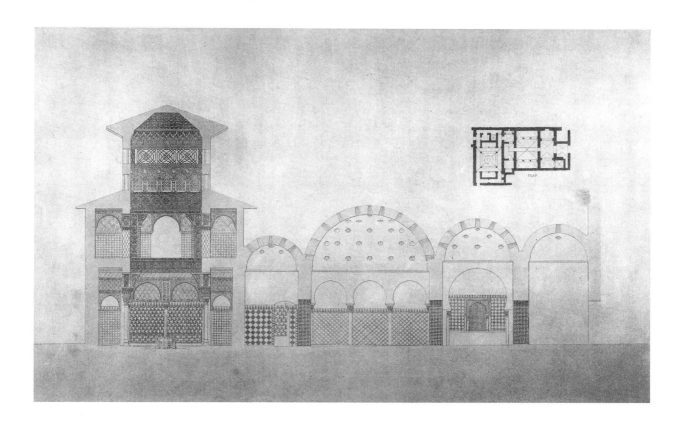

Alhambra: the Baño Real, or Royal Bathhouse
This bath, also known as the Baño del Palacio de Comares, dates back to the time of Yûsuf I. It has been rebuilt on several occasions, and we now have a more accurate picture of the layout details of the medieval bathhouse than Owen Jones, who drew up this plan and elevation in the 19th century.

The bathhouse is wedged in, so to speak, between the Myrtle Court, the Lion Court and the Hall of the Two Sisters, and lies well below the floor level of these complexes. It can be reached from the lower garden of the Lion Court palace, now known as the Linderaja garden. The bathhouse is of the type usual in western Islam during the Middle Ages, and is conspicuous only on account of its elegant decoration. The contemporary bathhouses of eastern Islam were generally of a more complicated layout.

square and seldom round (in the Generalife). Often the fresh water flows over a round, shallow dish into the pool below. The theme of water is pursued in the living quarters and reception rooms: in the "Hall of the Abencerrajes" and in the "Hall of the Two Sisters" the channels of the Lion Court are extended into the rooms inside, where the water splashes gently into indoor pools. One is reminded of the Paradise described in the Koran, with its gardens, its cool springs, and its "chambers where streams do flow." The quartered garden with its sunken beds, its symmetrically-placed pavilions, its pools and its channels is unmistakably an integral part of the reception suite; the enjoyment of nature is thus transformed into a status symbol. Of course this enjoyment of nature is not experienced directly: the foot of the visitor never walks on soil or grass; the flowers are out of reach, unpluckable; to lie down on the grass would be unthinkable. One walks on marble paths, high above the sunken beds, savouring the scent of the flowers and the orange blossom as it wafts upward; from the carpets and sofas of the reception room, open to the patio, one feasts one's eyes on the *hortus conclusus* and one's ears on the rippling of the fountains.

In these reception suites, the basilical halls of Madînat al-Zahrâ' have given way to domed rooms. The cupolas in the state-rooms are never of masonry; they consist of massive wooden vaulting as in Yûsuf I's Ambassadors' Hall, or of stucco *muqarnas* vaulting composed of countless tiny elements as in Muhammad's state-rooms. Always, they are built into pyramidal roofs. The rooms are relatively small and arranged into living quarters; adjacent to the domed room are side-rooms, alcoves, anteroom and portico. No hard-and-fast scheme of room arrangement seems to have been the rule either under Yûsuf I or under Muhammad V; one feature that is constant, however, is the fragmentation of the roof area. Every room has its own ceiling and roof-structure (which accounts for the kaleidoscopic appearance of the whole when viewed from above). All the same, the main room is unmistakably dominant. The hierarchical arrangement within every unit is likewise unmistakable: it is probable (though no longer demonstrable, the dwellings of the ordinary people not having been preserved), that there was an overall hierarchical arrangement of units, too, based on position, layout and decoration. Compared with Madînat al-Zahrâ', which opens the architectural period that the Alhambra closes, the latter exhibits a further evolution of fragmentation, more variety in room layout, and the preservation and refinement of hierarchical arrangements.

One individuality of the Alhambra consists in the way that the massive defensive towers are, so to speak, turned into summer palaces. The basic theme is still a large square or rectangular tower, with centrally-planned galleried spaces or rooms on each storey. The central space is sometimes converted into a courtyard, or rather into a shaft to admit light. This arrangement is by no means new; the conversion of a fortified tower into a prestige building has a very long tradition, as seen for example in Algeria, in the Manâr Tower in the Zirid Qal'a of the Banû Hammâd, dating from the late 11th century.[190] What is new is the gracefulness of the interior architecture, the intimacy of these apartments, far removed from the loudness of the Zirid Manâr Tower, which in certain respects lives on in the Comares Tower. The names that were later given to these towers, such as "Peinador de la Reina" ("The Queen's Hairdressing Room") and "Torre

The Patio de la Acequia in the Generalife
This long garden, like the Lion Court, also has raised paths in the form of a cross with a fountain at the centre.

de las Damas" ("The Ladies' Tower"), along with the legends collected by Washington Irving, in which beautiful, sorrowful Arab princesses languish for their lovers, show clearly that the Christian conquerors were struck just as forcefully as we are today by the contrast between their outward appearance and interior design.

The communication systems are extraordinarily complicated and likewise clearly hierarchical in arrangement. A good example is provided by the approach to the Comares complex through the "Cuarto Dorado". The south façade of the latter, which separates the public, administrative part of the palace from the private and reception suites, has two doors: the right-hand one gave access to the ruler's private chambers, while that on the left led through to the Comares complex, the palace's reception area. This passage, with three sharp bends, contained niches for the sentries along with doors which opened in opposite directions to facilitate surveillance. The private entrance was considerably more complicated still. The two were strictly separated the one from the other, and both forced the entrant along a pre-determined path from which no deviation or exit was possible.[191] The separation and demarcation of access routes according to category of user can be seen yet more clearly in later and better-preserved palace cities,[192] although such features were in all likelihood already present in Madînat al-Zahrâ'. To summarise the most important functional aspects of this palace city, one can safely say that defence was the overwhelming consideration, and that the prestige and reception functions led to new and specific solutions. At first sight, the religious function seems omnipresent, represented by a (no longer extant) Friday mosque, a large number of smaller prayerhalls, and the obligatory religious inscriptions, which, in this case, however, have to share space with historical and poetic texts.[193] The little private prayerrooms with their simple, square groundplan are far removed from the former palace oratories with their sophisticated symbolic planning and execution, and one has the general impression that the religious function here was less important than in many other Islamic palace cities. The symbolic function of the decoration has often been commented upon: there is no doubt at all that the domes with their geometric *muqarnas* and stellate decoration conjure up associations with the starry heavens, but one cannot really pursue the interpretation any further.[194]

Many questions remain unanswered even today, for example that concerning the relationship between the Comares complex and the Lion Court complex. Were they summer and winter residences? Or reception and private suites? Or simply two princely buildings built one after the other, aiming at confident self-presentation? Another open question concerns stylistic evolution. Thus in the "Patio del Haren" (in the Lion Court complex) there is some wall decoration in the Almohad style dating from the time of Muhammad V; it is quite different from the kind of decoration usual at this period, and forces us to re-think our ideas about the prevailing style.[195]

In general, one can observe a continual process of refinement in the execution of existing formal elements. Thus Muhammad V's columns are not new creations in themselves, but their rhythmical arrangement around the Lion Court had not been seen before. Completely innovatory and totally surprising are the three large paintings in the Kings' Hall, which

Granada: Façade of the Corral del Carbón
This former *funduq*, a kind of inn, storehouse and trading centre, lay in the centre of the city of Granada, close to the Great Mosque and the market (the Arab *sûq*). The interior of this early 14th-century building has been largely destroyed, but its fine brick façade is still preserved in an alleyway in the old quarter.

seem to be the work of some Christian studio whose masters may have been trained in Avignon.[196]

Nasrid Architecture in the City and Sultanate of Granada

The city and sultanate of Granada also witnessed the constructions of new buildings under the Nasrids, some of them still standing today. The "Cuarto Real de Santo Domingo", later occupied for a time by Torquemada, the Grand Inquisitor, was originally a palace, built in the reign of Muhammad II. Also in the "Potters' Quarter" is the "Casa de los Girones", probably also dating from the 13th century. The Alcázar Genil is situated further to the south, outside the city of Granada, not far from the Hermitage of Saint Sebastian, originally a Nasrid mausoleum. In the Alcázar Genil, which once had two pools, there is still a hall with two alcoves and a portico, whose decoration dates from the time of Yûsuf I. In the Poor Clares' Convent of Santa Isabel la Real, on the Alcazaba Qadima, a small palace has been preserved, known as the "Daralhorra", which is attributed to the 15th century. In the same neighbourhood is another convent, Santa Catalina de Zafra, with the remains of a 15th-century Islamic house. The remains still exist of a number of *munyas* in the district, for example in Cortijo del

View from the Vela Tower looking east towards the Alcazaba, the Torre de Homenaje and the Torre Quebrada
The heavily-fortified Alcazaba is the oldest part of the Alhambra. Within it are the ruins of a residential quarter, the Barrio Castrense (military quarter), which once had seventeen dwellings, a bathhouse, a well, storehouses, barracks and stables.

211

Madrasa: cupola in the prayer room
Above the square prayer room rises a wood and *muqarnas* cupola on an octagonal base.

Granada: mihrâb façade in the Madrasa
Yûsuf I founded a *Madrasa*, or college of theology and law, which was destroyed after the Christian reconquest but restored in the 19th century. In the square prayer hall the *muqarnas* squinches make the transition to the octagonal base of the cupola.

Cobertizo, and somewhat to the south, in the Cortijo de la Marquesa, the so-called "Darabenaz", probably also from the 15th century.[197] In Ronda, elements from the Islamic period are still preserved in the Casa de los Gigantes.[198]

Remains of the numerous Nasrid *hammâms* have been found in Granada and Taifa, and also near the village of Zubia and in Churriana. The *hammâm* in Ronda is also one of these Islamic bathhouses, even though the town was never under Nasrid rule during this period, but belonged to the Marînids. The *hammâms* of western Islam remained strangely archaic in comparison with the more advanced versions in the Near East. They are square in plan, with the changing room, cold room, temperate room and hot room following one upon the other. Separate cubicles were often incorporated into both the changing room and the sudatorium. Heating continued to be by means of hypocausts. The changing and relaxation room is bigger than the others and usually has a cupola, faïence decoration and sometimes galleries too.

In the city of Granada Muhammad V had a *mâristân* built, in other words a hospital for the poor with a psychiatric department; it was demolished in 1843.[199] Its rectangular inner court had a pool with two sculptured lions guarding a fountain; these latter are now in the Partal. The foundation stone with its inscription is now kept in the Alhambra museum. In general, this *mâristân* is simpler than its Near Eastern contemporaries. The present-day Corral del Carbón, a *funduq*, was built in the early 14th century near the *qaysâriyya* and the Great Mosque; it served as a warehouse, a wholesale outlet and an inn. Its monumental gatehouse has been preserved, but its interior appointments have not; however the ground plan, with its rectangular inner courtyard, its galleries and cells and its first floor, is still recognizable.

Many hilltops and ridges in the sultanate are crowned even today by the remains of fortresses, in most cases antedating the Nasrids, but restored and used during the Nasrid and Marînid periods. Some, like Tabernas, had primarily strategic functions, while others were either watch-towers or refuges, like Alcaudete, La Guardia near Jaén and Moclín; others again were fortified settlements or towns, like Archidona, Antequera and Ronda. The massive, rectangular corner-towers of this period suggest the influence of Christian fortresses. The Calahorra in Gibraltar and the keeps in Málaga and Antequera are in this category.

Of the religious buildings not much has been preserved. The Chief Mosque of the Alhambra had a nave and two aisles, the nave probably being higher and wider than the aisles; Christian influences have been detected. The much older (Zirid) Chief Mosque in Granada, which was demolished to make way for the Cathedral, also had a basilical prayer hall with a nave and aisles. Some minarets have been converted into church towers, for example the tower of San Juan de los Reyes in Granada, that of the no longer extant Church of St Sebastian in Ronda, and the minarets of Archez and Salares in a remote valley in the coastal mountains of Málaga province. Still preserved in Ronda is the *mihrâb* arch of the former Chief Mosque, whose site is now occupied by the church of Santa María; the rich stucco decoration is actually more typical of the Marînid period than of the Nasrid. In Granada Yûsuf I founded a university (*madrasa*) which was largely

destroyed during the 18th century and restored at the end of the 19th; of the original structure the patio and the square prayer hall with its *mihrâb* and dome on *muqarnas* squinches can still be seen. It is the sole more or less surviving madrasa in the Sultanate of Granada.

In Fiñana,[200] a fortified town *(hisn)* on the road from Almería to Granada, the remains of a Nassid mosque have been preserved in a hermitage on the same site. Four octagonal columns border nine bays. The prayer room is today very simple. The surviving *mihrâb*, by contrast, is richly carved, and may have been the work of one of Granadá's leading workshops.

Nasrid Architectural Ornamentation

Faïence mosaic: detail

Granada: faïence dish from the Alhambra, 14th century; in the Museo Nacional de Arte Hispanomusulmán

Nasrid architectural ornamentation is dominated by marble panels, sculptured stucco in coloured settings, and polychrome faïence. Wood, too, is used for ornamental purposes in ceilings, canopies, corbels and doors; the ornamentation takes the form of carving, painting or inlay work. Turned wooden bars are found above all in window and door openings and on balconies. The coloured upper lights of the windows, set in stucco, were just as common in Andalusia as they were in Marînid Morocco.

The Alhambra employs a great variety of arch shapes, from the horseshoe arch of the Caliphate via the simple round arch to flat and pointed arches and multi-lobed and *muqarnas* arches. The generously-proportioned forms of the Almohad period were now broken up into smaller elements. Broad imposts are inserted between the capitals and the springers; the visible surfaces are often sculpted. The capital itself is a logical consequence of the start made under the Caliphate: the lower, cylindrical section is totally contrasted with the upper, square section, resulting in a simpler silhouette; the internal ornamentation nevertheless grows increasingly detailed and prolific. The cylindrical section of the capital has, almost without exception, the same pattern: a kind of wavy ribbon, already present in the Almohad period as a schematization of the simple or double smooth leaf-crowns of the capitals of the Caliphate. The upper section, with its compact arabesque decoration, is more varied. The Alhambra also has pure *muqarnas* capitals. Many of the graceful marble columns reveal rings towards the top of their shaft, thus preparing the way, so to speak, for the capital itself. Octagonal columns are not infrequent; like other prismatic shafts, they may be clad in colourful faïence.

The Nasrid inventory of motifs attaches particular importance to epigraphy and in particular to cursive script forms. The Kufic script is now only used for repetitive religious formulas, among which one is used as a kind of heraldic device: "wa-lâ ghâliba illá'llâh", "there is no victor but God". The characters are intermingled with arabesques and a wide variety of other decorative forms.

The walls of the halls are often covered with horizontal strips and panels that provide an axis for the ornamental composition. The asymmetric semi-palmette, pennate or smooth, and a whole variety of different bud shapes combine with the circles of the leaf-stalks to form a dense, repetitive pattern of small elements for the coverage of surfaces. Small palmettes along with four and five-petalled flowers and a kind of trefoil lily are mingled with the semi-palmettes. Pine cones continue to occur, albeit

Fiñana: mihrâb converted into altar niche
Fiñana, a little mountain town to the south-east of Granada, was once a fortified Islamic settlement. On the site of its mosque there stands today an *ermita*, in which the remains of the Nasrid building are preserved. The finely-carved stucco panels of the *mihrâb* façade are of Nasrid making, and they bear witness, as do so many Spanish churches, to the constancy of sacred sites.

mostly only in a setting evolved from the semi-palmette. Geometric and vegetal elements are now almost indistinguishable. Interlocking arches form criss-cross lozenge patterns with dense internal ornamentation, using the same fusion of vegetal and geometric elements. The plaited star patterns are employed to cover ever greater areas; in spite of their apparent complexity, the basic scheme is quite simple, because it always comes back to the square in the end: the starpatterns are non-convex polygons with four, eight, twelve, sixteen or twenty-four points; five and six-pointed stars are virtually never used.

New elements of Christian, in most cases contemporary, origin in the architectural ornamentation of the Nasrid period and in particular of Muhammad V's Alhambra are obvious enough, but neither they nor the newly imported pointed arches can be said to lead to any real innovation. Nor do the plans and elevations produced by the Nasrid architects contribute any really new ideas; the house arranged around its rectangular patio and its galleries, the basilical form for religious architecture and the domed hall as the central feature of secular buildings – all these were well-tried formulas. In consequence, the Nasrid period has often, and with a certain justification, been written off as uncreative and decadent. But yet, in the search for refinement, in which "an ideal of elegance replaces that of strength,"[201] one can discern values which are altogether positive: harmony in place of pomp; lifestyle in place of bombastic sabre-rattling. The crowds of tourists who flock to the Alhambra are proof enough that our age is peculiarly receptive to the specific character of the Nasrid artistic outlook.

Ronda: springer of the mihrâb arch in the present-day cathedral
These stucco carvings may date back to the late 13th century and might reflect some Marînid influence.

Conclusion

Like Athene, Andalusian architecture presents itself from the hour of its birth in full possession of all its faculties. The original Friday Mosque in Cordova betrays no uncertainties, no doubts; it does not represent the first faltering steps of a beginner. The evolution which led up to this state of affairs had not taken place on Spanish soil, but in the Near East, where Umayyad art and culture arose, grew and matured from the mid-7th century to the mid-8th. In the Near East, this thread snapped in 750, only to be taken up once more in Spain thirty years later. Round about this time a new development started in the Near East, which in the context of a profound Orientalization of the Umayyad heritage was to lead to new forms and principles of design. On the Iberian peninsula, by contrast, this heritage was enriched, but not diluted, by an unavoidable confrontation with the cultures of the Romans and the Visigoths, cultures which had put down roots long before.

Is it then possible to discern specific features of Hispano-Islamic architecture which characterize it from its beginnings right until its end, and make it unmistakable in the more general context of Islamic architecture? Without a doubt, the answer to this question is: yes. The artistic province of Andalusia does possess a local style all of its own, which remains characteristic throughout all the changes of the passing centuries. It is a result on the one hand of the material realities; on the other, of the initial impulses. To the Visigothic artistic scene, with its Byzantine and Germanic features and its large proportion of provincial Roman culture, were imported those Umayyad ideas which in their turn were formed of Byzantine, Classical Mediterranean, and Sassanid elements juxtaposed.

Andalusia's geographical isolation is probably the most important factor in its individualistic stylistic development, and primarily responsible for its profound conservatism. As far as secular architecture is concerned, there is no challenge to the patio house with its inner courtyard, with or without portico, with or without side courts, with or without garden: the basic pattern is unmistakably a Roman legacy. The basilical structure informs the whole of sacred architecture; even the innovations of the Almohad period do not depart essentially from it. The Friday mosques of Andalusia remain true to Medina; the model is developed, but never really abandoned. The confrontation with the domed hall and the *ivân*, which is characteristic of architectural developments in the East from the time of the Seljuks onwards, never got through to Andalusia; nor does this assertion really have to be qualified by the experience of Cordova in the 10th

Alhambra: faïence mosaic, detail
These endless star patterns in faïence mosaic (and less extravagant faïence techniques too) have been used, since the building of the Alhambra, to cover square kilometre upon square kilometre of wall space throughout the Moorish world, albeit seldom attaining the quality of the work in the Alhambra.

century or Granada in the 14th; the former led to no structural innovations, but dissipated in ornamentation, while the latter was restricted to domes of wood and stucco within the roof-truss.

As far as ornamentation is concerned, one can observe a homogeneous and fairly linear development, which diverged from that of eastern Islam from the very outset. The forms and motifs derived from the Romans, the Orient and the Visigoths[202] can be clearly distinguished until well into the 10th century. It is actually not until the *taifa* period that they fuse into a homogeneous and highly sophisticated artistic idiom, one that was not shy of creating effects, and whose vegetal elements had largely liberated themselves from their natural models and instead gradually gave up their identity in a union with geometric forms. It was an artistic idiom aimed at elegance; underlying these fragmented, decorative compositions was an exact mathematical schema; repetition became a stylistic element in its own right. In the crafts, particularly, one finds lively and often humorous figurative motifs; they are as it were embedded in the superordinate geometric arrangement, without threatening to burst it.

The trial of strength with the North African Berber dynasties, who gave a new direction to taste, sensibility and sense of purpose in the field of

Alhambra: Cuarto Dorado, façade detail; 19th century print

The Patio de la Acequia in the Generalife

artistic creativity, led to fresh impulses from the early 12th century onwards. At first the African conquerors appear unambiguously as recipients, but soon the relationship changed, and Andalusia itself became the
recipient for a brief period. The cultural links with the Islamic Near East
were never actually severed; oriental ideas were continually being received
in the Islamic West, albeit in a peculiar and eclectic fashion; during the
period of Berber domination these ideas comprised both the latest achievements, such as *muqarnas*, for example, alongside very much older elements
such as certain stucco motifs from the Abbassid Samarra of the 9th century.
Nasrid art, while taking over much from the Almohad period, abandoned
the latter's all-permeating master vision. The artistic thrust of this last
period of Islamic rule and Islamic patronage on Iberian soil was directed
towards an intimacy and a harmony which have little in common with the
ambitious programmes of the Almohads. The integration of individual
motifs from the European world into the inventory of forms of this period
should perhaps be seen in exactly the same way as the incorporation of
Islamic motifs in the architectural ornamentation of the Christian palaces
in Seville, namely as the symbolic prelude to a new epoch, which, in spite
of the Inquisition and the Expulsion Edicts, did not renounce the Islamic
legacy, and for which Goethe's timeless lines from the *Westöstlicher Diwan*
are entirely appropriate:

"In splendour did the Orient
Cross the Mediterranean Sea;
You must know and love Háfiz
If you are to know the songs of
Calderón."

PAGE 220:
*View of the north façade of the Myrtle Court,
Romantic print*
The artist has discreetly omitted the palace of
Emperor Charles V, which looms over the Nas-
rid buildings.

Notes

1. A dinar kept in the Museo Arqueológico Nacional in Madrid.

2. Halm, H.: Al-Andalus und Gothica Sors, in: Welt des Orients, 66, 1989, pp. 252–63.

3. Bonnasié, P.: Les temps des Wisigoths, in: Bennasser, B.: Histoire des Espagnols, VIe–XVIIe siècle, Paris 1985, p. 50 f.

4. Claudio Sánchez-Albornoz speaks of an altogether fanatical cult of the memory of the Visigothera practised by the warriors of the Reconquista. Sánchez-Albornoz, C.: L'Espagne Musulmane, Publisud, [4]1985; idem: Espagne préislamique et Espagne musulmane, in: Revue historique, 1967, pp. 295–338.

5. de Palol, P.: Regard sur l'art Visigoth, Paris 1979. Also the relevant chapter in: Terrasse, H.: Islam d'Espagne. Une rencontre de l'Orient et de l'Occident, Paris 1958, pp. 15–25; see also Fontaine, J.: L'art préroman hispanique, la Pierre-qui-vire, in: Zodiaque (ed.), La Nuit des Temps, 38, 1973.

6. Actually, Madînat al-nabî, the Town of the Prophet. On the subject of the founding of Medina and the first Islamic state: Noth, A.: Früher Islam, in: Haarmann, M. (ed.): Geschichte der arabischen Welt, Munich 1987, pp. 11–100.

7. Ibn 'Idhârî al-Marrakûshî: Kitâb al-bayân al-mughrib, [2]II, 58–60, quoted from Hoenerbach, W.: Islamische Geschichte Spaniens, Zurich and Stuttgart 1970, pp. 65, 525.

8. This anecdote is always cropping up, but only in the literature of Andalusia. Ibn al-Khatîb in the a'mal al-a'lam takes it over from the Akhbar Majmû'a and the Bayan, [2]II, 59, 60, quoted from Hoenerbach, W., op.cit. (note 7), p. 64.

9. Singer, H. R.: Der Maghreb und die Pyrenäenhalbinsel bis zum Ausgang des Mittelalters, in: Haarmann, M. (ed.), op.cit. (note 6), p. 275.

10. According to Wasserstein, D.: The Rise and Fall of the Party-Kings. Politics and Society in Islamic Spain, 1002–1086, Princeton 1985, p. 23, the Christians did not start converting in large numbers to Islam until the mid-10th century.

11. Ibn al-Qûtiyya: Ifitâh al-Andalus, quoted by Sánchez-Albornoz, C., op.cit. (note 4), pp. 38–40.

12. Guichard, P.: Naissance de l'islam andalou, VIIIe–début Xe siècle, in: Bennasser, B., op.cit. (note 3), pp. 79, 81.

13. Sourdel, D.: Wazîr et hâjib en Occident, in: Etudes d'orientalisme dédiées à la mémoire d'E. Lévi-Provençal, Paris 1962, pp. 749–755.

14. ibid.

15. Vernet, J.: Die spanisch-arabische Kultur in Orient und Okzident, Zurich and Munich 1984, p. 37.

16. Lévi-Provençal, E.: Histoire de l'Espagne Musulmane, 3 vols., Paris 1950–67, vol. 1, pp. 193–278.

17. Although, at the latest since the excavation by C. de Mergelina (Bobastro, Memoria de las excavaciones realizadas en las Mesas de Villaverde, El Chorro [Málaga], Madrid 1927), the location of Bobastro in the Serranía of Málaga, on a hilltop overlooking the Guadalhorce valley, has been perfectly clear, disputes concerning it continue to break out: Vallve Bermejo, J.: De nuevo sobre Bobastro, in: Al-Andalus, 30, 1965, pp. 139–74. This author would place Bobastro in Marmuyas, which has, however, proved to be a Nasrid settlement. See: Fernandez López, S.: Marmuyas (Montes de Málaga). Análisis de una investigación, in: Actas de I Congreso de Arqueología Medieval Española, vol. III, Saragossa 1986, pp. 163–180.

18. Both are said to have been founded by a certain Hanash al-San'anî. Lévi-Provençal, E., op.cit. (note 16), p. 344; Ibn 'Idhârî al-Marrakûshî, op.cit., (note 7), pp. 98, 156.

19. Torres Balbás, L.: Arte Hispanomusulmán. Hasta la caída del califato de Cordoba, in: Menéndez Pidal, R. (ed.): Historia de España, vol. IV, Madrid 1957, p. 341, quoting Ibn al-Qûtiyya, op. cit., (note 11), p .11.

20. ibid., p. 370, after: Ibn al-Athîr, K. al-Kâmil fî l-târîkh, ed. and transl. by Fagnan, E.: Annales, p. 379, and transl., p. 101, and Maqqarî, Nafh al-tîb, ed. and transl. by Dozy, R.: Analectes, I, p. 358.

21. Reported in any case by Ibn 'Idhârî al Marrakûshî; however, he wrote his al-Bayân al-mughrib in the late 13th century, and his facts are not always reliable. The pre-history of the Great Mosque of Cordoba is still unclear. There is an outstandingly precise summary in Ewert, C.: Spanisch-islamische Systeme sich kreuzender Bögen. I. Die senkrechten ebenen Systeme sich kreuzender Bögen als Stützkonstruktionen der vier Rippenkuppeln in der ehemaligen Hauptmoschee von Córdoba, Berlin 1968 (Madrider Forschungen, 2) p. 1. See also: Ocaña Jiménez, M.: Precisiones sobre la Historia de la Mezquita de Córdoba, in: Cuadernos de estudios medievales IV–V, Granada 1979, pp. 275–82.

22. Creswell, K.A.C.: Early Muslim Architecture, vol. 2, New York [2]1979, p. 157, refers to Ibn al-Qûtiyya, Bibliothèque Nationale, Paris, Ms. arab., 1897, fols 27, 31, transl. by Cherbonneau, Journal Asiatique, 5e série, vol. VIII, p. 475.

23. As Creswell does, op.cit. (note 22), vol. I/1, pp. 198–201; vol. II, p. 156.

24. Bloom, J.: Minaret, Symbol of Islam, Oxford 1989, p. 33.

25. Cressier, P.: Les chapiteaux de la Grande Mosquée de Cordoue (oratoires d'Abd al-Rahmân I et d'Abd al-Rahmân II) et la sculpture de chapiteaux à l'époque émirale, in: Madrider Mitteilungen, 25, 1984, pp. 257–313, plates 63–72, and 26, 1985, pp. 216–81, plates 72–82.

26. Ewert, C., and Wisshak, J. P.: Forschungen zur almohadischen Moschee. I. Vorstufen. Hierarchische Gliederungen westislamischer Betsäle des 8. bis 11. Jahrhunderts: die Hauptmoscheen von Kairouan und Córdoba und ihr Bannkreis, Mainz 1981 (Madrider Beiträge 9).

27. Schlumberger, D.: Qasr al-Heir el-Gharbi, Paris 1986, p. 24.

28. Torres Balbás, L., op.cit. (note 19), p. 377.

29. Terrasse, H.: L'art hispano-mauresque des origines au XIIIe siècle, Paris 1932, p. 153.

30. al-Idrîsî, Description de l'Afrique et de l'Espagne, ed. and transl. by Dozy, R. and de Goeje, J., Leiden 1866, pp. 182, 220 f., after Torres Balbás, L., op.cit., (note 19), p. 385.

31. The disunity and isolation of the sons of 'Umar ibn Hafsûn led to the fortress eventually falling into the lap of the Emir like an overripe fruit. See Lévi-Provençal, E., op.cit. (note 16), vol. 2. pp. 16–24.

32. According to Gómez-Moreno, M.: El arte árabe español hasta los Almohades – Arte mozarabe, in: Ars Hispaniae III, p. 63, 'Abd ar-Rahmân III had a new fortress built there. Likewise Terrasse, H., op.cit. (note 29), p. 158, who refers to Ibn 'Idhârî al Marrakûshi, op.cit. (note 9), p. 333. See also the excavation report by de Mergelina, in: La iglesia rupestre de Bobastro, in: Arch. esp. de Arte y Arqueología, vol. II, Madrid 1925, and Torres Balbás, L.: Ciudades yermas hispanomusulmanas, Madrid 1957, pp. 182–195.

33. de Mergelina, C.: op.cit. (note 32); see also Gómez-Moreno, M., op.cit., p. 356.

34. Thus Ibn al-Khatîb, op.cit. (note 7), p. 109.

35. ibid., p. 130.

36. Guichard, P., op.cit. (note 12), p. 75; see also Wasserstein, D.: op.cit. (note 10), p. 237. The "Cordova Calendar" by Rabî 'Ibn Zayd or Recesmund is written in Arabic; bible trans-

lations into Arabic were also made at this time. While Latin texts were still being written during the 9th century, there are none extant from the 11th.

37 Glick, T. F.: Islamic and Christian Spain in the Early Middle Ages, Princeton, 1979, pp. 33–35, 282. Also: Bulliet, R.W.: Conversions to Islam in the Medieval Period. An Essay in Quantitative History, Cambridge, Mass. and London 1979.

38 Guichard, P., op.cit. (note 12), p. 76, who quotes a text by Ibn Hawqal in this connexion.

39 Ayalon, D.: On the Eunuchs in Islam, in: Jerusalem Studies in Arabic and Islam, 1, 1979, pp. 67–124.

40 Wasserstein, D., op.cit. (note 10), p. 25; also Lévi-Provençal, E., op.cit. (note 16), vol. 2, pp. 126 f.

41 Mamlûk: "unfree" ("property of another"), mostly applied to soldiers. Ayalon, D.: Mamlûk, in: Encyclopédie de l'Islam, vol. VI, 1987, pp. 299–305.

42 Miles, G.C.: The Coinage of the Umayyads of Spain, 2 vols., New York 1950.

43 Al-Maqqarî, Shihâb al-Dîn Abû l-'Abbâs Ahmad b. Muhammad Ahmad b. Yahyâ al-Qurashî al-Tilimsanî al-Fâsî al-Mâlikî (e. 1577–1632), Nafh al-tîb, publ. in Cairo 1949 (10 vols.), partially transl. by de Gayangos, P.: The History of the Muhammadan Dynasties in Spain, London 1840, new ed. New York 1964, vol. I, p. 232.

44 There was over the main entrance of various Umayyad palaces a statue of a man, possibly the ruler; Baghdad, too, is said to have had equestrian statues above the dome of the central palace and over the cupolas of the four city gates. The status of women in Islam makes it extremely unlikely that even a favourite wife would be glorified in the form of a statue over a city gate. However, what cannot be totally discounted is that al-Hakam had a classical statue placed above the gate, because he is known to have admired and collected antiquities.

45 Thus Ibn al-Khatîb, op.cit. (note 8), p. 122; also al-Maqqarî, op.cit. (note 43), vol. I, pp. 232 ff.

46 Hitherto only the northern parts of the city, the palaces and government buildings on the uppermost terrace, have been excavated, and even here work is not complete. The broad expanse below is totally untouched. Since the publication in 1965 by Klaus Brisch of a comprehensive summary of the existing literature (Medinat az-Zahra in der modernen archäologischen Literatur Spaniens, in: Kunst des Orients, 4, 1965, pp. 5–41), a num-

ber of more recent publications have appeared, which cannot all be listed here; among the more noteworthy are: Pavón Maldonado, B.: Memoria de la excavación de la mezquita de Medinat al-Zahra, Excavaciones Árqueológicas en España, Nº 50, 1966; López-Cuervo, S.: Medina az-Zahra. Ingeniería y forma, Madrid 1983; Hernández Giménez, F.: Madinat al-Zahra, Granada 1985; the first number of the new journal Cuadernos de Madînat al-Zahrâ' (1987) is a promising start. Also very useful is the short work, chiefly intended for tourists, by Castejón y Martinez de Arizala, R.: Medina Azahara, León ²1982.

47 As evidenced, for example, by the Colloquia which have taken place regularly since 1987, and the journal, mentioned above, entitled Cuadernos de Madînat al-Zahrâ'. The curator is Antonio Vallejo Triano.

48 al-Idrîsî, op.cit. (note 30), p. 212, transl. p. 163.

49 The names for the individual buildings are due to those conducting the excavation; there is no standardization in the archaeological literature.

50 Ibn al-Khatîb, op.cit. (note 8), p. 123; after Ibn 'Idhârî al-Marrakûshî, op.cit. (note 7), p. 231, who, however, talks of only 800 loaves.

51 Castejón y Martinez de Arizala, R., op.cit. (note 46).

52 This journey is also known from a Latin text: Johann, Abbot of St Arnulph, in his biography of Johann von Gorze, his predecessor in that office; Monumenta Germaniae Historica, Script. IV, p. 335 ff.

53 Castejón y Martinez de Arizala, R., op.cit. (note 46), p. 42 f.

54 Lévi-Provençal, E., op.cit. (note 16), vol. 2, p. 163 ff.

55 Marble plate to the right of the Puerta de la Palmas; Lévi-Provençal, E.: Inscriptions arabes d'Espagne, Leiden and Paris 1931, p. 8 f.

56 Creswell, K.A.C., op.cit. (note 22), p. 141.

57 Hernández Giménez, F.: El Alminar de 'Abd al-Rahmân III en la Mezquita mayor de Córdoba. Génesis y repercusiones, Granada 1979.

58 Brisch, K.: Die Fenstergitter und verwandte Ornamente der Hauptmoschee von Córdoba. Eine Untersuchung zur spanisch-islamischen Ornamentik, Berlin 1966 (Madrider Forschungen, 4), p. 28, note 5; also Ewert, C., op.cit. (note 21), p. 5.

59 See the excellent stylistic and technical analysis by Ewert, C., op.cit. (note 21), pp. 7–11, 67–74.

60 Thus for example in the library at Haghbat, and in three other 13th-century halls. Der Nersessian, S.: L'Art Arménien, Paris 1977, p. 171. See also Thierry, J.-M. and Donabédian, P.: Les Arts Arméniens, Paris 1987, p. 534 f. Incidentally also in the Armenian Church of St James in Jerusalem: Narkiss, B.: Armenian Art Treasures of Jerusalem, Jerusalem 1979, pp. 120–122.

61 There are good, clear analyses of this technique already in Reuther, O.: Ocheîdir, Leipzig 1912; see also Godard, A.: Voûtes iraniennes, in: Athar-é Irân, 1949.

62 Ewert, C., op.cit. (note 21), p. 74.

63 ibid., p. 75.

64 Stern, H.: Les Mosaïques de la Grande Mosquée de Cordoue, Berlin 1976 (Madrider Forschungen, 11), with an essay by Duda, D.: Zur Technik des Keramiksimses in der Großen Moschee von Cordova in: Madrider Forschungen, II, 1976, p. 53 f.

65 A technique that was also known to the master mosaicist of the Umayyad Dome of the Rock. See van Berchem, M.: The Mosaics of the Dome of the Rock and the Great Mosque in Damascus, in: Creswell, K.A.C., op.cit. (note 22), vol. 1, pt. 1, pp. 223–372.

66 Stern, H., op.cit. (note 64), pp. 36–38.

67 Ibn 'Idhârî gives this year, but it is not clear whether it refers to the beginning or the completion of the building work. For Torres Balbás, L., op.cit. (note 19), p. 571, it is the beginning, for Creswell, K.A.C., op.cit. (note 22), vol. 2, p. 144, the end.

68 Cf. the convincing arguments of Bloom, J., op.cit. (note 24).

69 Even if the number simply stands as symbolic for a very large quantity, it was nevertheless probably "the most important library in the western world", Vernet, J., op.cit. (note 15), pp. 47, 386.

70 Ewert, C.: Die Moschee am Bâb Mardûm in Toledo – eine "Kopie" der Moschee von Córdoba, in: Madrider Mitteilungen, 18, 1977, pp. 278–354. On Islamic Toledo: Delgado Valero, C.: Toledo islámico: ciudad, arte e historia, Toledo 1987, pp. 283–302.

71 Ewert, C., op.cit. (note 70), pp. 339–49. Amador de los Ríos, J.: Toledo pintoresca o descripción de sus más célebres monumentos, Toledo 1845, p. 307 f.; Gómez-Moreno, M.: Arte Mudéjar Toledano, Madrid 1916, p. 5 f.; idem, op.cit. (note 32), pp. 210–12. Several authors attribute the building to the 12th century, and consider it mudéjar in origin. On this, see the (as far as I know) most recent – and excellently documented – work by Delgado Valero, op.cit. (note 70), pp. 303–17, who supports the earlier dating.

72 The remains of various other religious buildings of the 10th and 11th centuries in Toledo are being investigated by Delgado Valero (note 70); a more detailed treatment of them is beyond the scope of the present work.

73 Ewert, C.: Der Mihrâb der Hauptmoschee von Almería, in: Madrider Mitteilungen, 13, 1972, pp. 287–336. He regards a three-nave layout as probable; Torres Balbás, L.: La Mezquita Mayor de Almería, in: Al-Andalus, 18, 1953, pp. 412–43; he thinks the mosque had five naves.

74 Cressier, P.: Le décor califal du mihrâb de la Grande Mosquée d'Almería, in: Madrider Mitteilungen, 31, 1990. I should like to thank the author for showing me the manuscript of the (then) still unpublished article. The restoration leading to the exposure of the arcades was carried out in 1987 by the Junta de Andalucía under the direction of L. Fernández Martínez and L. Pastor Rodríguez.

75 Abû 'Ubayd al-Bakrî was a famous 11th-century Andalusian geographer, who spent most of his life in Seville, Almería and Cordova. Regarding the south-west of Andalusia, he had access to extremely reliable sources, as his father was the ruler of Huelva and Saltés, where he himself had spent his youth. One of his major works on geography is the Kitâb al-mamâlik wa-l-masâlik, which has only been partly edited and translated. For North Africa, see Mac Guckin de Slane: Description de l'Afrique septentrionale, Algiers 1857, Fr. transl. in: Journal Asiatique, 1857–58. For Andalusia, see Lévi-Provençal, E.: La Péninsule Iberique au Moyen-Age, Leiden 1938. A new Spanish translation: Vidal Beltrán, E.: Abû 'Ubayd al-Bakrî, Geografía de España (Kitâb al-masâlik wa-l-mamâlik), Saragossa 1982 (Textos Medievales, 53).

76 Jiménez Martín, A.: La mezquita de Almonaster, Instituto de Estudios Onubenses "Padre Marchena", Diputación Provincial de Huelva, 1975; an important argument for the earlier dating is contained in this interesting monograph on the archaic character of the mihrâb.

77 ibid., p. 22.

78 Lévi-Provençal, E., op.cit. (note 55), p. 85 f., plate 20; also illustrated in: Kühnel, E.: Maurische Kunst, Berlin 1924, plate 18a.

79 Azuar Ruiz, R.: La Rábita Califal de las Dunas de Guardamar. Excavaciones Arqueológicas, Alicante 1989 (Museo Arqueológico); idem: Una rábita hispanomusulmana del Siglo X, in: Archéologie Islamique, 1, 1990, pp. 109–45.

80 Codera, F.: Inscripción árabe de Guardamar, in: Boletín de la Real Academia de la Historia, vol. XXXI, 1987, p. 31 ff.; also Lévi-Provençal, E., op.cit. (note 55), p. 93 f., plate XXIId; and Torres Balbás, L.: Rábitas hispano-musulmanas, in: Al-Andalus, 13, 1948, pp. 475–491.

81 The fortified structures of Islamic Spain have inspired various interesting research projects in recent years, for example Bazzana, A., Cressier, P. and Guichard, P.: Les châteaux ruraux d'Al-Andalus. Histoire et archéologie des husûn du sud-est de l'Espagne, Madrid 1988; Bazzana, A.: Eléments d'archéologie musulmane dans al-Andalus: caractères spécifiques de l'architecture militaire arabe de la région valencienne, in: al-Qantara, 1, 1980, pp. 339–363. Cressier, P.: Las fortalezas musulmanas de la Alpujarra (provincias de Granada y Almería) y la división política administrativa de la Andalucía oriental, in: Arqueología Espacial, Coloquio sobre distribución y relaciones entre los asentamientos, Teruel 1984, Actas, vol. 5, pp. 179–199; Zozaya, J.: Evolución de un yacimiento: el castillo de Gormaz (Soria), Castrum, 3, 1988; Acién Almansa, M.: Poblamiento y fortificación en el sur de al-Andalus. La formación de un país de Husûn, in: III Congreso de Arqueología Medieval Española, Oviedo 1989, Actas, pp. 137–50; Zozaya, J. and Soler, A.: Castillos Omeyas de planta cuadrangular: su relación funcional, ibid.; Giralt y Balagueró, J.: Fortificacions andalusines a la Marca Superior: el cas de Balaguer, in: Setmana d'Arqueologia Medieval, Lleida, pp. 175–193.

82 Nice examples in the volume of photographs by Reinhard Wolf, Castillos, Munich 1982.

83 Bazzana, A.: Un fortin omayyade dans le Sharq al-Andalus, in: Archéologie Islamique I, 1990, pp. 87–108.

84 Terrasse, H., op.cit. (note 29), p. 158.

85 Terrasse, M.: La fortification oméiyade de Castille, in: Revista del Instituto de Estudios Islamicos en Madrid, 14, 1967/68, pp. 113–127.

86 Delgado Valero, C., op.cit. (note 70), pp. 184–195.

87 The Puerta del Puente oder Bâb al-Qantara, ibid., pp. 140–48.

88 Torres Balbás, L., op.cit. (note 19), pp. 638–642; also op.cit. (note 32), pp. 52–60. I would like to thank the director of excavations, Ricardo Izquierdo Benito, for kindly providing the two photographer of Vascos (p. 121); see Izquierdo Benito, R.: La cerámica hispano-musulmana decorada de Vascos (Toledo), in: Homenaje a Prof. Martin Almagro Basch IV, Madrid 1983, pp. 107–115; idem: Tipología de la cerámica hispano-musulma-na de Vascos (Toledo), in: II Coloquio Internacional de Cerámica Medieval en el Mediterráneo Occidental, Toledo 1981, publ. 1986, pp. 113–125; idem: Los Baños Árabes de Vascos (Navalmoralejo, Toledo), in: Noticiario Arqueológico Hispánico, 28, 1986, pp. 195–242; idem: Una ciudad de Fundación musulmana: Vascos, in: Castrum, 3, 1988, pp. 163–172.

89 Berges Roldan, L.: Baños árabes del Palacio de Villardompardo Jaén, Jaén 1989.

90 Marçais, G.: L'architecture musulmane d'occident. Tunisie, Algérie, Maroc, Espagne, Sicile, Paris 1954, p. 228; the author erroneously assumes that stucco did not appear in Andalusia until later.

91 Cf. Brisch, K., op.cit. (note 58).

92 On this subject, see Ewert, C.: Elementos decorativos en los tableros parietales del salón Rico de Madînat al-Zahrâ', in: Cuadernos de Madînat al-Zahrâ', 1, 1987, pp. 27–60; also Golvin, L.: Note sur un décor en marbre trouvé à Madînat al-Zahrâ', in: Annales de l'Institut d'Etudes Orientales, XVIII–XIX, 1960/61, pp. 277–299; Terrasse, H.: Les tendances de l'art hispano-mauresque à la fin du Xe et au début du XIe siècle, in: al-Mulk, 3, 1963, pp. 19–24; idem: La formation de l'art musulman d'Espagne, in: Cahiers de Civilisation Médiévale, 8, 1965, pp. 141–158. On the capitals: Marinetto Sánchez, P.: Capiteles califales del Museo Nacional de Arte hispanomusulmán, in: Cuadernos de Arte, XVIII, Granada 1987, pp. 175–204.

93 See Gonzalez, V.: Origine, développement et diffusion de l'émaillerie sur métal en occident islamique, doctoral thesis, Université de Provence I (Aix-Marseilles), 1982, 2 vols., vol. I, p. 104 ff.

94 Beckwith, J.: Caskets from Córdoba, London 1960; Kühnel, E.: Die Islamischen Elfenbeinskulpturen, VIII. bis XIII. Jahrhundert, Berlin 1971.

95 Torres Balbás, L., op.cit. (note 19), p. 745 ff.

96 ibid., p. 772 ff.; Retuerce, M. and Zozaya, J.: Variantes geográficos de la cerámica omeya andalusí: los temas decorativos, in: La ceramica medievale nel Mediterraneo occidentale, Congresso Internazionale della Università degli Studi di Siena, 1984, Proceedings, Florence 1986, pp. 69–128.

97 Torres Balbás, L., op.cit. (note 19), p. 782 ff.; Serjeant, R.B.: Islamic Textiles (Material for a History up to the Mongol Conquest), Beirut 1972, ch. XVII: Textiles and the Tirâz in Spain, pp. 165–176.

98 Kubisch, N.: Das kalifale Becken des Museo Arqueológico Nacional von Madrid (mit weiterführendem Literaturverzeichnis), in:

Madrider Mitteilungen, 33, 1992 (in preparation). I should like to thank the author for showing me the manuscript. See also Gómez-Moreno, M.: Marmoles califales, in: Ars Hispaniae III, 1951, pp. 180–191; Kühnel, E.: Antike und Orient als Quellen spanisch-islamischer Kunst, in: Madrider Mitteilungen, 1, 1960, pp. 174–181, ill. plate 55.

99 See note 94. Also Ettinghausen, R. and Grabar, O.: The Art and Architecture of Islam, 650–1250, 1987, pp. 145–155.

100 Lévi-Provençal, E.: Un manuscrit de la bibliothèque du Calife al-Hakam II, in: Hespéris, 18, 1934, p. 198 ff.

101 Wasserstein, D., op.cit. (note 10), p. 57.

102 Idris, H. R.: Les Zîrîdes d'Espagne, in: Al-Andalus, XXIX, 1964/1, p. 42. See also Wasserstein D., op.cit. (note 10), p. 99.

103 Wasserstein, D., op.cit. (note 10), p. 113.

104 ibid., p. 137.

105 ibid., p. 198. The power of the Jews in Granada ended with the pogrom, which claimed the life not only of Samuel's son Jehoseph ben Naghrîla (also vizier and tax-gatherer for the Berber princes), but of 4,000 other Jews too.

106 The Muwashshahât, a verse form in stanzas in which the rhyme scheme can change from one stanza to the next. Stern, S.M.: Les Chansons Mozarabes. Les Vers Finaux (Kharjas) en espagnol dans les Muwashshas arabes et hébreux. Palermo 1953. See also Pérès, H.: La poésie andalouse en arabe classique au XIe siècle, Paris 1953.

107 Guichard, P., op.cit. (note 12), p. 110.

108 de Epalza, M. and Guellouz, S.: Le Cid, personnage historique et littéraire (Anthologie de textes arabes, espagnols, français et latins avec traductions), Paris 1983.

109 Wasserstein, D., op.cit. (note 10), p. 265 f.; Menéndez Pidal, R.: La España del Cid, 2 vols., Madrid 1969, vol. I, pp. 234–238, vol. II, pp. 727–733; MacKay, A. and Benaboud, M.: Alfonso VI of Leon and Castile, 'al-Imbratûr dhû'l-Millatayn', in: Bulletin of Hispanic Studies, 56, 1979, pp. 95–102.

110 There are good reasons for assuming that cries of help had gone out from *taifa* rulers to Yûsuf bin Tâshufîn as early as 1081–82; see Huici Miranda, A.: Al-Hulal al-Mawshiyya, crónica árabe de las dinastías almorávide, almohade y benimerín, Tetuan, Colección de crónicas árabes de la Reconquista, 1952. Also Wasserstein, D., op.cit. (note 10), p. 284. Probably Yûsuf was in no position at that time to undertake an expedition on this scale.

111 Idris, H.R., op.cit. (note 102), p. 73.

112 Lévi-Provençal, E.: La fondation de Marakech (462–1070), in: Mélanges d'Art et d'Archéologie de l'Occident Musulman, vol. 2, Algiers 1957, pp. 117–120.

113 In Ibn al-Khatîb, op.cit. (note 8), p. 336.

114 See Bazzana, A., Cressier, P. and Guichard, P., op.cit. (note 81), p. 130 ff. on the connexion between fortification and the administrative division of the country. See also note 81.

115 The Puerta Antigua de Bisagra in Toledo has often been adduced as evidence for the "straight" plan into the *taifa* period. Delgado Valero, however, gives good reasons for thinking this gate to be older: op.cit. (note 70), pp. 172–181.

116 Nevertheless, careful analysis of the literary evidence along with searches on the site have produced results; see Delgado Valero, C., op.cit. (note 70), pp. 195–229, in particular p. 211 ff. See also idem: Materiales para el estudio morfológico y ornamental del arte islámico en Toledo, Toledo 1987.

117 Cressier, P. and Lerma, J.V.: Un chapiteau inédit d'époque Taifa à Valence, in: Madrider Mitteilungen, 30, 1989, pp. 427–431.

118 Ewert, C.: Spanisch-islamische Systeme sich kreuzender Bögen. III. Die Aljaferia von Zaragoza, 3 vols., Berlin 1978 (Madrider Forschungen, 12), an exemplary architectural analysis. The excavation material has been for the most part published in Martín-Bueno, M., Erice Lacabe, R. and Sáenz Preciado, M.P.: La Aljafería. Investigación Arqueológico, Saragossa 1987.

119 They were directed by the architect Francisco Iniguez Almech, whose publications are listed in Ewert, C., op.cit. (note 118).

120 Ewert, C.: Hallazgos islámicos en Balaguer y la Aljafería de Zaragoza, con contr. de Duda, D. y Kirchner, G., Madrid 1979. See also Esco, C., Giralt, J. and Senac, P.: Arqueología islámica en la Marca Superior de al-Andalus, Huesca 1988. On the history of Balaguer, see Sanahuja, F.P., OFM: Historia de la ciudad de Balaguer, Balaguer ²1984.

121 Pérès, H., op.cit. (note 106), p. 142 ff.; Seco de Lucena Paredes, L.: Los palacios del taifa almeriense al-Mu'tasim, in: Cuadernos de la Alhambra, 3, 1967; Lazoro, R. and Villanueva, E.: Homenaje al Padre Tapia. Almería en la Historia, Almería 1988, pp. 173 ff.; Cara Barrionuevo, L.: La Almería islámica y su alcazaba, Almería 1990.

122 Ibn al-Khatîb, op.cit. (note 8), p. 366.

123 Torres Balbás, L.: "Hallazgos arqueológicos en la Alcazaba de Málaga" in: Al-Andalus, 2, 1934, pp. 344–357; idem: Excavaciones y obras en la alcazaba de Málaga, in: Al-Andalus, 9, 1944, pp. 173–190; Gómez-Moreno, M., op.cit. (note 32), pp. 244–253; Ewert, C.: Spanisch-islamische Systeme sich kreuzender Bögen. II. Die Arkaturen eines offenen Pavillons auf der Alcazaba von Málaga, in: Madrider Mitteilungen, 7, 1966, pp. 232–253.

124 Gómez-Moreno, M., op.cit. (note 32), p. 225 ff.; Seco de Lucena Paredes, L.: El barrio del Cenete, las alcazabas y las mezquitas de Granada, in: Cuadernos de la Alhambra, 2, 1966, p. 46 ff.; Huici Miranda, A. and Terrasse, H.: Gharnâta, in: Encyclopédie de l'Islam, vol. II, ²1977, pp. 1035–1043. For the history of Granada, see Peinado Santaella, R.G. and López de Coca Castañer, J.E.: Historia de Granada, II: La Época Medieval. Siglos VIII–XV, Granada 1987. See also note 179.

125 This thesis is forcefully defended by Bargebuhr, F.P.: The Alhambra Palace. A Cycle of Studies on the Eleventh Century in Moorish Spain, Berlin 1968, p. 90 ff. See also Pavón Maldonado, B.: La alcazaba de la Alhambra, in: Cuadernos de la Alhambra, 7, 1971, pp. 3 ff., 29.

126 Gómez-Moreno, M.: El Baño de la Judería en Baza, in: Al-Andalus, XII, 1947, pp. 151–5. For the first Zirid buildings, see Torres Balbás, L.: El alminar de la iglesia de San José y las primeras construcciones de los zîrîes granadinos, in: Al-Andalus, VI, 1941, pp. 427–444. On the Bañelo, see also Pavón Maldonado, B.: Tratado de Arquitectura Hispano-Musulmana. I. Agua, Madrid 1990.

127 Torres Balbás, L.: Ciudades hispano-musulmanas, 2 vols., Madrid, n.d., vol. 2, p. 490. Interesting new results are published in the lecture by Guerrero Lovillo, J.: Al-Qasr al-Mubârak, El Alcázar de la bendición. Discurso de recepción en la Real Academia de Bellas Artes de Santa Isabel de Hungria, 19 November 1970, Seville 1974, pp. 83–109.

128 Al-Qasr al-Zâhir, on the other side of the river, al-Qasr al-Zâhî, on the east bank of the river, and al-Qasr al-Mukarram, a city palace to the north of Qasr al-Mubârak. See Guerrero Lovillo, J., op.cit. (note 127).

129 ibid., p. 98 f.

130 Dickie, J.: The Islamic Garden in Spain, in: The Islamic Garden, Dumbarton Oaks, Washington D.C. 1976, pp. 87–106, p. 97 f.

131 It is however not very easy to say which parts of this garden stem from al-Mu'tamid and which from the Almohads.

132 Baer, E.: The "Pila" of Játiva. A Document of Secular Urban Art in Western Islam, in: Kunst des Orients, 7, 1970/71, pp. 142–166. On Játiva, see Torres Balbás, L.: Játiva y los restos del Palacio de Pinohermoso, in: Al-Andalus, XXII, 1958, pp. 143–171.

133 In Bayâd wa Riyâd and also in the al-Sûfî manuscript in the Vatican: Bibl. Apost., Ms. Ar. 368 and Ms. Siriaco 559.

134 Lagardère, V.: Le Vendredi de Zallâqa. 23 Octobre 1086, Paris 1989; see also the rather older description by Bosch-Vilá, J.: Los Almorávides (Historia de Marruecos V), Tetuan 1956.

135 The famous story of the beautiful Zaynab is not easy to unravel. Zaynab bint Ishaq al-Nafzawiya was a radiant beauty of outstanding intelligence, wealthy and of noble birth to boot. From among her countless suitors she chose first of all the lord of Aghmat, a prince of the tribe of the Maghrâwa. Abû Bakr ibn'Umar, the commander of the Almoravid army, succeeded in taking the mountain fortress and thereby won Zaynab's heart. The marriage took place towards the end of 1068. The next year the Almoravid army conquered large areas of Morocco. Abû Bakr however was soon recalled to the Sahara, whereupon he separated from his wife, whom he – whether immediately or later, voluntarily or otherwise – left to his nephew Yûsuf ibn Tashufin, later the sole ruler and at that time growing steadily in power.

136 On the possibility of matrilinear Almoravids social structures, see Lagardère, V., op.cit. (note 134), p. 28. Also Guichard, P.: Structures Sociales "Occidentales" et "Orientales" dans l'Espagne Musulmane, Paris and The Hague 1977.

137 Wasserstein, D., op.cit. (note 10), p. 282; see also Singer, H. R., op.cit. (note 9), p. 297.

138 On Ash'arism, see Watt, W.: "al-Ash'ari" and "Ash'a-riyya" in: Encyclopédie de l'Islam, vol. I, ²1975, pp. 715–718. On the Almohads, see Huici Miranda, A., op.cit. (note 10); idem: Historia política del Imperio Almohade, 2 vols., Tetuan 1956/57; also Le Tourneau, R.: The Almohad Movement in North Africa in the 12th and 13th centuries, Princeton 1969.

139 Watt, M.W. and Cachia, P.: A History of Islamic Spain, Edinburgh 1977 (Islamic Surveys, 4), p. 108.

140 Guichard, P.: Les Musulmans de Valence et la reconquête (XIe – XIIIe siècles), Damas 1990, pp. 139–145.

141 Terrasse, H., op.cit. (note 29), p. 225 ff.

142 See note 112.

143 First published by Berthier, P.: Campagne de fouilles à Chichaoua, de 1965 à 1968, in: Bulletin de la Société d'Histoire du Maroc, 2, 1969, pp. 7–26. See also the most recent findings by Ewert, C.: Der almoravidische Stuckdecor von Shûshâwa (Südmarokko). Ein Vorbericht, in: Madrider Mitteilungen, 28, 1987, pp. 141–178.

144 I should like to thank Mr Abderrahman Khelifa, Director of the Agence Nationale d'Archéologie et du Patrimoine in Algiers for his kind help when I was viewing Nedroma.

145 Ewert, C.: Die Moschee von Mertola, in: Madrider Mitteilungen, 14, 1973, pp. 217–246.

146 Gómez-Moreno, M., op.cit. (note 32), p. 279.

147 Navarro Palazón, J. and García Avilés, A.: Aproximación a la cultura material de Madînat Mursiya, in: Murcia Musulmana, Murcia 1989, pp. 253–256, 298; Navarro Palazón, J.: Arquitectura y artesania en la cora de Tudmir, in: Historia de Cartagena, vol. V, 1986, pp. 411–485, p. 416 ff.; Torres Balbás, L.: Monteagudo y "El Castillejo" en la Vega de Murcia, in: Al-Andalus, II, 1934, pp. 366 – 370; and Marçais, G., op.cit. (note 90), p. 214. All these authors had suggested this attribution, although Marçais deals with the complex in connexion with Almoravid palace architecture.

148 Ibn al-Khatîb, op.cit. (note 8), p. 463. The text continues: "he was in the habit of inviting great heroes, famous knights and old warhorses to his table, pouring out their wine with his own hands and passing them the goblet. Sometimes he was seized with an attack of excessive generosity, when he would give away the goblets and indeed the complete furnishings of the room. He was not averse to the pleasures of the flesh: he shared his sleeping quarters with more than two hundred slave-girls under one blanket. He had a tendency to adopt Christian customs, and he used Christians for purposes of state. He had dwellings built for them in Murcia, with taverns and churches. His precarious financial position compelled him to exploit his subjects mercilessly." The cruelty of this ruler towards his own family (for example banishing the daughter of his father-in-law after the latter's treason, and having his children by this marriage killed, as well as having his own sister killed, because her husband had deserted him) has been attributed by some historians to "western behavioural structures". Guichard, P., op.cit. (note 136), p. 111 f. On Muhammad ibn Sa'd ibn Mardanîsh idem: op.cit. (note 140), pp. 116 –124, and on his successor Zayyân ibn Mardanîsh, pp. 146 –149.

149 Bazzana, A., Cressier, P. and Guichard, P., op.cit. (note 81), p. 139 ff.

150 E.g. in Kühnel, E., op.cit. (note 94).

151 Illustrated in: The Arts of Islam, Catalogue of the 1976 London Exhibition, The Arts Council of Great Britain, London 1976.

152 Basset, H. and Terrasse, H.: Sanctuaires et forteresses almohades, Paris 1932; Terrasse,

H.: Minbars anciens du Maroc, in: Mélanges d'histoire et d'archéologie de l'occident musulman, Hommage à Georges Marçais, vol. 2, Algiers, 1957, pp. 159–167; idem: La mosquée al-Qaraouiyin à Fès, Paris 1968.

153 See Duda, D.: Spanisch-islamische Keramik aus Almería vom 12. bis 15. Jahrhundert, Heidelberg 1970; also Flores Escobasa, I., Muñoz Martín, M. and Dominguez Bedmar, M.: Cerámica Hispanomusulmana en Almería, Almería 1989. On the subject of the pottery of this period, see also Bazzana, A.: La cerámica islámica en la ciudad de Valencia. I. Catálogo, Valencia 1983; Puertas Tricas, R.: La Cerámica Islámica de cuerda seca en La Alcazaba de Málaga, Málaga 1989. There are interesting Almoravid and Almohad inscriptions in the Málaga museum; see Acién Almansa, M. and Martínez Nuñez, M.A.: Museo de Málaga: inscripciones árabes, Málaga 1982.

154 Navarro Palazón, J.: Excavaciones arqueológicas en la ciudad de Murcia durante 1984, in: Excavaciones y Prospecciones Arqueológicos, Servicio Regional de Patrimonio Histórico, Murcia 1989, fig. 13 and p. 264 f.

155 Soustiel, J.: La céramique islamique, Fribourg 1985; Llubia, L.M.: Cerámica medieval española, Barcelona 1968.

156 The reasons for the demolition of the Almohads' first Friday mosque and the subsequent building of a slightly re-oriented but otherwise almost identical mosque are unknown. The usual explanation, namely that the first mosque was wrongly oriented, is not satisfactory, seeing that the later structure departs even further from the true qibla orientation. See Ewert, C. and Wisshak, J.P., op.cit. (note 26), p. 3 note 28.

157 Idem: Forschungen zur almohadischen Moschee II: Die Moschee von Tinmal, Mainz 1984 (Madrider Beiträge, 10).

158 Wirth, E.: Regelhaftigkeit in Grundrißgestaltung, Straßennetz und Bausubstanz merinidischer Städte: das Beispiel Fes Djedid (1276 n. Chr.), in: Madrider Mitteilungen, 32, 1991. I should like to thank the author for sending me the manuscript prior to publication.

159 See Ewert, C. and Wisshak, J.P., op.cit. (note 157), p. 80 ff.

160 See Valor Piechotta, M.: Algunos ejemplos de cerámica vidriada aplicada a la arquitectura almohade, in: II Congreso de Arqueología Medieval Española, Madrid 1987, vol. III, pp. 194–202.

161 Cf. the re-use of Hispano-Umayyad capitals in the Kutubiyya and in the Qasaba mosque in

Marrakesh; Basset, H. and Terrasse, H., op.cit. (note 152); Terrasse, H.: Chapiteaux oméiyades d'Espagne à la Mosquée d'al-Qarawiyyîn de Fès, in: Al-Andalus, 28, 1963, pp. 211–220.

162 Idem: La grande mosquée almohade de Séville, in: Mémorial Henri Basset, 1928, pp. 249–266.

163 As far as I know, no comprehensive research on the building of these two complexes has been carried out. See Marín Fidalgo, A.: Arquitectura Gótica del Sur de la Provincia de Huelva, Huelva 1982, Santa María de la Granada, pp. 60–64, San Martín, pp. 64–65. In Puerto Santa María (province of Cádiz) there is another mosque still extant, with the usual multi-nave (in this case, three) structure, whose building history is unclear. It is assumed to date from the 11th or possibly the 12th century. See Torres Balbás, L.: La mezquita de al-Qanatir y el Sanctuario de Alfonso el-Sabio en el Puerto de Santa María, in: Al-Andalus, 7, 1942, p. 149 ff.

164 Jiménez, A.: Arquitectura Gaditana de Epoca Alfonsí, in: Cádiz en el siglo XIII, Acta de las Jornadas Commemorativas del VII Centenario de la Muerte de Alfonso X el Sabio, Cádiz 1983, pp. 135–158; see also Pavón Maldonado, B.: Jérez de la Frontera, Ciudad Medieval. Arte Islámico y Mudéjar, Asociación Española de Orientalistas, Madrid 1981, pp. 15–18; Menéndez Pidal, J.: La Mezquita-Iglesia de Santa María la Real (Alcázar de Jérez), in: Bellas Artes 73, no 19, p. 8 f.; Alcocer, M. and Sancho, H.: Notas y Documentos referentes al Alcázar de Jérez de la Frontera, en los siglos XIII a XVI. Publicaciones de la Sociedad de Estudios Históricos Jerezanos, no 7, 1940, pp. 9–29.

165 Torres Balbás, L.: Arte Almohade. Arte Nazarí. Arte Mudéjar (Ars Hispaniae IV), Madrid 1949, p. 30 f.

166 ibid., p. 31, fig. 20.

167 This result derives from pollen examination carried out by Rafael Manzano Martos. See Dickie, J., op.cit. (note 130), p. 98.

168 ibid., p. 97.

169 See note 161.

170 In the water on the right bank of the Guadalquivir in Cordova stands the ruin of what is presumably an Almohad palace, but one which is so poorly preserved that nothing can be said about its fitments or decoration. See Torres Balbás, L., op.cit. (note 165), p. 30 and fig. 16.

171 On the Valencia region, see Bazzana, A. et al., op.cit. (note 81), p. 157 ff.; for Alicante, see Azuar Ruiz, R.: Castellogía medieval alicantina: area meridional, Alicante 1981; for Murcia, see Navarro Palazón, J.: Aspectos

arqueológicos, Historia de la región murciana, vol. II, 1980, pp. 64–107.

172 Other polygonal towers besides the Torre del Oro in Seville are the Torre Redondada and the Torre Desmochada in Cáceres, one tower in the north-west corner of the town wall of Reina (between Seville and Badajoz), in Badajoz itself, the Torre Espantaperros; in Écija and in Jérez de la Frontera there are several polygonal towers. On Islamic Badajoz, see Valdés Fernández, F.: La Alcazaba de Badajoz. Síntesis de la historia de la ciudad, Badajoz 1979; idem: Ciudadela y fortificación urbana: el caso de Badajoz, in: Castrum, 3, 1988, pp. 143–152.

173 E.g. in Velefique. In Senés, the date of building cannot be established; studies of the building materials and techniques employed have produced no conclusive results. I would like to thank Patrice Cressier for showing me this excavation. See Bazzana, A. et al., op.cit. (note 81), p. 281.; Angelé, S. and Cressier, P.: Velefique (Almería): un exemple de mosquée rurale en al-Andalus, in: Mélanges de la Casa de Velázquez, 26, 1990, pp. 113–30.

174 Sing. burdj, hisn, qal'a, qulay'a, qarya, qasaba. These Arabic terms for the highly varied forms of fortified settlement with or without an administrative centre can be found in Spanish placenames even now, most frequently al-qal'a and its diminutive al-qual'aya: Alcalá de Henares, Alcalá la Real, Calahorra, Alcolea del Cinca. See also Lautensach, H.: Maurische Züge im geographischen Bild der Iberischen Halbinsel, Bonn 1960, pp. 11–33.

175 See Murcia musulmana, Murcia 1989, in particular: Navarro Palazón, J. and García Avilés, A., op.cit. (note 147), and Barnabé Guillamón, M., Fernández González, F. V., Manzano Martínez, J. et al.: Arquitectura doméstica islámica en la ciudad de Murcia, pp. 233–252. See also Navarro Palazón, J.: Arquitectura y artesania en la cora de Tudmir, in: Mas García, J. (ed.): Historia de Cartagena, vol. V, 1986; idem: El cementerio islámico de San Nicolás de Murcia. Memoria preliminar, in: Actas del I Congreso de Arqueología Medieval Española, Saragossa 1986, vol. IV, pp. 7–37; idem: op.cit. (note 154), pp. 307–320; idem: Hacia una sistematización de la cerámica esgrafiada, in: 2 Coloquio Internacional de Cerámica Medieval en el Mediterraneo Occidental, Toledo (1981) 1986, pp. 165–178; idem: Murcia como centro productor de loza dorada; Navarro Palazón, J. and Picon, M.: La loza de la Province de Murcie, étude en laboratoire, in: Congreso Internationale delle Universitá

degli Studi di Siena, 1986, pp. 129–143, 144–146; Navarro Palazón, J.: Nuevas aportaciones al estudio de la loza dorada andalusí: el ataifor de Zavellá, in: Les Illes Orientals d'al-Andalus, Palma de Mallorca 1987 (V Jornades d'estudis histórics locals), pp. 225–238; idem: Formas arquitectónicas en el mobilario cerámico andalusí, in: Cuadernos de la Alhambra, 23, 1987, pp. 21–65.

176 The town is being excavated under the supervision of J. Navarro Palazón. See his Siyâsa, una madîna de la cora de Tudmîr, in Areas, 5, Murcia 1985, pp. 171–189, idem: La conquista castellana y sus consecuencias: la despoblación de Siyâsa, in: Castrum, 3, 1988, pp. 208–214. I am most grateful to Julio Navarro Palazón, Director, for welcoming me so kindly to the Centro de Estudiar Árabes y Archeológicos "Ibn Arabi" in the city of Murcia, which houses the most important finds excavated in the region , and for showing me these excavations.

177 See Kubisch, N.: Die Ornamentik von Santa María la Blanca in Toledo, doctoral thesis, Munich 1991 (MS).

178 Torres Balbás, L.: Las Yeserías descubiertas recientemente en las Huelgas de Burgos, in: Al-Andalus, 8, 1943, pp. 209–254; see also Iñiguez, F.: Las yeserías descubiertas recientemente en Las Huelgas de Burgos, in: Archivo Español de Arte, 14, 1940, pp. 306–8, with twelve illustrations.

179 On the history of the Nasrid sultanate of Granada see the comprehensive work by Arié, R.: L'Espagne musulmane au temps des Nasrides (1232–1492), Paris 1973, new ed. Paris 1990. See also the publications listed in note 124, and in addition Torres Delgado, C.: El antiguo reino nazarí de Granada (1232–1340), Granada 1974. The chief town of the upper Genil valley and the surrounding mountainous country had previously been Elvira, and until the 11th century there is no mention of anything but a kûra of Elvira. Granada at that time was a small place of no political significance and largely settled by Jews, until its fortification by the Zirids. After these latter were ousted, Granada was ruled first by the Almoravids and then by the Almohads. The expeditions of Ibn Mardanîsh and later of Ibn Hûd led to relatively short occupations of Granada. Shortly after the latter was murdered, his enemy Ibn al-Ahmar succeeded in taking power in the city in 1237. See Peinado Santaella, R.G. and López de Coca Castañer, J.E., op.cit. (note 124), p. 32, for a discussion of the various hypotheses which have been formulated regarding the birth of Granada and its connex-

ion with Iliberis, the Municipium Iliberrita-
num and Madînat Ilbîra.

180 Hoenerbach, W., op.cit. (note 7); see also
Arié, R., op.cit. (note 179), p. 303.

181 ibid., p. 336.

182 Hoenerbach, W., op.cit. (note 7), p. 413.

183 The Alhambra is one of the most-visited
places in the world. There are many excellent
publications and guides, among which the
most recent is particularly precise and informative: Bermúdez Lopéz, J.: The Alhambra
and the Generalife, Granada, n.d. An outstanding work of documentation is: Plan especial de protección y reforma interior de la
Alhambra y Alíjares, Granada 1986. I would
like to thank Mr Jésús Bermúdez López for
his generosity in allowing us to work in the
Alhambra and the Generalife.

184 Bermúdez Pareja, J.: El baño del Palacio de
Comares en la Alhambra de Granada. Disposición primitiva y alteraciones, in: Cuadernos de la Alhambra, 10/11, 1974/75, pp. 99–
116.

185 The origin of this name has not been completely satisfactorily explained: García
Gómez, E.: Foco de antigua luz sobre la Alhambra. Desde un texto de Ibn al-Jatîb en
1362, Madrid 1988, p. 187, says that it arose
as a result of the participation of craftsmen
from Comares in the decoration of the hall;
more probably, and more usual, is the derivation from qamariyya, "light from above"
(from al-qamar, "moon").

186 The basin bears an inscription quoting a
poem by Ibn Zamraq, a Nasrid court poet
(1333–1393); its themes of water as a work of
art, of lordly power, as symbolized by the
lions, and of the Holy War are altogether appropriate to this fountain. Frederick Bargebuhr has discovered a poem by an 11th-cen-
tury Granada Jew, Salomo ben Gabirol, in
which the "Bronze Sea" of the Temple of
Jerusalem and Solomon are quoted in connexion with a lion fountain in a palace. Salomo ben Gabirol was the protégé of the Zirids' Jewish minister, Yehoseph ben Naghrîla, who is thought to have had a palace on the
site of the present Alcazaba. Bargebuhr con-
cludes that at least the lower part of the lion
pool came from this Jewish palace. Oleg
Grabar follows Bargebuhr's arguments,
which, while seductive, do not seem to be
conclusive, there being too many missing
links. Quite a part from this, in all probability the lions date not from the 11th but
from the 14th century. See Bargebuhr, F. P.,
op.cit. (note 125), idem: Salomo Ibn Gabirol.
Ostwestliches Dichtertum, Wiesbaden 1976;
Grabar, O.: The Alhambra, London 1978.

187 Torres Balbás, L.: Paseos por la Alhambra: la
Rauda, in: Archivo Español de Arte y Arqueología, 6, 1926, pp. 261–285.

188 Andrea Navagiero, an Italian envoy, who in
1526 went to see the Alhambra, Granada and
Seville, and whose detailed travel journal sur-
vives as Navagiero, A.: Il viaggio fatto in
Spagna et in Francia . . ., Venice, Domenico
Fani, 1563. See also Barrucand, M.: Gärten
und gestaltete Landschaft als irdisches
Paradies: Gärten im westlichen Islam, in:
Der Islam, 65, 1988, pp. 244–267.

189 Bermúdez Pareja, J.: El Generalife después
del incendio de 1958, in: Cuadernos de la Alhambra, 1, 1965, pp. 9–39.

190 See Golvin, L.: Les influences artistiques
entre l'Espagne musulmane et le Maghrib. La
Torre de la Vela de l'Alhambra à Grenade et
le donjon du Manâr de la Qal'a des Banû
Hammad (Algérie), in: Cuadernos de la Alhambra, 10/11, 1974/75, pp. 85–90.

191 See Fernández-Puertas, A.: La Fachada del
Palacio de Comares. I. Situación, Función y
Génesis, Granada 1980, in particular Fig. 2,
p. 5 ff. Emilio García Gómez has recently
put forward a new hypothesis regarding the
façade of the Comares Palace: it was, he says,
formerly the façade of the main gateway to
the Alhambra, and thus occupied the site on
which the Palace of Emperor Charles V now
stands, before being dismantled in 1538
and moved to the Cuarto Dorado. This
hypothesis was convincingly refuted by
Darío Cabanelas Rodríguez during the
"Encuentros de la Alhambra" in April 1991.
See García Gómez, E., op.cit. (note 185),
and Cabanelas Rodríguez, D., OFM: La Fachada de Comares y la llamada "Puerta de la
Casa Real", lecture, Alhambra, 26 April
1991.

192 Barrucand, M.: L'urbanisme princier en
islam. Meknès et les villes royales islamiques
postmédiévales, Paris 1985 (Bibliothèque
d'Etudes Islamiques, 13).

193 See the series by Cabanelas Rodríguez, D.,
OFM and Fernández-Puertas, A.: Inscripciones poéticas de la Alhambra, in: Cuadernos de la Alhambra: Partal y Fachada de Comares: 10–11, 1974/75, pp. 117–200; Generalife: 14, pp. 3–86; Fuente de los Leones: 15–
17, 1981, pp. 3–88; Tacas en el accesso a la
Sala de la Barca: 19–20, 1983/84, pp. 61–149.
See also Rubiera, M.J.: De nuevo sobre los
poemas epigráficos de la Alhambra, in: Al-
Andalus, 41, 1976, pp. 453–73; and García
Gómez, E.: Poemas árabes en los muros y
fuentes de la Alhambra, Madrid, 1985; also
the rather older work by Nykl, A.R.: Inscripciones árabes de la Alhambra y del

Generalife, in: Al-Andalus, 4, 1936–39,
pp. 174–194.

194 Bargebuhr, F.P., op.cit. (note 125), and Grabar, O., op.cit. (note 186) attempt by means
of symbolic references to penetrate further
into the "iconology" of the Alhambra.

195 Aguilar Gutierrez, J.: Restauración de pinturas murales en la Alhambra. Patio del Harén
y Retrete de la Sala de la Barca, in: Cuadernos
de la Alhambra, 25, 1989, pp. 204–211.

196 Bermúdez Pareja, J.: Pinturas sobre piel en la
Alhambra de Granada, Granada 1987.

197 Manzano Martos, R.: Darabenaz: una alquería nazarí en la Vega de Granada, in: Al-Andalus, 26, 1961, pp. 201–218; idem: De nuevo
sobre Darabenaz, in: Al-Andalus, 26, 1961,
p. 448 f.

198 Torres Balbás, L.: La acropolis musulmana
de Ronda, in: Al-Andalus, 9, 1944, pp. 469–
474; and Miró, A.: Ronda. Arquitectura y
Urbanismo, Málaga 1987 (pp. 73–106 deal
with the Islamic period).

199 Arié, R., op.cit. (note 179), p. 398 ff.; Torres
Balbás, L.: El Maristán de Granada, in: Al-
Andalus, 9, 1944, pp. 198–481; García Gra-
nados, J.A., Girón Irueste, F. and Salvatierra
Cuenca, V.: El Maristán de Granada. Un
Hopital Islamico, Granada 1989.

200 I am grateful to Patrice Cressier for drawing
my attention to this still unpublished building.

201 Marçais, G., op.cit. (note 90), p. 359.

202 Kühnel, E., op.cit. (note 98), pp. 174–181.

Glossary

This glossary has been compiled solely for the assistance of the non-specialist reader, and makes no claim to completeness or systematization.
The "index documentaire" in D. and I. Sourdel: La civilization de l'islam classique, Arthaud éd., Paris 1968, pp. 157–621 is remarkably concise, and includes art-historical subjects. The recently-published book by C. Glassé: Dictionnaire encyclopédique de L'Islam, Bordas éd., Paris 1991, deals chiefly with questions related to the religion; considerably more specialized and at the same time more comprehensive is the Encyclopaedia of Islam. However, the first edition (Leiden 1913 and 1936) is now dated, and the second edition (Leiden, since 1954) has only got as far "Mu".

Abbasids: Arabo-Islamic dynasty who ousted the Umayyads (q.v.) from the Caliphate (q.v.) in 750, retaining it in their hands until 1258. The Abbasids' Islamic empire was centred on Iraq, they themselves residing chiefly in Baghdad, which they founded in 762.

Acanthus: a Mediterranean thistle-like plant (*Acanthus spinosus*) whose broad jagged leaves were a favourite motif in Classical art from the 5th century B.C. onwards. Islamic art took over the motif, transforming it in its own way.

Aghlabids: largely independent Islamic dynasty, who ruled Ifrîqiya (q.v.) in the name of the Abbasids (q.v.) during the 9th century.

Alcazaba: Spanish, from the Arabic *al-quasaba*, fortress, fortified, fortified town, also administrative centre.

Alcázar: Spanish, from the Arabic *al-qasr*, fortified house or palace; the Arabic word in turn derives from Latin *castrum*, an army camp.

Alfiz: Spanish, a rectangular frame for an arch, probably deriving from Arabic *al-hayyiz*, a container (H. Halm).

Amîr: Arabic, commander, governor, ruler; in English often spelt "emir".

Amîr al-Mu'minin: Arabic, commander of the faithful; since 'Umar (the second Caliph) a title of honour reserved exclusively for the Caliph.

Baldiyyûn: Arabic, descendants of the first Islamic conquerors of the Iberian peninsula; often used in contrast to *shâmiyyûn* (q.v.).

Basilica: in the architectural sense used in this book, a rectangular building with a definite orientation, consisting of a central nave and side aisles separated by colonnades, with or without a transept or transverse aisle.

Caliph: from Arabic *khalifa*, representative or successor; used to designate the successor of the Prophet in the latter's capacity as temporal and spiritual leader of the Islamic community; the Caliphs did not claim to be successors of Muhammad in his capacity as Prophet.

Capital: head or crowning feature of a column, mediating between the latter and the load thrusting down upon it. It broadens the column's supporting surface area and offsets it against the parts to be borne.

Corral: Spanish, courtyard; Corral del Carbón, "coal yard", is the present-day name of the former Islamic *funduq* (q.v.) in Granada.

Dâr al-Imâra: Arabic, palace of a governor or ruler.

Dhimmî: Arabic, "protected by law"; non-Islamic communities within the population received contractual protection (*dhimma*) from their Muslim conquerors on payment of a tax. This protection covered life, property and the places and practice of worship; it was however only extended to "people of the Book", i.e. Jews and Christians, heathens being excluded.

Emir: see *Amîr*.

Friday Mosque: see *Mosque*.

Frigidarium: from Latin *frigidus*, cold; the room for cold baths in the bathhouses of Antiquity.

Funduq: Arabic, building serving as inn, warehouse and trading centre within a town; the word derives from the Greek *pandocheion*, inn, and is mostly found in Andalusia and the Maghreb; in the East, *khân* or caravanserai are more usual terms.

Hadj: from the Arabic *hajj*; ritual pilgrimage to Mecca forming one of a Muslims religious duties.

Hâjib: Arabic, treasurer. In Umayyad (q.v.). Spain, this title involved responsibilities and conferred prerogatives which raised its holder well above the status of a *vizier* (q.v.).

Hammâm: Islamic hot bath; right up to the present day, an indispensable element of Islamic culture, a legacy of Classical Antiquity.

Header: in masonry, brick or stone laid with the short end showing; contrast stretcher (q.v.).

Hisn: Arabic, fortress or castle, also administrative centre.

Hûdids: the dynasty of the Banû Hûd clan, one of the most important of the *taifa* period. Their main seat of government was Saragossa. A certain Muhammad ibn Yûsuf ibn Hûd al-Judhâmî al-Mutawakkil, who in the 12th century attempted to resist the Almohads and succeeded briefly in taking Granada, claimed to be descended from the Saragossa Hûdids.

Hypocaust: the Roman system of underfloor heating using hot-air ducts, especially in the hot rooms of public bathhouses. The system was adopted for the heating of Hispano-Islamic *hammâms* (q.v.).

Ifrîqiya: Arabic name for the eastern Maghreb; the geographical limits of the area thus known are somewhat blurred, but originally the term applied to the territory between Tangier and Tripoli. The word is derived from the Latin Africa.

Imâm: Arabic, example, leader; the term is applied to the prayer leader at public prayers, to the spiritual head of a congregation or school, and especially to the leader of the whole Islamic community.

Impost: a block, above the decorated capital, on which the springer (q.v.) of an arch rests.

Iwân: a rectangular, usually vaulted room, one of whose sides is entirely open to a forecourt or another hall. This type of structure was adopted by oriental Islam from Parthian or Sassanian architectural sources, and is not linked to any particular function, being found both in secular and in sacred buildings.

Jihâd: Arabic, Holy War; regarded by Muslims as a meritorious work, ensuring entry into Paradise. The word is derived from *jâhada*, to strive for something.

Jund: an Arabic word of Persian origin, referring in the Koran (q.v.) to any armed body of men; in Umayyad (q.v.) times it was applied to the Syrian military districts settled by Arabian warriors on constant alert, who were paid a fixed wage in addition to their share of booty.

Koran: Arabic *al-Qur'ân*, recitation; the holy scripture of Islam; it contains the revelation of the Prophet Muhammad, transmitted to him by God through the Archangel Gabriel.

Kutubiyya: the name of the Friday mosque (q.v.) in Marrakesh. It owes its name to the booksellers' market which lay in the vicinity (cf. p. 153 f.).

Lamtûna: a powerful nomadic Berber clan belonging to the Sanhâja tribe and inhabiting the western Sahara. The Lamtûna probably did not convert to Islam until the 9th century, after they had succeeded during the 8th in creating a king-

dom out of a confederation of Berber tribes, which they dominated until the early 10th century. As the vehicle of the Almoravid movement, they attained great historical importance in the 11th century.

Laqab: a name of honour; such names were at first only assumed by rulers, later by other high dignitaries too; initially fairly simple, these names grew in portentousness as time went by.

Leaf Arch: a kind of multi-lobed arch with vegetal motifs, particularly characteristic of Almohad architecture. It developed from the mixed-linear arch, with alternating broad and narrow lobes, with narrow scrolls at their base (C. Ewert).

Madrasa: "place of study", derived from the Arabic *darasa*, to read, to study. It is applied to public institutions of higher education specialising largely, but not exclusively, in Islamic law. They were supported by pious endowments which provided for the maintenance of teachers and students, and also allowed a measure of control to the benefactor. Organizationally and often physically they were close to the mosque (q.v.). Although the *madrasa* as an institution spread all over the Islamic world from the 11th century onwards, the various regions developed different forms of building in which to house it.

Mahdî: Arabic, "led by righteousness"; at first often no more than an honorific; however by the Shiites and under their influence it came to be applied to the expected religious leader of the Last Days, who, free from error and sin, will establish the rule of righteousness and faith, and rule a world united in Islam. Throughout the history of Islam, self-proclaimed *mahdîs* have appeared, one such being the founder of the Almohad movement, Ibn Tûmart.

Malikism: one of the four schools of law dating from the 8th and 9th centuries and recognized as orthodox by Sunni Muslims. It was founded by one Malik in Medina in the 8th century, and is characterized by conservatism and severity. Its influence was felt particularly in north-west Africa and in Spain.

Mameluke: "unfree" (lit., property of another), i.e. slave of non-Islamic origin. The term is chiefly applied to soldiers. In the Mameluke Sultanate of Egypt and Syria, which lasted from 1250 to 1517, this institution of military slavery led to centuries of rule by a "one-generation aristocracy" (D. Ayalon). In Spain no such development took place.

Maqsûra: place in the prayer hall of the Friday mosque (q.v.) near the *mihrâb* (q.v.), reserved for the Caliph (q.v.).

Mâristân: hospital; the word derives from the Persian *bîmâr*, sick, and the suffix *istân*, place. Hospitals endowed by pious benefactions are documented in the Islamic world from the late 8th century onwards. The oldest known *mâristân* in the Maghreb was founded by the Almohad Ya'qûb al-Mansûr in Marrakesh.

Masmûda: sedentary Berber tribe from the High Atlas, who attained historical importance through the Almohad movement, whose spiritual leader, the *mahdî* (q.v.) Ibn Tûmart, was one of their number.

Mawlâ, (plural, *mawâlî*); Arabic word of broad meaning, signifying usually, and in our context exclusively, non-Arabs who as freemen or freedmen have converted to Islam and thereby formally become members of an Arab tribe, whose "clients" they become.

Mexuar: Spanish, from Arabic *mashwar*; conference room. In the Maghreb, *mashwar* also refers to the open space in front of the main entrance to the palace complex, and is eventually expanded to include the entrance, too (e.g. in Rabat).

Mihrâb: Arabic; the niche in a prayer hall indicating the direction of Mecca.

Minaret: Tower used to call the faithful to prayer. While its origin, development and function remain unclear, it is thought to have evolved from the pre-Islamic signal tower (Arabic, *manâra*, place with light, i.e. lighthouse).

Minbar: staircase-like monumental pulpit in the Friday mosque (q.v.), from which the sermon is delivered.

Moors: from Greek *mauros*, dark; used by the Greeks for the aboriginal inhabitants of northwest Africa. In English usage, often used for the Islamic inhabitants of medieval Spain, whether of African or Near Eastern or mixed descent.

Mosque: Arabic *masjid*, "place where one prostrates oneself" (in prayer). The word has come into English, French and German via the Spanish *mezquita*. Islamic place of worship, in which the faithful gather for ritual prayer. A distinction can be made between small prayer halls, public or private, (*masjid*) and the Friday or Great Mosque (*masjid jâmi'*), in which the most important service of the week takes place at noon on Friday, consisting of collective prayers and a sermon; this service has a certain political importance.

Mozarabs: from Arabic *must'aribûn*, "Arabized"; Christians who lived as *dhimmîs* (q.v.) under Arabic overlordship. The word is used predominantly for the Christian communities in Islamic Spain.

Mudéjar: from Arabic *mudajjan*, domesticated. The term is applied to Muslims who remained in Spain after the Christian *Reconquista* (q.v.), paying tribute to the Christian rulers.

Muezzin: Arabic *mu'azzin*, one who calls the faithful to prayer on the five occasions each day as prescribed.

Munya: Arabic, country seat, villa.

Muqarnas: a honeycomb-like decorative motif consisting of numerous niches and niche fragments, first seen in the Islamic world in the 11th century, and quickly spreading. It is used primarily as an internal cladding for curved architectural elements, in domes, for example, and above all in the transitional zones between domes and their supports; also in *mihrâb* (q.v.) niches, tops of window openings, on capitals instead of tambours, and ledges.

Musâlimûn: Arabic, Christians who converted to Islam.

Musta'ribûn: see Mozarabs.

Muwalladûn: Arabic, "brought up, educated"; new Muslims, in particular the descendants of converted Christians in Spain.

Palaestra: Greek, a gymnasium for wrestling and athletics; one component of the bath-houses of Classical Antiquity which was not adopted in the Islamic *hammâm* (q.v.).

Patio: Spanish, an inner, roofless courtyard.

Qâdî: Arabic, judge. Appointed by the ruler, who always retained the final decision. His main function is the maintenance of public order through the application of the precepts of the Koran (q.v.).

Qaysâriyya: Arabic, central public-building complex in the commercial district of a town or city (see *sûq*). It contains shops, workshops and small warehouses, especially for luxury goods.
Closed on public holidays and in the evenings.

Qibla: Arabic, direction of prayer; originally Jerusalem, from 624 the Kaaba in Mecca. *Qibla* wall: the wall in the prayer hall of a mosque in which the *mihrâb* (which faces Mecca) is situated, and towards which the faithful turn when praying.

Quraysh: North-Arabian tribe which ruled Mecca in the early 7th century, comprising a number of families of different degrees of

wealth. Muhammad the Prophet, his descendants, the first four Caliphs (q.v.), the Umayyads (q.v.) and the Abbasids (q.v.) all belonged to this tribe.

Ramadan: The 9th month of the Islamic (lunar) year, during which every adult Muslim is required to fast. Fasting involves refraining from all food, drink and sexual intercourse between the hours of sunrise and sunset.

Reconquista: Spanish, reconquest; the term generally used for the Christian Reconquest of those parts of Spain occupied by the Moors.

Ribât: Arabic; a term to describe a fortified monastic foundation often established in the frontier areas of Islam as a base from which to conduct the Holy War, or else to serve as a place of religious retreat.

Sanhâja: one of the most important Berber tribes; they lived, often as nomads, all over the north-west of Africa from Kabylia in northern Algeria to the Atlantic coast of Morocco and Mauretania. They are recorded since pre-Islamic days. The Almoravid family belonged to the Lamtûna (q.v.), which was part of the Sanhâja tribe.

Saqâliba (sing.: *siqlabî* or *saqlabî*): medieval Arabic word for the inhabitants of eastern Europe, the "Slavs". In Islamic Spain the *saqâliba* ("slaves") were Europeans (not just from the eastern part) who had been captured in war; they were employed in the army or in the service of the court, and many attained senior positions. Not to be confused with the black slaves, who were known as *'abid*.

Shâmiyyûn: Arabic, Syrian; used here for those sections of the army who only arrived in Spain after the first conquest of Andalusia, as opposed to those Arabs "born in the country", the *baldiyyûn* (q.v.).

Spandrel: an approximately triangular area between for example the top of an arch and the rectangular frame or *alfiz* (q.v.).

Springer: the lowest voussoir (q.v.) of an arch.

Squinch: vault section, usually in the form of a semi-cone narrowing towards the top resting on the corners of a square or rectangular room and serving as intermediary between this and a round superstructure. The transition between square or rectangular rooms and round domes was one of the chief problems of Islamic architecture.

Stretcher: in masonry, a brick or stone laid with its long side showing; see header.

Sudatorium: Latin, sweat-room in a bathhouse; adopted and further developed in the Islamic *hammâm* (q.v.).

Sûq: Arabic, market; anglicized as souk, primarily applied to the commercial district of an Islamic town or city, but also used for other markets, e. g. outside the town.

T-plan: a concept from Islamic art history; it describes a type of mosque (q.v.) ground plan featuring a transept (q.v.) between the *qibla* (q.v.) wall and the end of the longstudinal nave and aisles.

Taifa: from Arabic *ta'ifa*, plural *tawâ'if*, separate group, party. *Mulûk al-tawâ'if* were "kings of small groups", petty kings, known in Spanish as *reyes de taifas*. After the fall of the Spanish Umayyads (q.v.) and until the coming to power of the Almoravids, Islamic Spain was ruled by a sizable number of petty dynasties. This period is known to history as the *taifa* period.

Transept: section of a building running at right angles to the nave. A common term in the history of Christian architecture, it is also applied to Islamic sacred architecture, e.g. to describe the *qibla* aisle at the top of the T-plan (q.v.), transverse to the main nave and aisles.

Tympanum: area above a porch within the arch; originally, the pediment of a classical temple.

Umayyads: first Islamic dynasty of Caliphs (q.v.), reigning from 660 to 750. Like the Prophets the Umayyads were Arabs who belonged to the *Quraysh* (q.v.) in Mecca; unlike him, however, they came from a leading family. The Umayyad dynasty was largely wiped out by the Abbasids (q.v.) in 750; one of their number succeeded however in fleeing to Spain and founding a dynasty which ruled in Cordova from 756 to 1031.

Vizier: from Arabic, *wazîr*, minister. In the Near East, the Prime Minister; in Islamic Spain, an honorific, not linked to any particular office.

Voussoir: one of the wedge-shaped elements in an arch; differential colouring, finish or materials for alternate voussoirs was an important motif in Islamic architectural decoration.

Bibliography

Acién Almanza, M.: La formación y destrución de Al-Andalus and Reino de Granada, in: Historia de los Pueblos de España, Barceló, M. (ed.), Tierras fronterizas (I), Barcelona 1984, pp. 21–56.

–: Madînat al Zahrâ' en el urbanismo musulmán, in: Cuadernos de Madînat al Zahrâ', 1, 1987, pp. 11–26.

–: Poblamiento y fortificación en el sur de Al-Andalus. La formación de un país de Husûn, in: III Congreso de Arqueología Medieval Española, Oviedo 1989, Actas, pp. 137–150.

Acién Almanza, M. and Martínez Nuñez, M.A.: Museo de Málaga. Inscripciones árabes, Málaga 1982.

Aguilar Gutierrez, J.: Restauración de pinturas murales en la Alhambra. Patio del Harén y Retrete de la Sala de la Barca, in: Cuadernos de la Alhambra, 25, 1989, pp. 204–211.

Alcocer, M. and Sancho, H.: Notas y Documentos referentes al Alcázar de Jérez de la Frontera, en los siglos XIII a XVI, Publicaciones de la Sociedad de Estudios Históricos Jerezanos, n° 7, 1940, pp. 9–29.

Amador de los Ríos, J.: Toledo pintoresca o descripción de sus más célebres monumentos, Toledo 1845.

Angelé, S. and Cressier, P.: Velefíqe (Almería): Un exemple de mosquée rurale en al-Andalus, in: Mélanges de la Casa de Velázquez, 26, 1990, pp. 113–130.

Arié, R.: L'Espagne musulmane au temps des Nasrides, Paris 1973; new edition Paris 1990.

Arts of Islam, The: Catologue of 1976 London exhibition, The Arts Council of Great Britain, London 1976.

Ayalon, D.: On the Eunuchs in Islam, in: Jerusalem Studies in Arabic and Islam, 1, 1979, pp. 67–124.

–: Mamlûk, in: Encyclopédie de l'Islam, vol. VI, 1987, pp. 299–305.

Azuar Ruiz, R.: Castellogía medieval alicantina: area meridional, Alicante 1981.

–: La Rábita Califal de las Dunas de Guardamar. Excavaciones Arqueológicas, Alicante 1989 (Museo Arqueológico).

–: Una rabita hispanomusulmana del Siglo X, in: Archéologie Islamique, 1, 1990, pp. 109–145.

Baer, E.: The "Pila" of Játiva. A Document of Secular Urban Art in Western Islam, in: Kunst des Orients, 7, 1970–71, pp. 142–166.

al-Bakrî, Abû'Ubayd, Kitâb al-mamâlik wa-l-masâlik. For Andalusia: Lévi-Provençal, E.: La Péninsule Ibérique au Moyen-Age, Leiden 1938. A new Spanish translation: Vidal Beltrán, E.: Abû 'Ubayd al-Bakrî. Geografía de España (Kitâb al-masâlik wa-l-mamâlik), Saragossa 1982 (Textos Medievales, 53).

Bargebuhr, F.P.: The Alhambra Palace. A Cycle of Studies on the Eleventh Century in Moorish Spain, Berlin 1968.

–: Salomo Ibn Gabirol. Ostwestliches Dichtertum, Wiesbaden 1976.

Barnabé Guillamón, M., Fernández González, F.V., Manzano Martínez, J. et. al.: Arquitectura doméstica islámica en la ciudad de Murcia, in: Murcia Musulmana, Murcia 1989, pp. 233–252.

Barrucand, M.: L'urbanisme princier en islam. Meknès et les villes royales islamiques postmédiévales, Paris 1985 (Bibliothèque d'Etudes Islamiques, 13).

–: Gärten und gestaltete Landschaft als irdisches Paradies: Gärten im westlichen Islam, in: Der Islam, 65, 1988, pp. 244–267.

Basset, H. and Terrasse, H.: Sanctuaires et forteresses almohades, Paris 1932 (Collection Hesperis V).

Bazzana, A.: Eléments d'archéologie musulmane dans Al-Andalus: caractères spécifiques de l'architecture militaire arabe de la région valencienne, in: al-Qantara, 1, 1980, pp. 339–363.

–: La cerámica islámica en la ciudad de Valencia. I. Catálogo, Valencia 1983.

–: Un fortin omayyade dans le "Sharq al-Andalus", in: Archéologie Islamique I, 1990, pp. 87–108.

Bazzana, A., Cressier, P. and Guichard, P.: Les châteaux ruraux d'Al-Andalus. Histoire et archéologie des husûn du sud-est de l'Espagne, Madrid 1988.

Bazzana, A. and Cressier, P.: Shaltish/Saltés (Huelva). Une ville médiévale d'al-Andalus, Madrid 1989 (Publications de la Casa de Velázquez, Etudes et Documents 5).

Beckwith, J.: Caskets from Córdoba, London 1960.

Berges Roldan, L.: Baños árabes del Palacio de Villardompardo Jaén, Jaén 1989.

Bermúdez López, J.: Die Alhambra und der Generalife, Granada, n.d.

–: Contribución al estudio de las contrucciones domésticas de la Alhambra: nuevas perspectivas, in: La casa hispano-musulmana. Aportaciones de la arqueología, Granada 1990, pp. 341–353.

Bermúdez Pareja, J.: El Generalife después del incendio de 1958, in: Cuadernos de la Alhambra, 1, 1965, pp. 9–39.

–: El baño del Palacio de Comares en la Alhambra de Granada. Disposición primitiva y alteraciones, in: Cuadernos de la Alhambra, 10–11, 1974–75, pp. 99–116.

–: Pinturas sobre piel en la Alhambra de Granada, Granada 1987.

Berthier, P.: Campagne de fouilles à Chichaoua, de 1965 à 1968, in: Bulletin de la Société d'Histoire du Maroc, 2, 1969, pp. 7–26.

Bloom, J.: Minaret. Symbol of Islam, Oxford 1989.

Bonnassié, P.: Le temps des Wisigoths, in: Bennasser, B.: Histoire des Espagnols. VIe-XVIIe siècle, Paris 1985, pp. 50–51.

Bosch-Vilà, J.: Los Almorávides (Historia de Marruecos, V), Tetuan 1956.

Brisch, K.: Madinat az-Zahra in der modernen archäologischen Literatur Spaniens, in: Kunst des Orients, 4, 1965, pp. 5–41.

–: Die Fenstergitter und verwandte Ornamente der Hauptmoschee von Córdoba. Eine Untersuchung zur spanisch-islamischen Ornamentik, 1966 (Madrider Forschungen 4).

Bulliet, R.W.: Conversion to Islam in the Medieval Period. An Essay in Quantitive History, Cambridge, Mass. & London 1979.

Cabanelas Rodríguez, D. OFM and Fernández-Puertas, A.: Inscripciones poéticas de la Alhambra, in: Cuadernos de la Alhambra: Partal y Fachada de Comares, n° 10–11, 1974–75, pp. 117–200; Generalife: p. 14, pp. 3–86; Fuente de los Leones: 15–17, 1981, pp. 3–88; Tacas en el accesso a la Sala de la Barca: n° 19–20, 1983–84, pp. 61–149.

Cabanelas Rodríguez, D. OFM: La Fachada de Comares y la llamada Puerta de la Casa Real, lecture, Alhambra 26. 4. 1991.

Cara Barrionuevo, L.: La Almería islámica y su alcazaba, Almería 1990.

Castejón y Martínez de Arizala, R.: Medina Azahara, Leon ²1982.

Codera, F.: Inscripción árabe de Guardamar, in: Boletín de la Real Academia de la Historia, vol. XXXI, 1897, pp. 31–35.

Chalmeta, P.: Al-Andalus: Musulmanes y cristianos (siglos VIII–XIII), in: Dominguez Ortiz, A. (ed.): Historia de España, vol. 3, Barcelona 1989, pp. 9–114.

Cressier, P.: Las fortalezas musulmanas de la Alpujarra (Provincias de Granada y Almería) y la división político administrativa de la Andalucía oriental, in: Arqueología Espacial, Coloquio sobre distribución y relaciones entre los asentamientos, Teruel 1984, Actas, vol. 5, pp. 179–199.

–: Le château et la division territoriale de l'Alpujarra médiévale: du hisn à la tâ'a, in: Mélanges de la Casa de Velázquez, 20, 1984, pp. 115–144.

–: Les chapiteaux de la Grande Mosquée de Cordoue (oratoires d'Abd al-Rahmân I et d'Abd al Rahmân II) et la sculpture de chapiteaux à l'époque émirale, in: Madrider Mitteilungen, 25, 1984, pp. 257–313, plates 63–72 and 26, 1985, pp. 216–281, plates 72–82.

–: Le décor califal du mihrâb de la Grande Mosquée d'Almería, in: Madrider Mitteilungen, 31, 1990.

Cressier, P. and Lerma, J.V.: Un chapiteau inédit d'époque Tâ'ifa à Valence, in: Madrider Mitteilungen, 30, 1989, pp. 427–431.

Cressier, P., Gómez Becera, A. and Martínez-Fernández, G.: Quelques données sur la maison rurale nasride et morisque en Andalousie-Orientale. Le cas de Shanash/Senés et celui de Macael Viejo (Almería), in: La casa hispano-musulmana. Aportaciones de la Arqueología, Granada 1990, pp. 229–246.

Creswell, K. A. C.: Early Muslim Architecture, 2 vols. (the first volume in two parts.), New York ²1979.

Der Nersessian, S.: L'Art Arménien, Paris 1977.

Delgado Valero, C.: Toledo islámico: ciudad, arte e historia, Toledo 1987.

–: Materiales para el estudio morfológico y ornamental del arte islámico en Toledo, Toledo 1987.

Dickie, J.: The Islamic Garden in Spain, in: The Islamic Garden, Dumbarton Oaks, Washington D.C. 1976, pp. 87–106.

Dozy, R.: see under al-Idrîsî.

Duda, D.: Spanisch-islamische Keramik aus Almería vom 12. bis 15. Jahrhundert, Heidelberg 1970.

–: Zur Technik des Keramiksimses in der Großen Moschee von Córdoba, in: Madrider Forschungen, 11, 1976, pp. 53–55.

de Epalza, M. and Guellouz, S.: Le Cid, personnage historique et littéraire (Anthologie de textes arabes, espagnols, français et latins avec traductions), Paris 1983.

Esco, C., Giralt, J. and Senac, P.: Arqueología islámica en la Marca Superior de al-Andalus, Huesca 1988.

Ettinghausen, R. and Grabar, O.: The Art and Architecture of Islam 650–1250, Penguin, 1987.

Ewert, C.: Spanisch-islamische Systeme sich kreuzender Bögen II. Die Arkaturen eines offenen Pavillons auf der Alcazaba von Málaga, in: Madrider Mitteilungen, 7, 1966, pp. 232–253.

–: Spanisch-islamische Systeme sich kreuzender Bögen I. Die senkrechtenebenen Systeme sich kreuzender Bögen als Stützkonstruktionen der vier Rippenkuppeln in der ehemaligen Hauptmoschee von Córdoba, Berlin 1968 (Madrider Forschungen, 2).

–: Die Moschee von Mertola, in: Madrider Mitteilungen, 14, 1973, pp. 217–246.

–: Der Mihrâb der Hauptmoschee von Almería, in: Madrider Mitteilungen, 13, 1972, pp. 287–336.

–: Die Moschee am Bâb Mardûm in Toledo – eine "Kopie" der Moschee von Córdoba, in: Madrider Mitteilungen, 18, 1977, pp. 278–354.

–: Spanisch-islamische Systeme sich kreuzender Bögen III. Die Aljafería von Zaragoza, 3 vols., Berlin 1978 (Madrider Forschungen, 12).

–: Hallazgos islámicos en Balaguer y la Aljafería de Zaragoza, con contr. de Duda, D. y Kircher, G., Madrid 1979.

–: Elementos decorativos en los taberos parietales del salón Rico de Madînat al Zahrâ', in: Cuadernos de Madînat al Zahrâ', 1, 1987, pp. 27–60.

–: Der almoravidische Stuckdekor von Shûshâwa (Südmarokko). Ein Vorbericht, in: Madrider Mitteilungen, 28, 1987, pp. 141–178.

Ewert, C. und Wisshak, J.P.: Forschungen zur almohadischen Moschee I. Vorstufen. Hierarchische Gliederungen westislamischer Betsäle des 8. bis 11. Jahrhunderts: Die Hauptmoscheen von Kairouan und Córdoba und ihr Bannkreis, Mainz 1981 (Madrider Beiträge, 9).

–: Forschungen zur almohadischen Moschee. II: Die Moschee von Tinmal, Mainz 1984 (Madrider Beiträge, 10).

Fagnan, E.: see under Ibn al-Athîr and Ibn 'Idhârî.

Fernandez López, S.: Marmuyas (Montes de Málaga). Análisis de una investigación, in: Actas del I Congreso de Arqueología Medieval Española, vol. III, Saragossa 1986, pp. 163–180.

Fernández-Puertas, A.: La Fachada del Palacio de Comares I. Situación, Función y Génesis, Granada 1980.

Flores Escobosa, I.: Estudio Preliminar sobre Loza Azul y Dorada Nazarí de la Alhambra, Madrid 1988 (Cuadernos de Arte y Arqueología, 4).

Flores Escobosa, I., Muñoz Martín, M. and Dominguez Bedmar, M.: Cerámica Hispanomusulmana en Almería, Almería 1989.

Fontaine, J.: L'árt préroman hispanique. La Pièrrequi-vire, Zodiaque (ed.), La Nuit des Temps, 38, 1973.

–: L'art mozarabe. La Pièrre-qui-vire, Zodiaque (ed.), La Nuit des Temps, 47, 1977.

Gabrieli, F.: Omayyades d'Espagne et Abbasides, in: Studia Islamica, 31, 1970, pp. 93–100.

Gamir Sandoval, A.: Reliquias de las defensas fronterizas de Granada y Castilla en los siglos XIV y XV, in: Miscelanea de Estudios Árabes y hebraicos, 5, 1956, pp. 43–72.

García Gómez, E.: Poemas árabes en los muros y fuentas de la Alhambra, Madrid 1985.

–: Foco de antigua luz sobre la Alhambra. Desde un texto de Ibn al-Jatîb en 1362, Madrid 1988.

García Granados, J.A., Girón Irueste F. und Salvatierra Cuenca, V.: El Maristán de Granada. Un Hopital Islamico, Granada 1989.

Gayangos, P. de: see under al-Maqqarî.

Giralt i Balagueró, J.: Fortificacions andalusines a la Marca Superior: el cas de Balaguer, in: Setmana d'Arqueología Medieval, Lleida, pp. 175–193.

Glick, T.F.: Islamic and Christian Spain in the Early Middle Ages, Princeton, N.J. 1979.

Godard, A.: Voûtes iraniennes, in: Athar-é Irân, 1949.

Golvin, L.: Note sur un décor de marbre trouvé à Madînat al-Zahrâ', in: Annales de l'Institut d'Etudes Orientales, XVIII–XIX, 1960–61, pp. 277–299.

–: Les influences artistiques entre l'Espagne musulmane et le Maghrib. La Torre de la Vela de l'Alhambra à Grenade et le donjon du Manâr de la Qal'a des Banû Hammad (Algérie),

in: Cuadernos de la Alhambra, 10–11, 1974–75, pp. 85–90.

Gómez-Moreno, M.: Arte Mudéjar Tóledano, Madrid 1916.

–: El Baño de la Judería en Baza, in: Al-Andalus, 12, 1947, pp. 151–155.

–: El arte árabe español hasta los Almohades – Arte mozarabe, Madrid 1951 (Ars Hispaniae, 3).

Gonzalez, V.: Origine, développement et diffusion de l'émaillerie sur métal en occident islamique, thesís, 2 vols., Université de Provence I (Aix-Marseilles), 1982.

Grabar, O.: The Alhambra, London 1978.

Guerrero Lovillo, J.: Al-Qasr-al-Mubârak, El Alcázar de la bendición, Discurso de recepción en la Real Academia de Bellas Artes de Santa Isabel de Hungria, 19 November 1970, Seville 1974, pp. 83–109.

–: Sevilla musulmana, in: Historia del urbanismo sevillano, Seville 1977.

Guichard, P.: Structures Sociales "Occidentales" et "Orientales" dans l'Espagne Musulmane, Paris-The Hague 1977.

–: Naissance de l'islam andalou, Apogée de l'islam andalou and Paysans d'Al-Andalus, in: Bennasser, B.: Histoire des Espagnols, Paris 1985, pp. 53–158.

–: Les Musulmans de Valence et la reconquête (XIe-XIIIe siècles), Damas 1990.

Halm, H.: Al-Andalus und Gothica Sors, in: Welt des Orients, 66, 1989, pp. 252–263.

Hernández Giménez, F.: El Alminar de 'Abd al-Rahmân III en la Mezquita mayor de Córdoba. Génesis y repercusiones, Granada 1979.

–: Madinat al-Zahra, Granada 1985.

Hoenerbach, W.: Islamische Geschichte Spaniens, Zurich and Stuttgart 1970.

Huici Miranda, A.: Al-Hulal al-Mawshiyya, crónica árabe de las dinastías almorávide, almohade y benimerín. Tetuan, Colección de crónicas árabes de la Reconquista, 1952.

–: Historia política del Imperio Almohade, 2 vols., Tetuan 1956/57.

Huici Miranda, A. and Terrasse, H.: Gharnâta, in: Encyclopédie de l'Islam, vol. II, ²1977, pp. 1035–1043.

Ibn al-Athîr, Kitâb al Kâmil fî l-târîkh, ed. and transl. by Fagnan, E.: Annales du Maghreb et de l'Espagne, Algiers 1901.

Ibn 'Idhârî al-Marrakûshî: Kitâb al-bayân al-mughrib, pt. 1, ed. by Colin, G.S. and Lévi-Provençal, E., Histoire de l'Afrique du Nord et de l'Espagne musulmane intitulée . . . , 2 vols., Leiden ²1948–1951; pt. 2: Lévi-Provençal, E., Al-Bayân al-mughrib. Tome 3ème. Histoire de l'Espagne musulmane au XIe lsiècle, Paris 1930. Transl. by Fagnan, E.: Histoire de l'Afrique et de l'Espagne intitulée . . ., 2 vols., Algiers 1901–1904.

Ibn al-Khatîb, Muhammad, Kitâb a'mâl al-a'lâm, pt. 2, ed. by Lévi-Provençal, E.: Histoire de l'Es-

pagne musulmane, Beirut ²1956; transl. of pt. 2 by Hoenerbach, W.: Islamische Geschichte Spaniens, Zurich and Stuttgart 1970.

Idris, H.R.: Les Zîrîdes d'Espagne, in: Al-Andalus, XXIX, 1964/1, pp. 39–145.

al-Idrîsî, Abû 'Abd Allâh Muhammad, Kitâb Nuzhat al-mushtâq; ed. and transl. in part by Dozy, R. and de Goeje, J., Description de l'Afrique et de l'Espagne, Leiden 1866.

Iñiguez, F.: Las yeserías descubiertas recientemente en Las Huelgas de Burgos, in: Archivo Español de Arte, 14, 1940, pp. 306 –308.

Izquierdo Benito, R.: La cerámica hispano-musulmana decorada de Vascos (Toledo), in: Homenaje al Prof. Martin Almagro Basch IV, Madrid 1983, pp. 107–115.

–: Tipología de la cerámica hispanomusulmana de Vascos (Toledo), in: II Coloquio Internacional de Cerámica Medieval en el Mediterraneo Occidental, Toledo 1981, publ. 1986, pp. 113–125.

–: Los Baños Arabes de Vascos (Navelmoralejo, Toledo), in: Noticiario Arqueológico Hispánico, 28, 1986, pp. 195–242.

–: Una ciudad de Fundacion musulmana: Vascos, in: Castrum, 3, 1988, pp. 163–172.

Jiménez, A.: Arquitectura Gaditana de Epoca Alfonsi, in: Cádiz en el siglo XIII, Acta de las Jornadas Conmemorativas del VII Centenario de la Muerte de Alfonso X el Sabio, Cádiz 1983, pp. 135–158.

Jiménez Martín, A.: La mezquita de Almonaster, Instituto de Estudios Onubenses "Padre Marchena", Diputación Provincial de Huelva, 1975.

–: Giralda (Exposición "La Giralda en Madrid"), Madrid 1982.

–: Los jardines de Madînat al-Zahrâ', in: Cuadernos de Madînat al-Zahrâ', 1, 1987, pp. 81–92.

Jiménez Martín, A.; Falcón, T., Morales, A.J. et. al.: La arquitectura de nuestra ciudad, Seville 1981.

Jones, O.: Plans, Elevations, Sections and Details of the Alhambra, London 1842; Details and Ornaments from the Alhambra, London 1845.

Kubisch, N.: Die Ornamentik von Santa María la Blanca in Toledo, thesis, Munich 1991 (MS).

–: Das kalifale Becken des Museo Arqueológico Nacional de Madrid (mit weiterführendem Literaturverzeichnis), in: Madrider Mitteilungen, 33, 1992, in preparation.

Kühnel, E.: Maurische Kunst, Berlin 1924.

–: Antike und Orient als Quellen spanisch-islamischer Kunst, in: Madrider Mitteilungen, 1, 1960, pp. 174–181.

–: Die Islamischen Elfenbeinskulpturen, VIII. bis XIII. Jahrhundert, Berlin 1971.

Labarta, A. und Barceló C.: Les fuentes árabes sobre al-Zahrâ': estado de la cuestión, in: Cuadernos de Madînat al-Zahrâ', 1, 1987, pp. 93–106.

Lagardère, V.: Le Vendredi de Zallâqa. 23 Octobre 1086, Paris 1989.

Lautensach, H.: Maurische Züge im geographi-

schen Bild der Iberischen Halbinsel, Bonn 1960.

Lazoro, R. and Villanueva, E.: Homenaje al Padre Tapia. Almería en la Historia, Almería 1988.

Le Tourneau, R.: The Almohad Movement in North Africa in the 12th and 13th centuries, Princeton 1969.

Lévi-Provençal, E.: see also under al-Bakrî, Ibn 'Idhârî, Ibn al-Khatîb.

–: Inscriptions arabes d'Espagne, 2 vols., Leiden and Paris 1931.

–: Un manuscrit de la bibliothèque du Calife al-Hakam II, in: Hespéris 18, 1934, p. 198.

–: Histoire de l'Espagne Musulmane, 3 vols., Paris Algiers 1950–67.

–: La fondation de Marrakech (462–1070), in: Mélanges d'Art et d'Archéologie de l'Occident Musulman. Hommage à Georges Marçais, vol. 2, Algier 1957, pp. 117–120.

López-Cuervo, S.: Medina az-Zahra. Ingenería y forma, Madrid 1983.

Llubia, L.M.: Cerámica medieval española, Barcelona 1968.

MacKay A. and Benaboud, M.: Alfonso VI of Leon and Castille, "al-Imbratûr dhû'l-Millatayn", in: Bulletin of Hispanic Studies, 56, 1979, pp. 95–102.

Manzano Martos, R.: Darabenaz: una alquería nazarí en la Vega de Granada, in: Al-Andalus, 26, 1961, pp. 201–218 and 448–449.

–: Poetas y vida literaria en los Reales Alcázares de la ciudad de Sevilla, Seville 1983.

al-Maqqarî, Shihâb al-Dîn, Nafh al-tîb min ghusn al-Andalus, publ. in Cairo, 1949 (10 vols.), transl. in part by de Gayangos, P.: The History of the Muhammadan Dynasties in Spain, 2 vols., London 1840–1843, new edition New York 1964.

Marçais, G.: L'architecture musulmane d'occident. Tunisie, Algérie, Maroc, Espagne, Sicile, Paris 1954.

Marín Fidalgo, A.: Arquitectura Gótica del Sur de la Provincia de Huelva, Huelva 1982.

Marinetto Sánchez, P.: Capiteles califales del Museo Nacional de Arte hispanomusulmán, in: Cuadernos de Arte, XVIII, Granada 1987, pp. 175, 204.

–: El capitel almorávide y almohade en la peninsula iberica, in: Estudios dedicados a Don Jesús Bermúdez Pareja, Granada 1988, pp. 55–70.

Martín-Bueno, M., Erice Lacabe, R. and Sáenz Preciado, M.P.: La Aljafería. Investigación Arqueológico, Saragossa 1987.

Menéndez Pidal, R.: La España del Cid, 2 vols., Madrid ⁷1969.

Menéndez Pidal, J.: La Mezquita-Iglesia de Santa María la Real (Alcázar de Jérez), in: Bellas Artes, 73, n° 19, 1973, pp. 8 f.

Mergelina, C. de: La iglesia rupestre de Bobastro, in: Archivo Español de Arte y Arqueología, 1925, p. 2.

–: Bobastro, Memoria de la excavaciones realizadas

en las Mesas de Villaverde, El Chorro (Málaga), Madrid 1927.

Miles, G.C.: The Coinage of the Umayyads of Spain, 2 vols., New York 1950.

Miró, A.: Ronda. Arquitectura y Urbanismo, Málaga 1987.

Navagiero, A.: Il viaggio fatto in Spagna et in Francia..., Venice, Domenico Fani 1563.

Navarro Palazón, J.: Aspectos arqueológicos, Historia de la región murciana, vol. II, 1980, pp. 64–107.

–: Siyâsa: una madîna de la cora de Tudmîr, in: Areas, 5, Murcia 1985, pp. 171–189.

–: Hacia una sistematización de la cerámica esgrafiada, in: 2 Coloquio Internacional de Cerámica Medieval en el Mediterraneo Occidental, Toledo (1981) 1986, pp. 165–178.

–: Arquitectura y artesania en la cora de Tudmir, in: Más García, J. (ed.): Historia de Cartagena, vol. V, 1986, pp. 411–485.

–: El cementerio islámico de San Nicolás de Murcia. Memoria preliminar, in: Actas del 1 Congreso de Arqueología Medieval Española, Saragossa 1986, vol. IV, pp. 7–37.

–: Nuevas aportaciones al estudio de la loza dorada andalusí: el ataifor de Zavellá, in: Les Illes Orientals d'al-Andalus, Palma de Mallorca 1987 (V Jornades d'estudis histórics locals), pp. 225–238.

–: Excavaciones arqueológicas en la ciudad de Murcia durante 1984, in: Excavaciones y Prospecciones Arqueológicas, Servicio Regional de Patrimonio Histórico, Murcia 1987, pp. 307–320.

–: Formas arquitectónicas en el mobiliario cerámico andalusí, in: Cuadernos de la Alhambra, 23, 1987, pp. 21–65.

–: La conquista castellana y sus consequencias: la despoblación de Siyâsa, in: Castrum 3, 1988, pp. 208–214.

–: Una Casa Islámica en Murcia. Estudio de su ajuar (siglo XIII), Murcia 1991.

–: Murcia como centro productor de loza dorada; idem and Picon, M.: La loza de la Province de Murcie, étude en laboratoire, in: Congresso Internazionale delle Università degli Studi di Siena, 1986, pp. 129–143 and 144–146.

Navarro Palazón, J. and García Avilés, A.: Aproximación a la cultura material de Madînat Mursiya, in: Murcia musulmana, Murcia 1989, pp. 253–356.

Noth, A.: Früher Islam, in: Haarmann, U. (ed.): Geschichte der arabischen Welt, Munich 1987, pp. 11–100.

Nykl, A.R.: Inscripciones árabes de la Alhambra y del Generalife, in: Al-Andalus, 4, 1936–1939, pp. 174–194.

Ocaña Jiménez, M.: Consideraciones en torno al prólogo de la obra Madînat al-Zahrâ'. Arquitectura y decoración de don Felix Hernández Giménez, in: Cuadernos de Madînat-Zahrâ', 1, 1987, pp. 107–124.

–: Precisiones sobre la Historia de la Mezquita de Córdoba, in: Cuadernos de estudios medievales IV–V, Granada 1979, pp. 275–282.

Palol, P. de: Regard sur l'art wisigoth, Paris 1979.

Pavón Maldonado, B.: Memoria de la excavación de la mezquita de Madinat al-Zahra, Excavaciones Arqueológicas en España, n° 50, 1966.

–: La alcazaba de la Alhambra, in: Cuadernos de la Alhambra, 7, 1971.

–: Jérez de la Frontera: Ciudad Medieval. Arte Islámico y Mudéjar, Asociación Española de Orientalistas, Madrid 1981.

–: Tratado de Arquitectura Hispano-Musulmana. I. Agua, Madrid 1990.

Peinado Santaella, R.G. and López de Coca Castañer, J.E.: Historia de Granada 2: La Época Medieval. Siglos VIII–XV, Granada 1987.

Pérès, H.: La poésie andalouse en arabe classique au XIe siècle, Paris ²1953.

Plan especial de protección y reforma interior de la Alhambra y Alíjares, Granada 1986.

Puertas Tricas, R.: La Cerámica islámica de cuerda seca en La Alcazaba de Málaga, Málaga 1989.

Retuerce, M. and Zozaya, J.: Variantes geográficos de la cerámica omeya andalusí: los temas decorativos, in: La Ceramica medievale nel Mediterraneo occidentale, Congresso Internazionale della Università degli Studi di Siena, 1984, Proc., Florence 1986, pp. 69–128.

Reuther, O.: Ocheïdir, Leipzig 1912.

Rosselló-Bordoy, G.: Algunas observaciones sobre la decoración cerámica en verde y manganeso, in: Cuadernos de Madînat al-Zahrâ', 1, 1987.

–: El nombre de las cosas en al-Andalus: une propueste de terminología cerámica, Palma de Mallorca 1991.

Rubiera, M.J.: De nuevo sobre los poemas epigraficos de la Alhambra, in: Al-Andalus, 41, 1976.

Sanahuja, F.P. OFM: História de la ciutat de Balaguer, Balaguer ²1984.

Sánchez-Albornoz, C.: L'Espagne Musulmane, Publisud ⁴1985.

–: Espagne préislamique et Espagne musulmane, in: Revue historique, 1967, pp. 295–338.

Schlumberger, D.: Qasr al-Heir el-Gharbi, Paris 1986.

Seco de Lucena Paredes, L.: El barrio del Cenete, las alcazabas y las mezquitas de Granada, in: Cuadernos de la Alhambra, 2, 1966, p. 46.

–: Los palacios del taifa almeriense al-Mu'tasim, in: Cuadernos de la Alhambra, 3, 1967.

Serjeant, R.B.: Islamic Textiles (Material for a History up to the Mongol Conquest), Beirut 1972.

Singer, H.R.: Der Maghreb und die Pyrenäenhalbinsel bis zum Ausgang des Mittelalters, in: Haarmann, U. (ed.): Geschichte der arabischen Welt, Munich 1987, pp. 264–322.

Sourdel, D.: Wazîr et hâjib en occident, in: Etudes d'orientalisme dédiées à la mémoire d'E. Lévi-Provençal, Paris 1962, pp. 749–755.

Soustiel, J.: La céramique islamique, Fribourg 1985.

Stern, H.: Les Mosaïques de la Grande Mosquée de Cordoue, Berlin 1976 (Madrider Forschungen, 11).

Stern, S.M.: Les Chansons Mozarabes. Les Vers Finaux (Kharjas) en espagnol dans les Muwashshas arabes et hébreux. Palermo 1953.

Terrasse, H.: La Grande mosquée almohade de Séville, in: Mémorial Henri Basset, Paris 1928, pp. 249–266.

–: L'art hispano-mauresque des origines au XIIIe siècle, Paris 1932.

–: Minbars anciens du Maroc, in: Mélanges d'histoire et d'archéologie de l'occident musulman, Hommage à Georges Marçais, vol. 2, Algiers 1957, pp. 159–167.

–: Islam d'Espagne. Une rencontre de l'Orient et de l'Occident, Paris 1958.

–: Les tendances de l'art hispano-mauresque à la fin du Xe et au début du XIe siècle, in: al-Mulk, 3, 1963, pp. 19–24.

–: Chapiteaux oméyades d'Espagne à la Mosque d'al-Qarawiyyîn de Fès, in: Al-Andalus, 28, pp. 211–220.

–: La formation de l'art musulman d'Espagne, in: Cahiers de Civilisation Médiévale, 8, 1965, pp. 141–158.

–: La mosquée al-Qarouiyin à Fès, Paris 1968.

–: La sculpture monumentale à Cordoue au IXe siècle, in: Al-Andalus, 34, 1969, pp. 409–417.

Terrasse, M.: La fortification oméiyade de Castille, in: Revista del Instituto de Estudios Islamicos en Madrid, 14, 1967–68, pp. 113–127.

Thierry, J.-M. and Donabédian, P.: Les Arts Arméniens, Paris 1987.

Torres, Balbás, L.: Paseos por la Alhambra: la Rauda, in: Archivo Español de Arte y Arqueología, 6, 1926, pp. 261–285.

–: Hallazgos arqueológicos en la Alcazaba de Málaga, in: Al-Andalus, 2, 1934, pp. 344–357.

–: Monteagudo y "El Castillejo" en la Vega de Murcia, in: Al-Andalus, 2, 1934, pp. 366–370.

–: El alminar de la iglesia de San José y las primeras construcciónes de los ziries granadinos, in: Al-Andalus, 6, 1941, pp. 427–446.

–: La mezquita de al-Qanatir y el Santuario de Alfonso el-Sabio en el Puerto de Santa María, in: Al-Andalus, 7, 1942, p. 149.

–: Las Yeserías descubiertas recientemente en las Huelgas de Burgos, in: Al-Andalus, 8, 1943, pp. 209–254.

–: Excavaciones y obras en la alcazaba de Málaga, in: Al-Andalus, 9, 1944, pp. 173–190.

–: La acropolis musulmana de Ronda, in: Al-Andalus, 9, 1944, pp. 469–474.

–: El Maristán de Granada, in: Al-Andalus, 9, 1944, pp. 481–498.

–: Rábitas hispano-musulmanas, in: Al-Andalus, 13, 1948, pp. 475–491.

–: Arte Almohade. Arte Nazarí. Arte Mudéjar, Madrid 1949 (Ars Hispaniae, 4).

–: La Mezquita Mayor de Almería, in: Al-Andalus, 18, 1953, pp. 412–43.

–: Arte Hispanomusulmán. Hasta la caída del califato de Córdoba, in: Menéndez Pidal, R.: Historia de España, vol. V, Madrid 1957.

–: Ciudades yermas hispano-musulmanas, Madrid 1957.

–: Játiva y los restos del Palacio de Pinohermoso, in: Al-Andalus, 22, 1958, pp. 143–171.

–: Ciudades hispano-musulmanas, 2 vols., ed. by Terrasse, H., Madrid, n. d.

Torres Delgado, C.: El antiguo reino nazarí de Granada (1232–1340), Granada 1974.

Uhde, C. (ed.): Baudenkmäler in Spanien und Portugal, Berlin 1892.

Valdés Fernández, F.: La Alcazaba de Badajoz. Síntesis de la historia de la ciudad, Badajoz 1979.

–: La Alcazaba de Badajoz. I. Hallazgos islámicos (1977–82) y testar de la Puerta del Pilar, Madrid 1985.

–: Ciudadela y fortificación urbana: el caso de Badajoz, in: Castrum, 3, 1988, pp. 143–152.

Vallejo Triano, A.: El baño próximo al salón de "Abd al-Rahmân III", in: Cuadernos de Madînat al-Zahrâ', 1, 1987, pp. 141–168.

–: La vivienda de servicios y la llamada casa de Ya'far, in: La casa hispano-musulmana. Aportaciones de la arqueología, Granada 1990, pp. 129–146.

Vallve Bermejo, J.: De nuevos sobre Bobastro, in: Al-Andalus, 30, 1965, pp. 139–174.

Valor Piechotta, M.: Algunos ejemplos de cerámica vidriada aplicada a la arquitectura almohade, in: II Congreso de Arqueología Medieval Española, Madrid 1987, vol. III, pp. 194–202.

Vernet, J.: Die spanisch-arabische Kultur im Orient und Okzident, Zurich and Munich 1984.

Vidal Beltrán, E.: see under al-Bakrî.

Wasserstein, D.: The Rise and Fall of the Party-Kings. Politics and Society in Islamic Spain, 1002–1086, Princeton 1985.

Watt, M.W. and Cachia, P.: A History of Islamic Spain, Edinburgh ⁴1977 (Islamic Surveys, 4).

Wirth, E.: Regelhaftigkeit in Grundrißgestaltung, Straßennetz und Bausubstanz merinidischer Städte: das Beispiel Fes Djedid (1276 n. Chr.), in: Madrider Mitteilungen, 32, 1991.

Wolf, R.: Castillos, Munich 1982.

Zanón, J.: Topografíía de Córdoba almohade a través de las fuentes árabes, Madrid 1989.

Zozaya, J.: Aproximación a la cronología de algunas formas cerámicas de época de Taifas, in: Actas de las Jornadas de cultura árabe e islámica (1978), Madrid 1981, pp. 277–286.

–: Evolución de un yacimiento: el castillo de Gormaz (Soria), in: Castrum, 3, 1988.

Zozaya J. and Soler, A.: Castillos Omeyas de planta cuadrangular: su relación funcional, in: III Congreso de Arqueología Medieval Española, Oviedo 1989, Actas.

Sources of Illustrations

Listed below are the photographers and archives on whom the publishers have drawn for additional illustrative material. The overwhelming majority of the photographs are new pictures by Achim Bednorz. The plans, elevations and maps have – with the exception of certain material from the publications of Christian Ewert – been newly drawn at the RZ-Studio für Werbung und Grafik Design, Hanover. The literary sources are listed below in short form; complete bibliographical details may be found in the Bibliography.

Manuel Armengol, Barcelona: pp. 18, 19, 65 right, 66 below, 70, 116, 120
Erwin Böhm, Mainz: pp. 34, 44 below
R. Izquierdo Benito: p. 101
Foto Mas, Barcelona: pp. 41,69 above, 100, 101 below, 187
Collection Viollet, Paris: pp. 13, 23, 43, 136, 142 above and below, 143, 144, 148 left and below, 150, 151, 162
R. Arié, L'Espagne musulmane: p. 180 above
R. Azuar Ruiz, La Rábita: p. 97
K. Brisch, Fenstergitter: pp. 44 left, 45
R. Castejón y Martinez de Arizala, Medina: p. 65 below
Encyclopédie de l'Islam: p. 27
C. Ewert, Islamische Funde in Balaguer: pp. 122 below, 123 above and below
–, Der Mihrâb der Hauptmoschee von Almería: p. 93 below
–, Die Moschee am Bâb Mardûm in Toledo: p. 73
–, Spanisch-islamische Systeme I (Cordoba): pp. 41 below, 74 below, 75, 86
–, Spanisch-islamische Systeme II (Zaragoza): pp. 117, 118
M. Gómez-Moreno, Ars Hispaniae, 3: pp. 69 below, 125, 146
A. Jiménez Martin, La arquitectura: pp. 98, 154 below
O. Jones, Alhambra, 2 vols.: illus pp. 10, 12, 15, 84, 184/185, 186, 207, 218, 220
S. López-Cuervo, Medina: p. 64
A. Marín Fidalgo, Arquitectura: p. 157 right, below
C. de Mergelina, La iglesia: p. 49
J. Navarro Palazón: Siyâsa: p. 172
H. Terrasse, La Grande mosquée: p. 157 right, above
L. Torres Balbás, Arte Hispanomusulmán: pp. 25, 46, 92, 170
–, Ciudades: p. 158
C. Uhde, Baudenkmäler: pp. 85, 89

General Map

Madînat al Zahrâ', Salón Rico

Mérida, Aqueduct

Cordova, Great Mosque

Almonaster la Real

Seville, Torre del Oro

Ronda, Puente San Miguel

Jérez de la Frontera, Alcázar

Granada, Lion Court in the Alhambra

Toledo, San Cristo de la Luz

Saragossa, Aljafería

Almería, Circumference Wall

Málaga, Alcazaba

Bobastro, Cliff Church

Burgos

Górmaz

Buitrago

Madrid

Toledo

Zaragoza

Balaguer

Teruel

Valencia

Guardamar
del Segura

Monteagudo

Murcia

Mérida

Córdoba

Almonaster la Real

Madînat al Zahrâ'

Alcaudete

Fiñana

Sevilla

Granada

Tabernas

Almería

Bobastro

Málaga

Ronda

Jerez de la Frontera

Index of Persons and Places